SOUTHALL 23 APRIL 1979

The Report of the
Unofficial Committee of Enquiry

Chairman: Michael Dummett FBA,
Wykeham Professor of Philosophy and Logic,
University of Oxford

D1612834

Published for the Committee by
the National Council for Civil Liberties
1980

Printed in Great Britain
by the Russell Press Ltd, Nottingham.

Contents

Membership of the Committee of Enquiry

Michael Dummett, Wykeham Professor of Philosophy and Logic, University of Oxford (chairman).

Roger Butler, Southall District Secretary, Amalgamated Union of Engineering Workers.

Stuart Hall, Professor of Sociology, Open University.

Patricia Hewitt, General Secretary, National Council for Civil Liberties.

Bill Keys, General Secretary, Society of Graphical and Allied Trades; Member, General Council of the TUC.

Joan Lestor, Member of Parliament for Eton and Slough.

Dick North, Member of the Executive Committee, National Union of Teachers.

Paul O'Higgins, Reader in Law, University of Cambridge.

Ranjit Sondhi, Director, Asian Resources Centre, Birmingham.

Rt Rev Hewlett Thompson, Bishop of Willesden.

Pauline Webb, Methodist Church.

Terms of Reference

To establish a full and accurate account of events in Southall on Monday 23 April 1979 and the night of 23/24 April relating to the National Front meeting in the Town Hall, and the background to those events, and to consider:

1. The decision to allow the National Front to hold an election meeting in the Southall Town Hall; the responsibilities of local authorities under the Representation of the People Act and the Race Relations Act; and the procedures used for taking such decisions.

2. The response of the community in Southall to that decision.

3. The presence of people from other areas, and their part in the original protest and subsequent events.

4. The reaction of the police to the decision to allow the meeting, and their response to representations from local community groups; the powers and responsibilities of the police under the Public Order Act and common law.

5. The development of confrontation on 23 April between the police and members of the public, including the use of police from outside the division and the role of the Special Patrol Group; the nature and extent of injuries suffered by police and public; the circumstances leading to the death of Blair Peach; and the procedures used by the police for the arrest and detention of suspects.

6. The treatment of these events by the press, radio and television.

7. Subsequent events in Southall.

And to make recommendations for the consideration of the relevant agencies.

1: Introduction

Southall has for many years had a large Asian population, predominantly Indian, with a much smaller number of people from the Caribbean. Probably because the Asian community is sufficiently numerous, and has sufficiently prospered, to make it relatively invulnerable to persecution, Southall has an excellent general record for race relations; the white people living there manifest very little hostility towards their neighbours from the Indian sub-continent and from the Caribbean. The Indian community is particularly well organised: the Indian Workers' Association (Southall), which is independent of either wing of the national organisation of the same name, is one of the largest black organisations in the country, and has for many years owned the biggest cinema in Southall; there are several other well-run and effective, though smaller, groups.

This is not to say that members of the ethnic minorities living in Southall inhabit a haven on which racial prejudice never impinges. They read the same newspapers, and hear the same broadcasts, as people elsewhere, and know as well as anyone else the climate of feeling that prevails in the country. They have suffered from the severity of the immigration laws which have been the principal official expression of hostility to black people and which have hampered many and frustrated some in their attempts to reunite their families. They have experienced the bussing of their children to distant schools, and the prejudice and ignorance of some teachers. They too have encountered, and fought against, discrimination by employers; and, during the racial hysteria which gripped the country in 1976, one of their number, a young boy, was stabbed to death in full daylight in a Southall street. They know very well in what sort of country they are living.

On 23 April 1979 the National Front, an unmistakably fascist political party whose leaders have expressed admiration for Hitler and whose principal appeal to voters lies in its openly proclaimed racialism, held an election meeting in Southall Town Hall. This meeting was only nominally designed to win support for the candidate representing the party in the constituency of which Southall forms part. Forty National Front members were brought in from outside the constituency to attend the meeting; of the twenty seats remaining, only five were occupied by ordinary members of the public. Even if the National Front had won the support of all five members of the general public present, it would have had little effect upon the election result. The meeting, held on St George's day, was plainly for symbolic effect. (The Council, with unbelievable crassness, flew the Union Jack, which the National Front has arrogated to itself as a party badge, over the Town Hall all that day, on the pretext that it was St George's day, actually the one day of the year when that particular flag is inappropriate.) The meeting was evidently intended as a calculated affront to the local black community, whose right to be in Britain at all the party vociferously denies.

The community decided, at a meeting open to all, that, if it proved impossible to persuade the local Council to rescind their permission for the National Front to hold its meeting, they must make a visible protest against what they saw, not merely as the propagation of views they hold abhorrent, but as an insult directed at them. This was to take three forms: a march for 'unity and peace' on the preceding Sunday; the closure, on 23 April, of shops and offices; and a peaceful sit-down in front of the Town Hall before the commencement of the meeting. The Southall Youth Movement, one of the few local groups not to co-operate in these plans, proposed an independent protest, in the form of a picket near the Town Hall in the early part of the afternoon. Both plans were communicated to the police; but the intentions of the police were not correspondingly conveyed to the community leaders. On 23 April, hours before the planned demonstrations, the Metropolitan Police force arrived in Southall two and three-quarter thousand strong, and proceeded to occupy the whole centre of the town, rendering any demonstration impossible; the community leaders and the stewards of the demonstration found themselves rendered incapable of fulfilling their role of exercising leadership, or even of finding one another in order to make an alternative plan. The outcome was a day of frustration for the local community, and for those, proportionately not very many, who had come to Southall, principally from other parts of London to register their disapproval of the actions of the National Front. Members of the local community had intended to execute a dignified protest at the presence in their midst, indeed in their Town Hall, of a political group dedicated to the open advocacy of racialism and there for no other apparent purpose than to humiliate them. Instead, they found themselves rendered impotent to register any protest whatever. Their role was to act as spectators of an occupying force which sealed off the centre of their town, into which the propagators of racial hatred were to be escorted. If the National Front's plan was to humiliate the community, it succeeded more than they could have hoped.

This was not, of course, the only outcome: nor was it the outcome to which the attention of the nation was directed by the reports of the media, or by the utterances of political leaders. Indeed, owing to the persistent use in such reports of the term 'the demonstration', it was difficult for the public at large to grasp that this had been one outcome. It cannot be emphasised too strongly that there was no demonstration. More than one had been planned, but the police saw to it that none could take place; there were would-be demonstrators, and there were manifestations of their anger and frustration, but there was no demonstration, a fact in itself essential for an understanding of what took place on that day and of subsequent reactions to it in Southall. Given that fact, it is not surprising that there was a further outcome, well known to everybody: at various times and places, there were severe breaches of public order, some of them involving considerable violence. In the course of these, many people were injured, both police and members of the public, some of them very seriously indeed, and one person, Blair Peach, lost his life. There can be no question that acts of violence were committed both by the police and by members of the public: an attempt will be made in this report to determine how much violence there was on each side, and who was provoked by whom.

In the days immediately following the disaster, spokesmen for the police and others several times observed that such an event must never be allowed to occur again. This presupposes that there is some way of preventing such occurrences consistent with the maintenance of legitimate rights to free speech. But surely almost everyone would agree that, if such a means can be found, it is of the utmost importance to prevent a recurrence of what happened in Southall on 23 April 1979. It is because we each hold this view, most strongly, that we agreed to undertake the enquiry whose conclusions are embodied in this Report. A recurrence will not be prevented by merely expressing the hope that it will not take place: if it is to be prevented, it must be established precisely what did happen at Southall, why it happened and whose was the responsibility for its happening; this done, it then becomes of urgent importance to decide what are the right steps to prevent its happening again, there or anywhere else. We believe that the events at Southall were of such gravity that the outgoing Government should immediately have instituted a full public inquiry, and, failing that, that the incoming Government should have done so. We have never seen our un-official enquiry as a substitute for an official one: in October 1979, we issued a Press statement supporting the continued demands for a full judicial enquiry, and wrote accordingly to the Home Secretary and the Attorney General. But, in default of such an enquiry, we have attempted, as far as can be done by a body with no official standing, to carry out the task a public enquiry would have undertaken: to determine what happened and why, and to consider what is needed if it is not to happen again.

To acknowledge that, if it is possible, then it is vital, to prevent a repetition of what occurred at Southall is in no way to prejudge the answer to the question: what were the causes and whose was the fault? It is perhaps important that the reader should reflect upon the need to avoid a recurrence of the disaster before looking at our analysis of the responsibility for it. So far, many have deplored the occurrence, but there has been no consensus on the steps necessary to prevent a repetition; the very question has largely faded from public consciousness. We hope that the publication of this Report will revive it and will stimulate both a general determination that such a thing must not occur ever again and an informed consideration of what is required to secure that end. It will not have that effect unless every reader is quite clear at the very outset about the magnitude of the disaster and the consequent need to make certain that it is not repeated. Some may find that they disagree with our analysis or our recommendations, though we hope that most will find them convincing; but those who disagree ought to have been clear from the start that they have a duty to propose an alternative analysis, consistent with the actual facts, and a corresponding alternative strategy for the future.

One reason, universally acknowledged, why a repetition of what took place at Southall must be prevented is the severity of the disturbance to the public peace and, particularly, of the injuries inflicted upon individuals; in one case, death, and in many, grave impairment of health. Such effects are not to be reckoned among the normal hazards of the electoral process: it is intolerable that they should be suffered either by ordinary citizens or by policemen, merely as a consequence of the holding of a meeting that the authorities saw themselves as powerless to prohibit and bound to protect.

There is, however, another reason, at least equally weighty, but seldom cited in public discussions of the episode. For individuals who were injured, and for their friends, for those who underwent a frightening and utterly unnerving experience, and for those who have been arraigned in court, the principal evil consequences of the event were, naturally, those that fell on them. For society at large, on the other hand, the most serious consequence has been the effect upon race relations in this country. These have been deteriorating steadily for the past two decades, largely as a result of the continued use by both major political parties of demands for and announcements of even harsher immigration controls as a ritual expression of hostility to black people. During this period there have been intermittent episodes, each of which has caused a sudden sharp deterioration. For example, the outburst of national hysteria in 1976 prompted, in the first instance, by the arrival of a Goan family with British citizenship precipitately expelled from Malawi and also culminating in a death on the streets of Southall. As long as there is no counteracting force effecting any compensating improvements in relations between black people and white, there is no alternative to the worsening of those relations as time passes. Of all the events which have in this way caused a sudden deterioration in race relations, we think that the disturbance in Southall is probably the gravest so far.

The immediate effect has, of course, been on the community in Southall itself. As already remarked, members of that community were already well aware of the racialist strains in British society as a whole; but, even with that knowledge, what happened in their town on 23 April came as a severe psychological shock. Many have observed to us that they had never conceived that the British police could behave as they saw them behave on that day; and those who

9

have said this were none of them previously disposed to unrealistically romantic notions about the police force. In order to accept this point you do not have to believe that the actions of the police were, in the circumstances, anything other than necessary, lawful and justified. Indeed, if the police were blameless, then it is the circumstances which need to be avoided in future. It is not even necessary, for the sake of appreciating the damage to community relations, to accept the eyewitness accounts of police behaviour. You could believe that, though sincere, they were distorted by the shock of the occasion. But of the sincerity of people's reactions, and the magnitude of the shock, there can be no doubt.

In the days which followed the disaster, the interpretation of it which became general in Southall was that, at some very high level, whether by senior police officers or by Government itself, a decision had been taken to use the opportunity provided by the National Front meeting to teach Southall a lesson; in effect, under cover of protecting an election meeting, to mount a punitive expedition. Many have testified to us of their belief that what occurred was a deliberate assault on the whole small community. Again, you do not have to believe this interpretation in order to recognise how sincerely and widely it is held in Southall, and to appreciate how grave a calamity it is that such a belief should have been formed.

On top of this have come the trials, dragging on for many months, held a great distance away, and resulting in a large number of convictions. If there had been any imaginative grasp by those in authority of the psychological wounds inflicted on 23 April on a racial minority already conscious of the degree of hostility towards them which finds such constant expression, the people of Southall would surely have been spared this further, and prolonged, ordeal. The disillusion with the British police engendered by the events of the day has now been crowned by disillusion with British justice. Many have said to us that, after the bitter experience of the 23 April, they had expected justice in the courts, and were utterly chagrined that they did not find it. It is possible to argue that the level of justice meted out by the magistrates' courts on this occasion was no lower than that dispensed by magistrates' courts in general; but only on the assumption that that is very rough justice indeed. It is very difficult to avoid the impression that some, at least, of the magistrates conceived of themselves as engaged in teaching a lesson to some group of which they took those who appeared before them to be members. There was, in many of the courts, an evident, and at least on one occasion avowed, bias in favour of police witnesses, whose testimony was presumed to be accurate and truthful in the face of any amount of contrary evidence from ordinary people, or at least from the sort of people taking part in a demonstration against the National Front or giving help to others doing so. What was completely absent was the most elementary grasp of how deep was the provocation that had been offered, to members of a racial minority already the targets of widespread prejudice, by the holding in their Town Hall of a meeting by a party openly propagating racialism and by a massive occupation of their town by uniformed ranks of policemen brought in from outside. An understanding of the depth of that provocation would have revealed both the wisdom and the justice of a lenient treatment of the cases, in place of an apparent disposition to severity; but it was not forthcoming. Above all, it would have shown the especial need for meeting the high standard of proof supposedly required in a criminal court. British justice is professedly founded upon the principle that it is far worse for the innocent to be convicted than for the guilty to go free for lack of sufficient proof. It is hard to believe that such a principle holds sway when a young boy is found guilty on the testimony of one policeman, contradicted by seven witnesses, including a lawyer and a doctor, who testified to his being elsewhere at the time. (The fact that his conviction was reversed on appeal is a tribute to the system of judicial process considered as a whole, but underlines the inequity of the magistrates' decision.)

The psychological effect of this experience upon people whose friends have been convicted of crimes they cannot imagine them committing, on parents whose children have for the first time acquired a court record, and on the young people themselves, has been gravely aggravated by the contrast with the way the police themselves have fared since 23 April. Many would admit that there was lawless behaviour on the part of some who were in the streets that day, but would maintain that many policemen, too, behaved lawlessly; yet there has been no public admission of the fact, and no policeman has, to anyone's knowledge, been disciplined or rebuked, let alone charged and tried in court. All that is known is that there has been an investigation carried out by the police themselves, concerning which the public has been officially told only of one fact, namely that, after studying its results, the Director of Public Prosecutions has concluded that there is insufficient evidence to bring any proceedings. In circumstances in which there is still grave suspicion that it was a policeman who killed Blair Peach, in which more than one witness has said to us that the police were lucky that there was only one death, and in which some policemen are known subsequently to have been discovered with illegal and lethal weapons in their possession, it is unsurprising that those who have been subjected to these long-drawn-out proceedings have conceived a bitter disillusion with that British justice in which they formerly had some faith. Once again, in order to understand this effect and appreciate how much danger it poses for the future health of society, you do not have to think the condemnation wholly just: you only have to grasp the effect and to perceive how inescapable it was, given the way in which things have been allowed to develop.

The result of all this has been a far deeper alienation of Asian and other black people living in Southall from society at large. Racialism, by its very nature, denies to members of the group it attacks the right to consider themselves as belonging to the general community or as being accepted as belonging to it; that is why exclusionist immigration policies are so apt an expression of racialism. Black people are vividly aware of the hostility to them of the nation's political leaders and of many other people. Many have nevertheless retained a trust in British institutions, and particularly in the law courts and there has been an assumption that there are limits beyond which the infection of the national life by racialism will not go. In Southall, unlike some areas, there was a general confidence in the police. These beliefs have now been eroded and, for some, shattered.

No more catastrophic effect can be imagined. Those who belong to racial minorities and face repeated public and private expressions of hostility need some rock to cling to, some social institution they can trust to operate impartially, if they are not to be reduced to despair. Of all institutions, those whose impartial operation it is most important to maintain are the police and the law courts. Deprive people of the sense that they enjoy the protection of the law and of the agencies that enforce and administer it, and you destroy their whole feeling of security and any sense that they might otherwise have preserved that they are part of the society within which they live. It is this process which was begun in Southall on 23 April, and continued in the courts at Barnet and elsewhere during the months that followed. Probably only a minority of people in Southall care to dwell on what happened there in April 1979; many, and probably most, find it painful to recall and would like, nearly a year afterwards, to put it out of their minds, an operation rendered difficult by the long agony of the court trials. But that is not at all to say that the effect has passed off; as one witness put it to us, it is like a broken leg that has been wrongly set. There remains a deep unease and insecurity caused by the occurrence of what most people would never have imagined could happen; a sense of hurt, and a disillusion with institutions they wanted to be able to respect, institutions whose agents have proved extra-ordinarily adept at identifying individual members of the community charged with sundry offences and glimpsed, in some cases, only momentarily, and yet apparently unable to identify and bring to justice whoever was responsible for the one death that took place. The effect has not, of course, been confined to Southall. Members of the ethnic minorities all over the country read not only the national press but newspapers serving their own communities, and many have friends or relatives living in Southall: the repercussions of such events are felt among black people everywhere in Britain.

We have dwelt at some length, in this introduction, on the consequence for community relations of the disturbance of 23 April because, unlike the public disorder which occurred, it remains generally unappreciated. To repeat, we shall not be concerned until later chapters to evaluate the ideas now prevalent in Southall about what happened to them: at this point, we are neither endorsing nor rejecting them, but merely reporting that they are held; we insist only that this effect, wholly foreseeable by anyone with the least understanding of the psychology of minorities, is of very serious consequence. That it has not been perceived is due to the rudimentary stage at which the understanding of racial problems remains in this country. The tacit assumption is always that what is called 'racial harmony' depends only upon the willingness of the white majority to tolerate the black minorities; or that, in so far as the attitude of the minorities is an obstacle, they must then be open to blame for 'not wanting to integrate' or for 'inverted racialism'. This is to ignore the effects upon the minorities of their past experience of rejection. It wounds his self-respect, which he can safeguard only by differentiating himself from the society that has rejected him and emphasising the distinctness of his heritage, even though at the outset he would have been happy to have been accepted as part of the general community; impatient of ignorant and uncomprehending 'toleration', he demands an earnest of respect for his group and its culture, recognition of his distinct individual needs and feelings and acknowledgement of the wrongs that have been done to him. For this reason, the longer racialism flourishes, the harder it becomes to create a unified society even after it no longer has a grip on the attitudes of the majority. For that reason, it becomes of more than usual importance that the racial minorities should not only be treated fairly, but given reason to believe they are being treated fairly. Their feelings matter, not only in themselves, but for the health of the whole society. It becomes of critical concern to that society that they should not construe mere clumsiness or harshness as yet one more manifestation of injustice directed specifically at them. It is altogether wrong to discount their reactions as due to exaggerated sensitivity: when this is present, it is due to past experience of hostility. Their feelings matter precisely because they have been treated in the past as though their feelings do not matter.

Many who would indignantly repudiate the suggestion that they were racially prejudiced remain quite blind to these considerations. They do so because, much as they might genuinely like to see the racial minorities treated fairly, they have tacitly accepted the assumption underlying most discussion of race and of immigration, that it is up to 'us' (the majority) to decide what to do with and about 'them' (the minorities), and so they have actually lost the habit of regarding members of the minorities as people with their own needs, wishes and viewpoints, which are as important as anybody else's. (This comes out clearly whenever politicians or journalists refer to the feelings of people in 'areas of high immigrant concentration', the feelings of the immigrants themselves never being considered as contributing to the resultant total.)

The Southall affair has therefore only very rarely been discussed in terms of its lasting effect upon the population of that town or on black people generally. In particular, the politicians have not seen it in this light. They have unanimously, and of course rightly, deplored the breach of public order. They have almost as unanimously laid the blame on the supposed arrival in large numbers of outside extremists who launched physical attacks on the police, or incited local residents to do so. They have all praised the police for their restraint and courage. While still Home Secretary, Merlyn Rees hinted at possible changes in the Public Order Act to prevent a recurrence, while Mrs Thatcher's recipe was to bring down 'the whole might and power of the law', presumably on those charged with offences.

But not one appears to have perceived the necessity for saying something to allay the feelings of alienation produced in the Southall community or even to express an understanding of the affront which the day's events had caused.

It was remarked earlier that almost everyone would agree on the importance of preventing a second such episode, if possible; but an exception should be made for the National Front itself. Those who share its views were probably the only people in the country not dismayed by what took place. They went to Southall to provoke and humiliate the people living there: those people were grievously provoked and bitterly humiliated. It is largely pointless, in such a report as this, to hand out rebukes to private individuals and unofficial organisations, since their behaviour will be unaffected and lies outside the scope of public policy: the propensities of various sections of the public to act in certain ways are among the data of the problem. But it would be improper to leave unmentioned the very great share of the blame to be accorded to the National Front. Their calculated insult to the people of Southall was the sole prime cause of all that subsequently happened; the responsibility of these men who stood on the steps of the Town Hall giving Nazi salutes is heavy indeed.

We now turn to the questions which form the main themes of this report.

The first question to be decided is this: Given that the National Front had applied to hold an election meeting in the Town Hall, and given the disposition of the various sections of the public to react as they did, was what happened inevitable? In the first place, was Ealing Council correct to say that it had no option, under the existing law, other than to grant the application? Secondly: given that the meeting was to take place, was the disaster then inevitable? Here the responsibility of each group of participants must be examined. Were the community leaders at fault in planning a demonstration of the kind they intended or of any kind? Were the police authorities at fault for failing to take those leaders into their confidence? Was the whole police strategy of a massive investment of force, which prevented a demonstration of any kind and sealed off the whole centre of the town, either wise or necessary? On the face of it, the outcome could not have been worse than it was: would some other plan have produced a better result? Given the plan devised by the senior officers, how far was the disaster due to the behaviour of the police on the ground, or of some section of them? Did individual policemen act with unwarranted roughness or ferocity? Did they behave unlawfully? If so, was there a breakdown of discipline, or were they following instructions? The responsibility of the protesters must equally be enquired into. Did they behave with exceptional aggressiveness? Was there a concerted plan to attack the police? If so, was it devised by outsiders or by people living in Southall, and by which group was it executed? All these questions are examined in this Report; the answers need not be anticipated here.

The second large question is, of course: How can such an event be prevented from occurring again? The answer to it depends upon those to the first batch of questions. If, given the existing law, what took place was *not* inevitable, the remedy must depend upon an analysis of what went wrong and who, after the National Front, bears the prime responsibility. If, in fact, the Council was not under any compulsion to allow the National Front meeting in the form in which it was held, or even at all, this fact should be established and made generally known. It would still be of great importance to determine to whom the responsibility should be assigned, given that the meeting was to be held. It is unfortunate that people's positions along the Left/Right axis of political opinion usually predispose them to judgements, independent of the particular facts of the case, on any disorder involving police and demonstrators. Those on the Left are quick to accuse the police of brutality and repression. Those on the Right equally automatically either regard all demonstrators as trouble-makers deserving whatever they get, or, if they have more regard for freedom of expression, suspect manipulation of the crowds by dedicated bands of revolutionaries intent on the deliberate provocation of disorder. As explained in chapter 8, the last of these three interpretations was that applied to Southall by a large section of the press and by the leaders of the two main political parties immediately after the event. It has also been vigorously advocated by Commissioner Sir David McNee; it represents his settled judgement, reiterated months after the original affair.

We consider that any such preconcerted action to provoke the police would be mischievous in the extreme, and that, if uncovered and brought home to identifiable individuals, would merit Mrs Thatcher's recipe of bringing down upon them the full severity of the law, by which, presumably, she meant exemplary sentences. Here the argument does require a little anticipation of our findings. We have in fact been unable, despite diligent enquiries, to discover any adequate ground for supposing that anything of the kind occurred in Southall. If it did the police are seriously at fault for having failed, either at the time or subsequently, to arrest the instigators or to uncover evidence of any conspiracy beforehand or any incitement during the event on the part of any group of 'extremists'. If there was no such group, from within or outside Southall, it follows that the violence perpetrated by some of the protesters was a reaction, however reprehensible, to the frustrations and humiliations of the day and to what was perceived or misperceived as hostile, contemptuous or aggressive behaviour by the police. We do not condone acts of serious violence, against the police or anyone else, however great the provocation. But we are not disposed to believe that stiff sentences, let alone convictions based on a low standard of proof, can serve to discourage a similar reaction to similar future occurrences: what is required is to avoid events of the sort that provoked such a reaction. Those newspapers which put about a baseless and distorted picture of what had happened, and those politicians who were quick to endorse that picture, may well have implanted erroneous preconceptions in the minds of some of the magistrates that would explain their policy in the cases that came before them.

We strongly deprecate the use of the word 'extremists' in this connection. Non-pejoratively employed, it would apply to anyone whose opinions on some matter stood at one end of some spectrum: among Christians, Quakers and Roman Catholics might thus be termed 'extremists'. They are never so called, because the term is unavoidably pejorative, suggesting fanaticism and unreason, and hinting at a propensity to violence. There is no general ground for associating opinions at the end of some scale with irrationality, still less with violence: what are probably extreme opinions about democracy or about free speech are probably held by a majority of people in Britain today. Sir David McNee has described the police in Southall as intervening between two rival groups of extremists. To reject racialism and feel a particular abhorrence of it is to stand at one end of a scale; it does not merit the use of an abusive term. Dropping the term in this connection would force each commentator to make explicit whether he means to attribute to those of whom he is speaking a propensity for violence, which is a proper concern of the police, or only the possession of certain opinions, which is not.

If what happened was, in the circumstances, inevitable, the only possible remedy is a change in the law. We look in this report at various possible such changes including measures designed to outlaw meetings such as that which provoked the whole affair. We are not, as a body, in favour of such measures. We reject the curtailment of what rights at present exist to give expression to ideals, beliefs or grievances and, indeed, in chapter 7, we suggest a strengthening of the law to protect public protest. But it is up to the society in which such rights are recognised to find a manner of handling public protest without precipitating public disorder. If the events in Southall were *not* inevitable, someone must be to blame. When public authorities are at fault, public recognition of the fact is a necessary and often a sufficient step towards its correction. This is not true of private individuals. Even though the 'outside extremists' theory is untenable, it could intelligibly be proposed, as a moral judgement, that the protesters who engaged in violence against the police were the most culpable of those involved. Whether right or wrong, such a judgement would be of no help in determining how to prevent a repetition of the disaster because it would carry no weight with those on whom it was passed. It is rather a factor to be taken into account that people placed under the psychological pressure to which those in Southall were subjected are liable to react as they did. As already remarked, we do not think that stiff sentences in the courts can do anything but make things worse: they certainly do not deter anyone from reacting in the same way in similar circumstances. It is the circumstances which must not be allowed to exist.

The original initiative for setting up an unofficial enquiry was taken by some of the community leaders in Southall when it had become quite clear that the Government had no intention of instituting an official one. They approached the National Council for Civil Liberties with the proposal, and asked them to organise it. The NCCL then approached various people, asking them to participate, and our Committee of Enquiry held its first meeting on 15 June 1979. We have in no way acted on behalf of the NCCL, however; that body is not bound by our views, nor are we responsible for any expressed by it. We have done our best to proceed in the same spirit as would an official body of enquiry. We have analysed press reports and viewed video-tapes of the events; we have taken statements from witnesses; we have monitored the court proceedings; and we have striven to arrive at as true a version of the facts as recollections that have sometimes been confused and testimony that has sometimes conflicted have allowed. We are acutely conscious that no unofficial enquiry can have the standing or authority of an official one; but we urge anyone disposed to doubt the accuracy of our factual reconstruction not to dismiss the results of months of investigation without solid reason. As for our recommendations of policy, all lies open to view and each reader must make up his mind for himself: we shall be content if our Report receives consideration of these issues and determination to find a solution.

We are deeply grateful to all those who have given evidence to us. With one large exception, all whom we have asked to do so have agreed. The exception is the police. Patricia Hewitt, who acted as Secretary to the Enquiry, wrote on 16 July 1979 to Assistant Commissioner W.H. Gibson of the Metropolitan Police, asking that police officers should give evidence to our enquiry. A reply dated 7 August refused in the following terms:

It is considered that your enquiry will delay the improvement in race relations in Southall and elsewhere in London which the Metropolitan Police is seeking to achieve. Metropolitan Police officers cannot under these circumstances therefore contribute in any way to your enquiry.

Members of the enquiry were dismayed by this decision and the cold tone in which it was conveyed, and unable to follow the reasoning behind it. Professor Michael Dummett, who acted as Chairman of the Enquiry, therefore wrote at length, urging a reconsideration of the decision.

We deeply regret the decision, conveyed in your letter, that no officers of the Metropolitan Police force shall give evidence to our enquiry. I am writing to urge, most strongly, that this decision be reconsidered. We are extremely anxious to arrive at as accurate a picture as possible of what took place on the day in question. Obviously the testimony of the police would be of the greatest assistance to our doing so. We find it hard to understand why the police should suppose that it will be of advantage to them or to the public that we should be denied the benefit of their evidence. If the decision is maintained, we shall naturally have to record in our report the fact that we were denied this co-operation; it is quite obvious that neither we nor you would then be able to prevent some members of the public concluding that the police felt they had something to hide. I am not in the least suggesting that that is in fact your motive; but you must know perfectly well that many people will inevitably draw that conclusion. If, as the result of your refusal to co-operate with us, our report contains conclusions that you feel to be unfair to the police, any protest that you make will be gravely weakened by the fact that you had refused to lay your evidence before us. We can understand that you have reasons for thinking it regrettable that our enquiry was launched; but that is not now the question at issue. Our enquiry has been announced and is well under way; there can therefore be no question of our not completing it. However much you may regret this, or, indeed, however good your reasons for doing so, we think that, on further reflection, you must agree that, as things now stand, it would be better for everybody if you reversed your decision and allowed officers of the Metropolitan Police to testify to our enquiry. We ask you, most earnestly, to do so.

We are happy to see that you do not, in your reply, in any way impugn the good faith of our enquiry. We assure you that all the members of the enquiry are concerned to arrive at conclusions based strictly on the evidence that is given to us and uninfluenced by any preconceptions. The members of the enquiry include a bishop, a Member of Parliament and two academics, and all of us have not only a personal commitment to integrity but professional reputations which would be damaged by any lapse from probity. You need therefore have no fear whatever that any testimony received from police officers would not be given due weight.

The reason you give for your decision not to allow officers of the Metropolitan Police to give evidence to us is that you think our enquiry will delay the improvement in race relations in Southall and elsewhere which we are happy to hear that you are seeking to achieve. We find this judgement surprising. You must be well aware that the events of 23 April seriously damaged race relations, in Southall and perhaps elsewhere. You must be anxious that similar events should not occur again. To attempt to discover exactly what did happen, and what were the causes of its happening, is surely an essential contribution towards avoiding a recurrence. Steps to prevent a recurrence will be the more likely if the general public does not forget what took place in Southall on that day; as you must surely know, the ethnic minorities are unlikely to forget.

However that may be, the ground that you give, even if correct, would be a reason against our holding the enquiry at all, not for your refusing to co-operate with it now that it is proceeding. If you had expressed your view, and given reasons for it, at the time when it was first announced that the setting up of such an unofficial enquiry was contemplated, we should have taken your arguments into consideration in deciding whether to proceed with the enquiry. Now, as I remarked above, the decision to hold the enquiry is beyond recall. We cannot see how you can possibly expect to improve race relations by refusing to let us have the evidence of the police. Such a refusal is unlikely to restore confidence in the police among those in whom such confidence has, fairly or unfairly, been weakened by what happened. Nor can we see any substance in the claim that that refusal would serve to improve race relations in any other way. We therefore beg you to reconsider your decision.

To this letter no substantive reply was received for some six weeks; when it came, it merely stated, without further explanation, that the Metropolitan Police saw no reason to alter their decision.

We deeply regret this decision, which continues to appear to us quite misguided. By their refusal, the police have undoubtedly weakened our credibility, since there has been an important source of evidence almost inaccessible to us; but, in so doing, they have, in our view, even more gravely damaged their own. We cannot think that damaging either theirs or ours is any service to the public. It makes it that much harder to arrive at a generally agreed understanding of what happened in Southall, and therefore harder to decide what is needed to prevent its happening again. If the police are not in fact at fault in their conduct on 23 April, it would surely have been better for them and for the public if they had done their best to convince us of the fact, even if they had only partially succeeded. If they were to any degree at fault, it would surely be wrong of them not to recognise or not to acknowledge that fault. If there were total public confidence in the police, it might be better not to weaken it by admitting some error or misconduct. Unhappily, that is far from so; and therefore confidence would be strengthened, not weakened, by a frank acknowledgement of mistakes and a declared intention of correcting them.

We have had a few means of discovering the police version of events: the testimony of police witnesses in court cases; the remarks of Sir David McNee immediately after the event and in a much later television interview; and the memorandum laid by the Home Secretary in the Library of the House of Commons and based on a report to him by the Commissioner. We are reasonably confident that, with these clues and the evidence of other witnesses, we have succeeded in making an accurate detailed reconstruction of events, despite being hampered by the refusal of the police to co-operate with us. If anyone is unconvinced of this, we hope that he will, for that very reason, support us in continuing to press, even at this late stage, for an official enquiry.

Our work has been delayed by adjournments in several court cases, particularly where the defendant was advised not to talk to us until after the case was heard. A special difficulty has been the repeated adjournments of the inquest into Blair Peach's death. At a stage when no new date for the inquest had been announced, we decided that we could not delay completion of our report until after the unforseeable date when the inquest would be finished. We have therefore had to publish this report with a chapter on Blair Peach's death containing only information so far made public. We may issue a further report on his death after the inquest is complete. But tragic as it was that such a death should have occurred, and grave as are the suspicions surrounding it, there are many other serious issues arising from the Southall affair which demand urgent consideration.

We owe many thanks to Alice Clover and Roger Smith, who worked full-time for the enquiry, with great diligence, intelligence and enthusiasm. Our thanks are also due to Milan Dulovic and Nigel Harris, who worked on the early part of the enquiry, and to Gareth Evans, who observed at a number of court hearings. We are grateful to the Indian Workers Association (Southall) and to the Southall district of the Transport and General Workers' Union, who provided meeting places for our enquiry. Without the readiness of the many witnesses on whose testimony we have relied to submit written statements and to be interviewed, sometimes more than once, and their patience in answering our questions, we obviously could not have done any work at all, and we thank them all most sincerely. We thank also the lawyers representing the various defendants, who gave us much assistance, and the reporters who did the same. Our particular thanks are due to the trust whose generous grant made it possible to conduct this enquiry and publish the results.

2: The Sequence of Events

Introduction

2.1 Southall is a small town situated in the south-west corner of the West London Borough of Ealing. According to the 1976 sample census, some 18% of Ealing's population either were born or were the children of parents born in the New Commonwealth and Pakistan, as compared with the national figure of 3.5%. An average of 46% of the population of the five wards of Southall were of such origin. Because of this relatively high concentration of people of Asian origin, Southall has become something of a national symbol of a British Asian town (although its absolute size is small), much as Brixton in South London is something of a symbol of those of West Indian origin. In both cases, the symbolism is potent for the extreme right.

2.2 In 1976, during a particularly tense sequence of racially-inspired incidents throughout the country, an Asian youth, Gurdip Singh Chaggar, was stabbed by white youths outside 'The Victory', a public house in Southall. While the judge at the subsequent trial ruled that the killing was not racially motivated, a strong feeling persists in the town that it was. The murder gave rise to the declaration by the then Chairman of the National Party, Kingsley Read: 'One down – a million to go'. In late 1977, Kingsley Read was acquitted by a jury under Judge McKinnon of an offence under the Race Relations Act 1965.

2.3 The Parliamentary constituency of Ealing, Southall has been held since 1966 by a Labour member, Mr Sydney Bidwell. On 3 May he defended his seat against a Conservative (Robert Patten), a Liberal (R. Harris), a National Front candidate (John Fairhurst) and three Asian candidates – Tariq Ali (Socialist Unity), Councillor S. Gupta (Independent) and an independent businessman, Sohan Singh Paul. The two neighbouring seats, Ealing, North and Ealing, Acton, are regarded as marginal seats.

2.4 It should be stressed that 23 April fell in the middle of a General Election period, when political interest and attention was greater than normal and when some political groups welcomed the opportunity to secure the maximum pub-

21

licity possible, even though this did not necessarily improve their chances of electoral success. Furthermore, the events in Southall formed part of a sequence of meetings and events organised by the National Front, leading up to the General Election (see Appendix 3). The campaign by the Front was relatively closely followed by the national press. Two days before 23 April, there had been clashes between police and demonstrators at Leicester and the Leicester experience may have influenced police behaviour in Southall.

Preparations for 23 April

2.5 23 April — St George's Day — is an important annual date for the National Front, when traditionally they hold a major function or march. The selection of Southall for the meeting on that day was, therefore, more than just a decision concerning a local election meeting. Nick Woolley, on the BBC1 programme, *Nationwide,* reported that Southall was eagerly anticipated by the National Front as 'the battle of the Khyber Pass'. On Thames Television on 24 April, Martin Webster, National Activities Organiser of the National Front, said: 'At the present time, the National Front is facing local councils banning the National Front from having halls, even when we've got candidates nominated. And so when the council at Ealing said we could have that hall we jumped at the chance . . . because we didn't know which other councils in West London were going to ban us'.

2.6 It was and remains the policy of Ealing Council not to let council-owned halls to the National Front. In view of the fact, however, that the National Front had nominated a candidate for the Ealing, Southall constituency, the Council took the view that they were required under the Representation of the People Act 1949 to allow that candidate facilities for a *bona fide* public meeting. On 11 April, the town clerk wrote to Ealing Community Relations Council, stating that 'no firm booking has been made for National Front use of the Southall Town Hall on 23 April and I am awaiting a reply to questions I have put to them before a decision is made'. The Council sought and obtained an assurance from the National Front candidate that one-third of the seating capacity in the hall was to be allocated in a block for members of the public other than the candidate's supporters. This assurance was, however, significantly qualified as follows: 'Members of the public who it cannot reasonably be considered would themselves disrupt the meeting will be entitled to be admitted subject to seats being available'.

2.7 It has been suggested that the Council, having decided that they were under an obligation to permit the National Front to hold an election meeting in Council property, could have required the National Front to hold that meeting in a less sensitively situated place than Southall Town Hall. In fact, however, the Council appears to have no such discretion under the terms of the Representation of the People Act. The Borough of Ealing contains three Parliamentary constituencies. A candidate in the Ealing, Southall constituency could not be required to hold his election meeting in one of the other two Ealing constituencies. Once the Council had decided in principle to permit the National Front candidate to hold a meeting, they furnished him with a list of Council-owned meeting places in the Southall constituency, in which he could hold his meeting. The decision to choose Southall Town Hall for the meeting was, therefore, made by the National Front. According to the then Home Secretary, Merlyn Rees, the electoral registration officer of each local authority is required to keep a list of meeting rooms and to make the list available on request to candidates and their election agents. Each candidate at an election is then entitled to use any meeting room on that list, provided reasonable notice is given and, for example, that the use does not conflict with a prior letting agreement. In a letter dated 23 April to Sydney Bidwell, Mr Rees stated that: 'The Act does not appear to empower a local authority to refuse use of a meeting room on public order grounds'.

2.8 We discuss fully in chapter 6 the question of whether Ealing Council could have refused to allow the National Front to hold a meeting at all in council-owned property under the Representation of the People Act.

2.9 The National Front did not publicise the fact that Ealing Borough Council had granted it permission to hold an election meeting on Monday 23 April in Southall Town Hall. By the first week in April, however, the news was already known in Southall. This was not because the Council had officially notified local organisations who might be expected to have an interest in the matter. Vishnu Sharma, the then President of the Indian Workers Association (Southall), appears to have been the first to learn of the meeting, on 7 April, when he accidentally met Chief Inspector Gosse, the local Police Liaison Officer after a meeting in the Dominion Cinema. Mr Sharma explained that: 'I was told quite incidentally about the National Front meeting by Chief Inspector Gosse'.

2.10 On the same day, 7 April, after discussion with Mr Khabra, the secretary, Mr Sharma sent out a letter on behalf of the Indian Workers Association (Southall), inviting representatives of local community organisations to attend a meeting on Wednesday 11 April, 'in order to discuss the implications of the National Front rally and to chalk out a clear, united strategy against fascism coming to Southall and to mobilise maximum turn-out for organising a peaceful resistance against it'. He also arranged an emergency meeting of the IWA's Executive for 10 April. At that meeting the Executive agreed a four point strategy:

1. To petition the Ealing Borough Council to request the cancellation of the booking of the hall for the National Front;
2. The petition to be put to the Council on the day before the demonstration, on Sunday 22 April, after a march from Southall to Ealing Town Hall;
3. That all business, restaurants, shops, etc. should shut down on 23 April from 1 pm onwards;
4. That the National Front meeting itself at the Town Hall should be ignored.

2.11 Energetic efforts were made to persuade the Conservative Leader of the Council, Mrs Beatrice Howard, to reconsider the decision. Ealing Community Relations Council and the Indian Workers Association (Southall) both wrote on 11 April to Mrs Howard, pointing out that Brent Council and the Inner London Education Authority had both refused the National Front permission to hold meetings, because there was evidence that any such meeting would not be a public meeting within the meaning of the Representation of the People Act 1949 and because the Council was therefore not under a statutory obligation to make meeting rooms available. The Town Clerk, who was also the Electoral Returning Officer, replied on the same day, stating: 'I must make it perfectly clear to you, however, that I and the Council are bound by the law on this matter and that no purpose can be served by a meeting of your representative with members of the Council on this issue.' Councillor Howard added: 'If we try to get around the law in the case of the National Front, we'd have to do it with all meetings of extremists. That would be banning freedom of speech'.

2.12 On 11 April, between 80 and 100 representatives of local organisations attended the meeting convened by the IWA (Southall). Amongst the organisations represented were the Ealing Community Relations Council, the local branch of the Anti-Nazi League and a wide range of political, religious and community groups. The first three points proposed by the IWA secured general agreement from the meeting. There was considerable disagreement about the fourth proposal to ignore the National Front. It was said at the meeting that the Anti-Nazi League had already announced, in a broadcast by one of its officers, Mr Peter Hain, that there would be a demonstration on 23 April to oppose the National Front meeting. This may not actually have been true. We have been unable to trace such a broadcast (see paragraph 8.7). It was strongly argued at the meeting on 11 April that, even if the meeting agreed with the IWA proposal that the National Front rally should be ignored, a demonstration would go ahead anyway and that the community organisations should intervene in that demonstration and give the lead. Mr Sharma, however, argued that, since the police would ensure that National Front members were able to attend their meeting and were kept away from demonstrators, any confrontation which took place would be between the demonstrators and the police. He therefore argued that there should only be a peaceful protest in the form of closing down of businesses. Eventually, however, it was agreed that at 5 pm on Monday 23 April, there should be a mass, peaceful sit-in on all the approach roads to the Town Hall. It was explicitly recognised that those taking part in the sit-in would be arrested for obstruction of the highway and it was agreed at the meeting that those present would offer themselves peacefully for arrest.

2.13 Martyn Grubb, then principal Community Relations Officer of Ealing CRC, told the Enquiry: 'I thought that the original IWA plan of meeting the National Front with a wall of silence was a good one. But it was obvious from the mood of the meeting on 11 April that this position could not be held, since most people in the room wanted to demonstrate their opposition to the National Front. Vishnu (Sharma) had to alter the plan to include a peaceful sit-down on the roads leading to the Town Hall. Ealing Community Relations Council officially supported this strategy'. Mr Sharma commented: 'There was an almost unanimous feeling from the floor of the meeting that the National Front should not be allowed to meet in Southall — the whole community was angry. There was, however, some difference of opinion over the legality of trying to stop this, Chamber of Commerce arguing that the Council might be legally obliged to let the hall for election purposes. The keynote of the meeting was peaceful resistance. We knew that by blocking the roads leading to the Town Hall, we would lay ourselves open to arrest for obstruction of the highways. We were prepared to offer ourselves for arrest, without resistance, and this strategy was made clear to the police'.

2.14 The meeting set up a Co-ordinating Committee, consisting of representatives of the main organisations concerned. Vishnu Sharma was appointed convener. That committee subsequently issued a leaflet setting out the four points of protest: the petition calling on the Council to cancel the fascist meeting; the march on Sunday 22 April; the shut-down of businesses, public transport, shops and other workplaces in Southall from 1 pm on Monday 23 April; and a huge, *peaceful* sit-down protest, starting at 5 pm at Southall crossroads, on Monday 23 April. Approximately 25,000 leaflets and 1,000 window posters were issued by the Co-ordinating Committee to publicise these four points.

2.15 One of the main community groups, Southall Youth Movement (SYM), and a smaller group, the Indian Workers Front, did not attend the meeting on 11 April. Nor did they participate in the Co-ordinating Committee's preparations for the Sunday demonstration — the March for Unity and Peace as it became known. The SYM argued that it was too late by then to influence the Council's judgement, that the Council building would be closed and that there would be no one to receive the petition, and that therefore the march was liable to be exploited for election purposes by particular candidates. However, SYM members participated fully in the demonstration on 22 April.

2.16 On 11 April, John Beeston, President of Southall Chamber of Commerce, wrote to all members saying that '. . . the Police have assured us they will do everything in their power to stop damage or injury to persons and property near the Town Hall'. Jointly with the police he recommended closing of all shops by 4.30 pm, the boarding up of shopfronts and the removal, where possible, of 'Asian signs', presumably to avoid damage by National Front sympathisers attending the meeting.

2.17 On 12 April, the Co-ordinating Committee appointed representatives to liaise with the police over the arrangements for 22 and 23 April. On 13 April, Ealing Community Relations Council wrote to all Councillors of the London Borough of Ealing, asking them to urge the Leader of the Council to withdraw permission for the National Front meeting.

2.18 On 17 April, solicitors wrote to the town clerk of Ealing Borough Council on behalf of the Indian Workers Association, urging the Council to reverse its decision to allow the National Front to hold a meeting and asking what steps would be taken, if the meeting went ahead, to ensure that it was a genuinely public meeting. In particular, the IWA's solicitors informed the Council that about 100 IWA members had expressed an interest in attending the meeting and, at the appropriate time, questioning the speakers. They asked for an assurance from the Council and the police that these people would be admitted to the meeting. The Council's reply of 19 April repeated the Council's view that the meeting was a *bona fide* meeting within the terms of the Representation of the People Act and stated that admission by members of the public would be limited to 20. The IWA instructed their solicitors to advise on the possibility of applying for an injunction to oblige Ealing Council to withdraw permission for the election meeting. The solicitors, however, advised against such proceedings.

2.19 All the publicity issued by the Co-ordinating Committee for the demonstration on 23 April stressed that the protest was to be peaceful. In their letter of 13 April, for instance, Ealing CRC informed Councillors that 'The community in Southall will stage a *peaceful, sit-down* demonstration outside Southall Town Hall'. The letter continues: 'The IWA meeting stressed that this demonstration should be *peaceful* and people would sit down in the street. Any provocation with the police etc. should be avoided *at all costs*'. Not all the publicity concerning the plans for 23 April, however, laid a similar stress on the peaceful nature of the protest. The Anti-Nazi League issued a leaflet in English and Punjabi, headed 'Stop the Nazi Meeting', which called on people to support 'a massive demonstration outside Southall Town Hall to stop the rally, beginning at 5 pm'. A leaflet issued by Socialist Unity and their candidate in the Southall election, Tariq Ali, announced a 'picket' at 5 pm on 23 April at the Town Hall. *Socialist Worker* on 21 April used the slogan 'Stop the Nazi meeting' and 'Shut Down Southall', calling on people to assemble at Southall Town Hall on Monday at 5 pm. Other articles in the same issue of the newspaper, however, stated that the demonstration would be at 6 pm at Southall Town Hall. In addition, *Socialist Worker* called on all members of the Socialist Workers Party in London and the Home Counties to support the demonstration. Publicity issued by the Socialist Workers Party, Socialist Unity and the Anti-Nazi League does not seem to have used the word 'peaceful' at all. It was therefore possible for different interpretations to be placed on the plans for a sit-down demonstration outside Southall Town Hall. In the event, however, no sit-down took place.

2.20 On 17 April, representatives of the Co-ordinating Committee met the Southall police station commander, Chief Superintendent Dee, Chief Inspector Gosse (X Division Community Liaison Officer) and a representative from Scotland Yard. The police also invited SYM and other organisations not on the Co-ordinating Committee. The meeting was amiable and no objection was made by the police to the plans for a peaceful sit-down protest. Martyn Grubb states:

'There was no indication from the police side of any of the police tactics which were in fact used. In retrospect, it was ominous that Chief Superintendent Dee said that he would not be in charge on the day and this rendered the meeting useless. When I asked the Scotland Yard representative who he was, he said he was just a sergeant, so in fact liaison between the community and the police was meaningless.' Vishnu Sharma told the Enquiry: 'The police statement after 23 April, that we were to be allowed to demonstrate in three areas, is complete humbug. The police did not tell us before 23 April whether we were to be allowed to demonstrate or not. We had made it clear to them what our plans were and they had not said that these plans could not go ahead. At the meeting, our impression was that the Council were determined not to cancel the National Front meeting and that the police were helpless and simply had a duty to enforce the law. We had no idea that the whole of Southall centre would be encircled by the police. If they had told us that, we would have organised ourselves entirely differently.' By 22 April, however, responsibility had been transferred from Chief Superintendent Dee to Assistant Deputy Commissioner Helm, head of A8 (Public Order Division), Metropolitan Police.

2.21 On 18 April, the Co-ordinating Committee met and established an inner group of Vishnu Sharma, Martyn Grubb, Rev. Jim Parkinson, S. Pulley (Southall Trades Council) and Balwinder Singh Rana (Southall Anti-Nazi League). Three members of this group with Yinnon Ezra (Ealing CRC and Secretary, Southall Rights) secured an interview with Merlyn Rees, the then Home Secretary, on the occasion of his visit to Acton for an election meeting, on 19 April. The group wanted to explain to him their desire for a peaceful demonstration and that all leaders of the Southall community were prepared to accept arrest without resistance. Vishnu Sharma reported on the meeting: 'Merlyn Rees took an entirely legalistic view that he could not ban a public election meeting. Neither at this meeting nor at the earlier one with the police did anyone give a satisfactory reply as to whether we could sit down peacefully. Merlyn Rees was interested when we told him that police-public relations had not been too bad locally (although there were certain irritations) and that we did not want all this destroyed on 23 April. He promised to speak to Commissioner McNee that very night. Either he did not do this or McNee did not take his advice because on the day we did not see a "low profile" of police, as we had pleaded for.' Vishnu Sharma also told the Enquiry: 'In private talk some police have admitted that they could not cope with a mass sit-down. If there were 3,000 people sitting in the road, they would have needed 6,000 police to arrest us all. They did not want to have to arrest community leaders, churchmen and Sikh temple leaders.' Martyn Grubb explained: 'We wanted the police to know our plans at the highest level. We thought that Merlyn Rees would not want community leaders arrested and that he might ask the Chief Constable to avoid it, as, in fact, the Chief Constable of Devon and Cornwall did the next day.'

2.22 The day before the meeting with Mr Rees, Ealing CRC sent a telegram to the Prime Minister, Home Secretary and the Chairman of the Commission for Racial Equality stating that violence was feared if the National Front meeting went ahead, that community leaders would take part in a peaceful sit-down demonstration in the street and would accept arrest if the police cleared the way for the National Front.

2.23 On 23 April, the Home Secretary wrote to Sydney Bidwell MP stating that the local Council had no power to offer an alternative meeting room to the National Front candidate. Mr Rees went on to say: 'The policing arrangements for this meeting will be an operational matter for the Commissioner and I have no power to intervene or give directions. I am in no doubt though that appropriate measures will be taken to preserve public order and prevent breaches of the peace.'

The March for Unity and Peace: Sunday 22 April

2.24 Police were patrolling Southall from early in the morning of 22 April. Reg Taylor, Chairman West London Co-ordinating Committee TGWU, stated: 'I had to attend a union meeting on Sunday 22 April at the TGWU offices in South Road and I had got there a bit early about 9.50 am. There was police activity even at that early hour, around the Town Hall and on five separate occasions I was asked by police (including two plain-clothes officers) what I was doing there, who was going to be present at the meeting etc. The meeting was not related to the demonstration and I did not think it was any of their business.'

2.25 The demonstration assembled in the car park at the back of the Dominion Cinema in Featherstone Road at 1 pm. Accounts vary as to how many people were on the march, but it probably grew from about 3,000 at the beginning to about 5,000 by the time it reached Ealing. The Commissioner of the Metropolitan Police estimated the number of police deployed in the march to be in the region of 1,200. The marchers, once on their way to Ealing Borough Town Hall, occupied the left-hand side of the highway, marching some five abreast with a single file of policemen on either side. The leaders, who included Rev. Jim Parkinson, Vishnu Sharma, Sydney Bidwell MP, and the leader of the Labour opposition on the Borough Council, Michael Elliott, stressed at the outset that the marchers were to adhere strictly to the principle of peaceful protest. The front of the march, which was accompanied by Chief Superintendent Dee and, apparently, police drawn from the Southall force was a reasonably amicable and lightly policed affair.

2.26 By contrast, the main body of the march was under the supervision of a far larger number of police commanded by the A8 division of Scotland Yard. The *Midweek Gazette* (Tuesday edition of the local newspaper, the *Ealing Gazette*) made the 'massive security operation' by the police the centre-piece of its report, with an accompanying photograph of two lines of police on either side of the marchers.

2.27 Many marchers have complained about the heavy density of police and the presence of mounted police at the assembly point in the Dominion Car Park. The first two arrests (for obstructing the police) occurred as the march was passing Southall police station (situated just east of the Town Hall on High Street). A steward, John Knight, was himself one of those arrested, but was subsequently acquitted of the charge of obstruction at the magistrates court. The police case was that he had been trying to stop the march, but the defendant argued that he had simply been trying to bring some order into the procession, by trying to stop the demonstrators shouting at the police and the police abusing the demonstrators. He had been arrested as he tried to run up to the front of the march to discuss this with Sydney Bidwell. The Chief Inspector in this case told the Court that he feared that the march would attack both the Town Hall and the police station, although it had been advertised as a peaceful march. Stewards halted the march immediately after the arrests and ordered the demonstrators to sit down in the road in protest. They did so and remained there seated until bail was granted to the two defendants. The march then resumed.

2.28 According to the accounts of several participants, the march was poorly organised and stewarded. Mr Sydney Bidwell stated in the House of Commons (Hansard 25 May 1979) that: 'That march became something of a shambles . . . elements in that supposedly peaceful anti-National Front march helped to spoil an effective, peaceful demonstration by dragging their feet, halting the march and in some respects provoking the police during its early stages'. Mr Bidwell himself admits, however, that, being at the front of the march, he was unable to find out exactly what was going on further back. He does not seem to have appreciated the reason for the delay.

2.29 Other witnesses complained of unnecessary police force and some harassment. Councillor Cotter noted: 'The police presence was heavy but no worse than on other marches I've been on. I could not see reasons for the arrests. They just seemed to be for shouting and running in and out of the march. Those arrested were not going quietly. There were three or four police manhandling one person and using what seemed excessive force. They were not particular how they got people into the vans. There were two young policemen near me, who seemed very much on edge. They must have been warned that there would be a lot of trouble'. The marchers arrested, apparently, were those who wanted to stop marching and hold a protest. Just such an arrest occurred when the marchers concerned had passed under the Iron Bridge and reached Hanwell, with the effect of dividing the march into two and sometimes more distinct groups. The person arrested was over half-way back along the march and the front section continued on its way to Ealing, apparently unaware that the marchers behind had once again sat down in protest at this latest arrest. Vishnu Sharma stated: 'There were two arrests at the start of the march . . . I went to discuss it with the police since I knew that there was a strong likelihood of further disorder and of the march not proceeding at all because of indignation at the arrests. The senior police officer there told me not to intervene and that I myself could be arrested. I thought that this seemed to be a quite arbitrary use of the power of arrest and that the police officer showed that he had no idea of keeping a march under control and orderly, if he was so eager to arrest its leaders'. A participant, Jeanette Thomas, commented: 'The march passed a group of National Front youths, wearing swastikas etc., who started shouting and swearing at us, "Bloody blacks go home" and other racial abuse. One of the black kids in the demonstration got really upset and started swearing back and shaking his fist. The police grabbed him but did not do anything to the boys on the other side of the road, even when one of them drew a knife'. Several witnesses remarked on the enormous numbers of police at Ealing Town Hall where the petition was handed in, with police filling every step up to the hall. Mr Bhatia states: 'I could not understand why there were so many police there at all as no trouble was expected and the presence of mounted police was quite uncalled-for . . . the police were being very objectionable. Just pulling people out of the procession for no reason except that they might have stepped slightly out of line. I saw two people arrested being hit by the police and one having his head pushed into the side of the police van'.

2.30 The march was reported in the local newspaper, but was covered in the national press only by the *Morning Star.* Participants frequently contrasted the police tactics employed on Sunday with those used in the first March of Peace and Unity (June 1976) in protest at the killing of Gurdip Singh Chaggar. Then the police were said to have been exceedingly co-operative, to have closed off the main roads, and to have been relatively little in evidence during the march.

2.31 The Home Secretary's Memorandum on the events of 22/23 April (appendix 2) attributes the difficulties of the Sunday march to two causes. The march was disorganised, and there was obvious friction between different organisations. The evidence available suggests that inadequate organisation and poor stewarding was compounded by police tactics, such as the presence of mounted police at the assembly point and their use in one particular incident when they went through the march in order to apprehend a demonstrator who had 'broken ranks'. Although the Southall Youth Movement had disagreed with the plan to hold the march, 'friction' between different groups on the march does not account for the hostility between marchers and the police, nor for the arrests which took place.

Monday 23 April

2.32 Although the demonstration outside the Town Hall was not due to take place until 5 pm and a separate Southall Youth Movement picket not due to begin until 3 pm, both the police and some demonstrators began to arrive in Southall early in the morning. A police officer from the Special Patrol Group in Leytonstone told the court on 6 November that his group had been in Southall since 10 am on Monday 23 April. One member of Ealing Socialist Workers

Party, who was also active in the Anti-Nazi League, told the Enquiry that she and others arrived in Southall at about 10 am on Monday 23 April, in a lorry loaded with placards, badges and other ANL material. They parked outside 6 Park View Road, which they understood was to be the distribution point and took the badges and other material inside. It has also been reported that SPG vans were present from early in the morning to keep an eye on 6 Park View Road, premises occupied by a local community group called Peoples Unite.

2.33 By about 12.30 pm police were stationed outside the Town Hall. By that time also, groups of young people were clustered on the pavement outside the Three Horse Shoes pub, on the corner of High Street and South Road, immediately opposite the Town Hall. Representatives of the legal advice centre, Southall Rights, advised them to keep moving.

2.34 By 1 pm most of the shops and business premises in the central part of the town had closed down. At about the same time, workers from a number of different local places of employment left work and came to Southall.

2.35 The Southall Youth Movement (which had not taken part in the Co-ordinating Committee's plans for a sit-down demonstration later that afternoon) met on Monday morning to consider the likely course of events. Rumours had been circulating that the police either had already smuggled, or might attempt to smuggle, National Front members into the Town Hall well before the advertised time of the meeting; indeed, one rumour had it that a coach containing people in civilian clothes with a police escort had been seen on the M4 motorway in the small hours of 23 April. It was decided by the SYM to establish a picket on the opposite side of the road to the Town Hall in order to ensure that no one was admitted to the National Front meeting before the scheduled time for the demonstration, 5 pm. At about 12.30 pm, some 30 or 40 members of the SYM began to walk from their offices south of the railway bridge (on Featherstone Road) northwards to the town centre.

2.36 This departure of the SYM was earlier than had been notified to the police. The Police Community Liaison Officer, Chief Inspector Derek Gosse, had visited the SYM premises in the week preceding 23 April and was told then that the SYM would begin a peaceful picket opposite the Town Hall as from 3 pm. However, since Chief Inspector Gosse accepted the 3 pm time without objection, it was not thought unreasonable to revise the starting time and inform him as soon as he could be found. Balraj Purewal records: 'There was no question of the police being taken by surprise by our tactics. We have the closest of liaison with the police'.

2.37 The group of SYM members, now perhaps some 50 in all and carrying the banner of the organisation, proceeded northwards. They were outside the DHSS office (before reaching the railway) when a police van going south passed them, did a U-turn, and returned to draw up alongside the group. Southall-based

31

policemen got out, and attempted to arrest one member of the group, alleging that a warrant existed for his arrest in respect of non-attendance at court the previous week for failure to pay a fine. The police were asked for the warrant, but said they did not have it with them and did not need to show it. There was considerable anger at this, something of a scuffle, and another member of the group was promptly arrested. In fact, the police did not need to be in possession of the warrant at the moment of arrest although SYM did not know this at the time. Despite this, the group continued northwards until they reached the crossroads and the Town Hall.

2.38 Here, they endeavoured to stand on the pavement opposite the Town Hall. However, they were not permitted to do this by the police on duty there, nor to stand anywhere within the vicinity of the Town Hall. Some arrests took place. Other supporters were joining the original group as it progressed. The group grew to about 200 and was split into smaller sections. At the same time, police strength was rapidly augmented, with possibly 100 officers round the Town Hall and other concentrations on the four main highways. No information was given to the demonstrators as to where they might stand without attracting police intervention.

2.39 At various stages, leading representatives of the demonstrators endeavoured to reach Mr Gosse to arrange some agreement about the maintenance of the picket. The first visit to Southall Police Station by two leading members of the SYM at about 1.15 pm was fruitless since it proved impossible to find Mr Gosse. A second visit by three SYM members was more successful. After discussion, Mr Gosse gave permission for the SYM to mount a picket outside the Town Hall. The SYM leaders then returned to the junction and instructed their supporters to form a single file along the pavement. A senior officer of the police intervened, ordering them to move on. The SYM representatives explained that Mr Gosse had given them permission to maintain a picket but the police officer is said to have replied: 'Who the fuck's Gosse! I am in charge here. Move!'

2.40 A third visit to the police station took place a little later, by a group including both SYM members and Yinnon Ezra of Ealing Community Relations Council. The deputation was redirected to Commander Richardson, head of X division and joint chairman of the ECRC police liaison committee, outside the Town Hall. Mr Ezra records what happened: 'I explained to him that the police were using very heavy tactics, and some 40 people, most of whom were SYM members, had been arrested. He was not really wanting to discuss this, and gave me all the usual remarks about "doing their duty" etc'. Other members of the party put the same points. Another member of the group states: 'We also asked him to let us try and control our own people. Most of us were on the borders of panic' (due to worries about the worsening situation). The party decided to go to see Balraj Purewal on the Broadway to collect the latest figures on arrests, and Commander Richardson agreed to remain where he was until they returned. But while they were on their way, a major police effort began to clear the area and they were unable to return to Commander Richardson.

2.41 The Co-ordinating Committee had agreed to meet at Southall Rights Centre at about 1 pm. By the time they met, however, the events referred to outside the Town Hall were already taking place. Because of the arrests which were being made, Southall Rights required their space to organise legal advice for defendants, so the meeting of the Co-ordinating Committee was transferred to the offices of the National Association of Asian Youth at 46 High Street. Both Vishnu Sharma and the Chief Steward, Balwinder Singh Rana, were delayed in arriving. A substitute, Peter Alexander, was therefore nominated to replace Balwinder Singh Rana as Chief Steward until his arrival. Also attending the meeting were Martyn Grubb, Rev. Jim Parkinson and Rev. Roy Smith.

2.42 According to all participants in the meeting, the main discussion was about how to ensure that the demonstration would be peaceful and orderly, and all present were warned not to carry anything about them which might be construed as an offensive weapon. Stewards were appointed, including four senior stewards for the four main roads converging at the Town Hall: Paul Croft for Uxbridge Road West; Clarence Baker for Uxbridge Road East; Eve Turner for Lady Margaret Road; and John Knight for South Road. Eve Turner described the function of the stewards as 'to tell people of their rights, to observe police behaviour, to keep a track of any people arrested and to keep in touch with Southall Rights'. They were thus assigned no active organising role. Red arm bands were distributed to the stewards. It was agreed that the communications centre for the demonstration would be 46 High Street. Legal advice would be available at Southall Rights a few doors away. A first aid centre with a doctor and ambulance man was established at Peoples Unite at 6 Park View Road, about five minutes away from Southall Rights and the National Association of Asian Youth, to the north of Uxbridge Road. The loudhailers promised by the Indian Workers Association had not arrived and the only one available at that time was with Clarence Baker. The members of the Co-ordinating Committee therefore agreed that they would remain close to the street loud-speaker which had been set up above the shops on the opposite side of the road to the Town Hall.

2.43 Outside, others were seeking to assemble at the town centre. At the Liberty cinema on the western side of South Road, a group of Asian youths were giving out leaflets, when the police attempted to move them on on the grounds that they were obstructing the highway. Mohammed Asghar, Co-ordinator of Southall Rights, commented: 'I saw a group of youths on South Road, by the bus stops, being quite encircled by the police so that they could not move anywhere. The boys were shouting but did not appear to be using any physical violence'. Phil Cohen, a journalist, came to the Town Hall at about 1.30 pm after interviewing Sydney Bidwell. He says: 'There were a number of arrests and the police seemed to be using exceptional force in collaring people and literally dragging them away. I discussed the number of arrests with a TV reporter at the junction with the Broadway, then called the office and confirmed an ugly situation was developing. There was already this air of the police involved in a major operation with blanket policing the operative method'. The two Asian youths carrying the SYM banner were arrested for what seemed to be that reason only. The accounts given later in court by both police and defence suggest that there were some 200 demonstrators milling across the road and that many people were being pushed and shoved in a confused melee. The failure of the police to advise the demonstrators as to where they could peacefully demonstrate, together with the lack of unity in the police command, increased the confusion and frustration among the demonstrators.

2.44 With reinforcements from the eastern sector of High Street (where the police station was located), the police began a sustained drive to clear the area. People were pushed forcibly outwards from the junction, along the four main highways. The police apparently issued no warning or explanation of their intentions. At the same time as clearing the pavement area in the centre, the police endeavoured to keep the streets open to traffic. The Chief Steward and others appealed for calm. Surprisingly, here and elsewhere during the demonstration, the police made no effort to use the stewards of the demonstration to assist them in controlling the crowd. Balwinder Singh Rana, Chief Steward, said that he went over to where the police were clearing demonstrators from the area and 'tried to calm the situation down. I told a Chief Inspector that I was the Chief Steward and I will ask the people to move'. He was given no opportunity to do so, and '. . . suddenly policeman started grabbing everyone and started arresting them'. With fairly rough police pushing, inevitably tempers were frayed and further arrests took place.

2.45 Thereafter, for the rest of the day, there was no possibility of a single demonstration nor of any effective unified leadership of the demonstrators. By 4 pm access to both Southall Rights and the communication centre at 46 High Street was denied by the police, who prevented people entering the premises but not from leaving. Most people found it impossible to reach the two offices as late as 8.30 pm that evening. John Witzenfeld, a solicitor, was however, after negotiation, permitted to cross the police cordon on Uxbridge Road (that is, the eastern end of High Street) and, with a police escort, go to Southall Rights just before 6 pm. Even local leadership was difficult to maintain since the police appeared to arrest first those who were stewards; for example, three Peoples Unite stewards had been arrested very early in the day (see paragraph 2.97).

2.46 By about 4 pm, therefore, police cordons had been established at four points to the north, south, west and east of the crossroads on which the Town Hall is situated. Members of the public, including would-be demonstrators, were forced to congregate in groups outside those cordons. There is clear evidence that many of those caught in the crowds were residents endeavouring to return to their homes. D.S. Ghiani, former President of the IWA, found that as early as

3 pm there were between 100 and 200 people trapped near the railway station unable to go home who congregated round himself and other known leaders. Mr Dhesi, who lives within the cordoned area, was arrested when he protested that he wanted to go home. In the main the central area was kept empty of all but police. Phil Cohen remembered: 'The fact that police appeared to be defending the Town Hall like a fortress probably exaggerated the desire to breach it, as a symbolic protest . . . The police, by their vast numbers and high visibility had already assumed the role of allies of the fascists in the eyes of the demonstrators . . . The Town Hall was sealed off from all four directions giving Southall the appearance and face of a ghost town. An eerie silence descended on the area around the Town Hall'. Dilbagh Chana makes the point: 'The Union Jack had been flying over the Town Hall all day, which I thought was a bit unfortunate, considering the way in which it is used by the National Front. I had asked the staff there if they could not put up an English flag instead but they said they always did this on St George's Day. I think that the clearing of the roads was the main source of the disorder, since it increased the tension. From 2 pm to 7.30 pm, there was nothing to do. Frustrations were building up and there was no target but the police. If people had been allowed to demonstrate near the Town Hall, there would have been a lot of noise but little real trouble'.

2.47 We now turn to examine in some detail events in the three areas in which the police and would-be demonstrators were concentrated: the Broadway and Uxbridge Road West; Uxbridge Road East; and South Road. In reading the following sections, it should be borne in mind that events were taking place simultaneously in different parts of the area and that events in one place may have influenced those in another.

The Broadway and Uxbridge Road West

2.48 By about 3.15 pm a group of SYM members were among a crowd of people being moved westward by the police along the Broadway. Evidence was given by police officers at the trial of Aulak and others that they formed a north-south cordon across the Broadway in an attempt to clear the crossroads outside the Town Hall of demonstrators whom they feared would stage a sit-down. Mr Aulak was pulled out of the crowd by two policemen for apparently no reason. He had a hand bandaged after an earlier accident with a glass. One of his arresting officers deliberately squeezed the wound and blood was seen to flow from it. The president of SYM, Gurmail Brard, went to protest at this conduct and was promptly arrested at the same time. Four other members of SYM were arrested at the same time. Mr Aulak was later acquitted on three charges of assault and one of threatening behaviour. Mr Brard was also acquitted. Only two of the six were convicted. The magistrate accepted that there was doubt over the veracity of the prosecution evidence given in all by 13 officers. He commented: 'The officers who gave evidence against Mr Aulak gave clear and specific accounts of what they saw him do. These included plain discrepancies which were con-

35

tradicted by Mr Aulak but without the discrepancies. Mr Aulak's own evidence was supported in part by medical evidence and in later stages by some of his co-defendants.

'Several witnesses made statements which we have no grounds to believe were conspired and which described violence by the police in the moments when the police say they were restraining Mr Aulak. The words 'restraint' and 'restraining' have been used so often in this case they are worthy of pause. They can mean the lawful quelling of a prisoner, whether arrested lawfully or unlawfully. But they can also mean the quelling of a prisoner by means which have passed from the lawful to the unlawful. What they may mean is a measure of retaliation. Both meanings have been vigorously canvassed here.

'The scene in Southall on 23 April 1979 was a battleground of police and demonstrators. The demonstrators were incensed and the police, as they well needed to be, were in a near-military disposition. There were grave tensions. In such a crowd there is plain leeway for confusion. There is plain leeway for mistake and there is plain leeway on both sides for anger and revenge.'

2.49 The police cordon moved westward and halted at the junction between Broadway and Greenford Avenue, leaving open Herbert Road to the south. At the same time, within the area held by the police, side roads were sealed off, so that people could not easily enter or leave the cordoned-off area. However, the police endeavoured to keep the roads open to traffic, holding demonstrators on the pavements.

2.50 At about 3.30 pm a number of demonstrators attempted to get on to a No.207 bus on scheduled service down the Uxbridge Road towards Ealing. Some of those who got onto the bus had realised that this was the only way to get through the cordon to the Town Hall. Others simply wanted to get out of the situation which was developing on the Broadway, or to get home along the Uxbridge Road to the east. The double-decker bus stopped at the last bus stop before the police line of control. The crowds were numerous on both sides of the road. There was a rush of demonstrators onto the bus. In court, a police inspector estimated that 60 people had got onto the bus, although the bus driver and conductor estimated that there were about 20 people. Some climbed to the upper deck and the police rushed on board. The police began to throw people off the bus. The driver gave evidence that the bus was immobilised by a switch outside, either by the police or someone else. One of the demonstrators on the top deck started to kick the bus windows out. London Transport later estimated the damage caused at £260.

2.51 One of those arrested, Mr Rihal, who was alleged to have kicked in bus windows and struggled with police officers, stated that he had not even got on the bus with the demonstrators at the Broadway, but had been a passenger since Hayes. He had three witnesses to the fact that he had been that afternoon to pick up his wages and P45 from his previous employer in Hayes, since he was changing jobs. He said that he had not wanted to be involved in the demonstration, since his wife was ill at home, having just come out of hospital, and he had to look after her. He was not believed and, in spite of having no previous convictions, was sentenced to three months' prison.

2.52 Other police broke from the police cordons to pursue those who had been ejected from the bus, chasing them into the crowd. Fighting broke out; bricks, stones and dustbin lids were thrown and there were further arrests. Balraj Purewal states: 'There were individuals trying to escape the police and officers running after them, tackling them and, when they were on the ground, kicking them. People tried to rescue them, so the fight spread. The cordon broke and it was a complete battleground'. This was the cue for the police to cut off the Broadway entirely. They halted any remaining traffic and the cordon pushed further westwards. The police ordered the bus onwards, carrying some of those arrested. Many of those in the crowd fled down Herbert Road and a connecting alley to South Road. Others took refuge in Greenford Avenue.

2.53 The crowd was now able to spread across the road freely. The police line advanced in stages westwards. A big advance was made at about 4.30 pm to cover the window of the Co-op store when it was broken by someone in the crowd. By 5.30 pm, both Greenford Avenue and Herbert Road were closed and by 6 pm St George's Avenue was shut off. At the same time, a second police cordon holding riot shields was set up west of the crowd, which, for a time, permitted people to enter the area between the cordons but not to leave it. Dilbagh Chana, Chairman of Ealing CRC, states: 'All the side roads were blocked except Alexandra Avenue. I sensed danger although there was nothing happening then. I thought it would only need that line of officers nearest the Town Hall with shields to move up and someone in the crowd to do something silly, like throw a bottle and the police horses would move in and fighting would break out . . . I thought this second cordon was unnecessary and that if they wanted people to move away they should open up the side roads'. For most of the evening, the only exit from this area was Alexandra Avenue giving access to Lady Margaret Road (north of Shackleton Road where police controls operated) and ultimately to Uxbridge Road East. However, as the main cordon moved westwards along Broadway, the other cordon, west of the crowd, was moving eastwards through the early evening, producing increasing pressure on the crowd between. The crowd, it should be noted, was not entirely composed of intending demonstrators. Many present were seeking to return from work to their homes, now beyond the police lines. Presumably the police intended, by the act of compression, to induce people to leave the area although it was never made clear to them by loudspeaker or otherwise how they could do so. Perhaps these compression tactics were also to prevent stone-throwing and make throwers more easily identifiable. The pressure became even more severe when Alexandra Avenue was encompassed by the western cordon. For a short time, several hundred people were held in a very narrow area. Rev. Dr D.L.E. Bronnert, Vicar of St John's told us: 'Throughout the evening I was in no danger from any section of the public (though the police were in danger from some sections of the public). I saw cans and bricks thrown. But it is also true that on a number of occasions, especially in the Broadway area, I felt in danger from the police; to stand in the middle of two serried ranks of police advancing towards each other is not a pleasant experience'. Malcolm Imray stood on the Broadway from about 5 pm to 6.30 pm. 'Most of that time the picket was more or less silent, apart from occasional speeches from Asian leaders and sporadic chanting. From time to time, the police would, apparently without reason, decide to push back sections of the picket from the pavement into the road in front — sometimes using riot shields as weapons. Riot shields were used in this way several times — only once did I see stone-throwing which would justify their use as protection.'

2.54 The police lines were held at various points on Broadway up to 7.30 pm or 8 pm. However, before that time, there were various other incidents. A little after 6.30 pm apparently after a push from the crowd towards them the police advanced forcefully from the east and some panic was engendered in the crowd. There was a sit-down and the police halted their drive. The sit-down — in rather wet and cold conditions — was peaceful, but came to an end after about 20 minutes. Shortly afterwards, the windows of the Safeway store were broken and the police moved to include the shop within the cordon. A few shop windows were broken in the Broadway. Some were undoubtedly broken deliberately by members of the crowd. Both Rev. Bronnert and the Bishop of Willesden state, however, that they saw accidental cracks in windows caused by pressure from the crowd rather than by missiles. A second sit-down followed to prevent this advance.

2.55 Peter Baker states that: 'At about 7.30 the good humour of the crowd on the Broadway was shattered . . . a roar went through the crowd, emanating from the rear. People turned and looked westwards down the street. I saw, to my amazement, a coach being driven fast straight into the back of the crowd. It was a private coach, an ordinary 30-40 seat char-a-banc. At a cautious estimate, I would put the speed of it at 15 mph, which is murderous when it is being driven into a crowd . . . How no-one was killed I just don't know . . . The coach had a civilian driver and a uniformed police officer standing beside him'. Martyn Grubb relates: 'A coach suddenly appeared, driving fast (from the west). I would say at about 25-30 mph straight at us'. The reaction of the crowd was first fear for their safety and then anger. Martyn Grubb said: 'Everyone got out of the way and I did also. If I had not done so, the coach would have run over me. I actually touched the coach as it went by . . . The crowd was very angry and several people started waving their fists at the police in the cordon, protesting that it was extremely dangerous to drive a coach like that at a crowd'. Peter Baker continued: 'The crowd was furious. Certainly, at this stage, some objects were thrown at it and the rear window was shattered as it went through the cordon. It was not damaged before it reached the crowd . . . It was a very dangerous piece of driving which inflamed and stunned the crowd'. Martyn

Grubb noticed the broken rear window and was told by an inspector standing near to him in the cordon that: 'The coach had been attacked by a fire-bomb and how could you expect the driver to do anything else other than get away by driving through the crowd?' Several witnesses have confirmed that a small flare or explosive charge, causing a flame three or four feet high for a few seconds, was thrown at the coach and flared up on the road, causing no damage to the coach or police, though several demonstrators had to jump out of the way. The passage of the bus through the crowd, which could have been unplanned, was followed by forays by police transit vans which were clearly part of a deliberate policy. Peter Baker said: 'Then from the back again a blue police transit van charged through at the same sort of speed, did a U-turn in front of the police cordon and waited there, ringing a bell. A second followed and did exactly the same thing. The two then drove westward through the crowd just in front of the kerb on either side of the street at such a speed that people had to jump for their lives on to the pavements. I was so angry as I had never seen anything like it in my life. By that time, the police inside the vans had identified one or two of those who had thrown bricks. The vans would squeal to a halt, police would rush out of the back, seize people, throw them in and drive off. A third van drove up, which was more heavily loaded. The policemen who got who out of this third one had plastic riot shields. The police swooped to seize several people.

'There was terrific anger among the crowd by this time and one or two people . . . started to smash shop windows . . . Throughout the events, the police cordon had stood still, good-humouredly maintaining a show of force. In my view, it was doing the correct thing. Nobody was going to penetrate the police line and nobody tried to. The cordon did not once charge the crowd and no missiles were thrown at it that I saw. Missiles that were thrown were reserved exclusively for the vans. People were provoked by the vicious driving. They threw missiles (mainly milk bottles, picked up on the spur of the moment) . . . I have never seen police behave this way in my life and I hope I never see such a thing again.'

One witness admitted to us that he had been provoked by the police action. 'There were three vans going up and down the road very fast, acting as sort of bait. Someone would throw something and the van would stop and pick on someone, not necessarily the person responsible. They had riot shields and truncheons. Someone from the church told me off for throwing stones but I felt I'd been provoked by their behaviour . . . we felt they had declared war on us.'

2.56 The incident with the police coach marked the beginning of what many observers considered to be the breakdown in police discipline on the Broadway. Councillor Brian Hudson reports: 'At about the time of the NF meeting the two further cordons withdrew. There were some senior police officers on the roof of the big supermarket there, with their walkie-talkie radios. Two green SPG vans came down from the Hayes end of the Broadway. They were 15 cwt vans going very fast (I'd say 40+ mph) and charging into the crowd, so that people had to scatter. There had been a bloke near me before with a bad bow-leg and it was lucky that he happened to be on the pavement when they came charging through. They turned around and did a second or maybe third run, considerably faster, since the street was now clear. By the second run, the people were throwing things at the vans, just litter not deliberately-brought missiles . . . People were frightened and shocked. I think the vans were directed by the senior officers on the supermarket. The vans were stopping in the Broadway and snatching people. They just went into a group and grabbed a few. There could not have been any arrestable offence committed at the time, although I could not say if there had been earlier.

'I saw one Asian boy, in particular, not struggling, just held by the back of the collar; the officer had a riot shield on his other arm and as he pulled the van door open he smashed the youth's face into it and shouted "Get in there, you black bastard!" It was all quite unnecessary since the boy was quiet. I was trying to get the officer's number when I was hit by a riot shield in my face, quite unnecessarily since I was in nobody's way . . .

'It all seemed quite planned, for instance, the vans hold about twelve but had only five police in them, who each arrested five youths.'

Father Thomas Lloyd, a Catholic priest, was convicted of obstruction. He got out of the way of the police vehicle, which was being pelted with small pebbles or gravel. He said, however: 'Though no bricks or larger missiles were thrown I was nevertheless nervous about my eyes (I wear glasses). I was then grabbed from behind by police, my arms twisted behind my back and I was pushed through the police cordon. I cannot see how I could have been obstructing when I was not facing the cordon at the time I was arrested and had no intention of breaking through the cordon. My arrest was not violent except for one or two policemen who kicked me as I went through their line'.

2.57 Just after 8 pm, Martin Brice, reporter for the *Ealing Gazette,* walked from the Park. He felt that tension was relaxing and the demonstration effectively over. He walked through the police cordon into the Broadway. 'I saw two SPG vans driving towards me, quite quickly. They stopped in the middle of the road and about 20 policemen got out. They charged across the road towards a group of people on the south footway. They chased these people down a road. I was rather surprised at the ferocity of the charge, which was out of touch with the atmosphere in the Broadway at that time. It amounted to a sudden escalation of the violence, I thought. When the officers had all returned to the van from this chase, one ran towards two Asian youths walking towards him. He shouted very loudly: "Go home". They ignored him and continued to walk along the Broadway. Just as they turned a corner to go down a side street the officer shouted again, "Go home" and ran to them, grabbed them by the scruff of the neck and banged their heads together, then shoved them very hard indeed, causing them to slip a few paces. They kept walking down the side road, then the officer stood watching them for a few seconds and then ran up behind them again and pushed them very hard in the back of their necks and shouted "Go home". They continued to walk along the road. I was quite unnerved by the severity of the police action. I had seen a totally unprovoked attack on two youngsters.' The reporter thought that he would be safer behind the police cordon and moved off towards it. He had walked a little way when two SPG vans pulled up and charged at a group of about eight youths on the same side of the street as he was walking. 'All I can remember of this incident is suddenly realising that about 20 police were charging towards me with their truncheons in their hands. It was perfectly obvious that anyone caught by the SPG would get very rough treatment indeed – and my press card would make very little impression on them. I ran for my life back up the Broadway and ducked into the doorway of the petrol station . . . I walked over to join the police sheltering under the canopy. I felt they would offer some protection from the SPG. They had moved forward onto the footway and were saying things like "What do those blokes think they are doing?"

'I had just walked up the Broadway and seen no trouble at all. Why were the SPG running around with their batons drawn? . . . I was astonished by their brutality. I can understand a young and inexperienced constable losing his temper during a demonstration. But the SPG are supposed to be highly trained and experienced officers. What I saw of their behaviour after the demonstration reminds me more of a gang of drunken hooligans.'

2.58 Paul Croft states: 'At about 8 pm, the police were issued with riot shields and 10-20 came through the cordon towards the crowd. People moved away instinctively, but the police pushed and charged people away, hitting some in the back with their riot shields, telling us to "Go home" and "piss off". Martyn (Grubb) sat down in protest. When I saw him, I did too, but the police just picked us up. Martyn was dragged along the street and I was put into a green police van . . . An officer asked me what I was doing there. I told him "I don't know if you don't!" He just told me to get out and kicked me up the backside . . .'

2.59 Jack Dromey, Transport and General Workers Union Officer, was on the Broadway about 8.15 pm. 'I must say that I have never seen such unrestrained violence against demonstrators nor such hatred on both sides. The SPG vans were making stupid forays into the crowd, turning round and coming back. Moving the cordon forward might have cooled the situation but this was just insane . . . The SPG started running down the pavement. There was abuse from the kids and the police suddenly pushed a dozen of them into a shop window very hard with their riot shields. The kids naturally retaliated. I spoke to a senior officer and said that what they had just done was insane. He just said "It is what they deserve" . . . I was on the Broadway for about half an hour and there was a stone thrown at the police about every ten minutes except when the vans came through, when there were far more stones thrown. The SPG were just running wild and in a far more unrestrained manner than at Grunwick. Their senior officers were sanctioning what took place and even taking part themselves in the melee . . . It was a very messy operation. At Grunwick the SPG had been heavy, but acted with a clear purpose although naturally, I did not agree with that purpose. But these operations were just pointless.'

2.60 Another witness, Gavin Hibbs, describes this: 'Suddenly there was a big rush of Asian kids pushing down Alexandra Avenue to get away from the Broadway. This happened twice and on the second time, I ran in front of it . . . In about the second house along there was an Indian woman standing in her garden inviting people in to shelter. I went in . . . three SPG officers pulled me out by my coat and pushed me in the back. I was told to go down the Broadway, so I offered no resistance and we had decided to leave because of the violence. There were three police coming down the road with riot shields. One punched me with his fist in the stomach as I passed and said "That is what bastards like you deserve". I was shocked and badly winded. Then the second one hit with the side of his riot shield, grazing my arm. The third one went to hit me with his shield, but I managed to fend it off.'

2.61 The crowd fled into Northcote Avenue and Saxon Road to the north, and Beechcroft Avenue to the south (Saxon Road is a cul-de-sac and Beechcroft Avenue leads into Orchard Avenue, from which the only normal exit is Herbert Road, at this time cordoned by the police). Councillor Bob Lewis noted: 'The SPG arrived about 7-7.15 pm. There were small groups of police coming down the road, deliberately provoking people. They were pushing people with riot shields and then when they said "Don't push me" they would arrest them. If you did not go faster than you were already walking, you got arrested. The SPG seemed quite out of control. There were a lot of people demonstrating who would not normally demonstrate and they seemed to be trying to make it so that they would not again.' Mrs Eileen Monaghan stood on the Broadway with her three children: 'Suddenly the cordon began to move westwards and the police charged with batons drawn. They hit a group of 5-10 people who were just standing there, over the head. I remember one particular incident. A young Indian gentleman, dressed very smartly in a business suit, was just standing on the pavement with his hands in his pockets. As the police charged, he was told to move and hit on the back of the head before being given a chance to do so. His glasses fell and he caught them just in time to save them from being broken. The police continued to belt people like cattle. He could not have been throwing anything. He had just been watching. His hands were in his pockets . . . We were all frightened. It could have been anybody. What disturbed me most was the fact that police were hitting people over the head with truncheons. I had always understood that they were to be used only to hit the shoulder.'

2.62 Colin Robins noted: 'There were windows being broken but no looting of the shops. The police seemed to be doing nothing about the young Asian kids who were breaking the windows . . . Lots of the people there were respectable, elderly Sikhs and their wives who were just watching . . . There were elderly Sikhs trying to restore order and shouting at the kids to stop, which they did.

It was only a minority of them doing it anyway. Whenever anything was thrown at the police, the cordon moved further forward but no arrests seemed to be made.' After a police van had been stoned there was a big push forward by the police and he ran into an Asian lady's house for shelter. 'I came out onto the street . . . the officer winded me by punching me in the stomach and then kneed me in the back. Another policeman punched me in the side by the kidneys . . . in that area they seemed to be going for white ANL people rather than Asians, although any stone throwing was being done by Asians there . . . On the Broadway, while I was there the atmosphere was fairly restrained until the incident with the bus and the bomb, when the police just seemed to panic. I was really taken aback to be attacked, since I had done everything that the police asked me to. They just seemed to be seeking revenge.'

2.63 Paul Croft's verdict was: 'Overall my impression was that the police were in total control of the situation from about 1 pm, while the demonstrators became more and more demoralised and depressed. None of the incidents I saw compared with the level of brutality on the part of the police, in pushing innocents and treating all with general disrespect. I was not at all surprised to hear of the death of Blair Peach, given the violence that I had seen.' The coach incident was, he thought, 'symptomatic of police over-reaction throughout. The scene was set by the police attitude on the Sunday march − a threat of arrest for obstruction hanging over every demonstration unless we kept moving. Yet, on the Monday, the police frustrated all attempts by people to keep moving, by blocking off all central roads and causing a fracas. We could not win either way . . . The police were generally abusive and told us all to go home, where we came from. That was ironic since we could not because of the cordons.' James Barton saw young Asians breaking shop windows on the Broadway at about 8.20 pm. '. . . the police were just standing there passively letting these boys (about 20 of them) do what they wanted. I tried to stop them since it was just anarchy and would feed the opposition. But then there was a police push through. However, they made no attempt to arrest those concerned, but they were just hitting everyone in sight, including old men in turbans who were just watching. I was hanging back from the demonstration but even so I got a punch in the mouth from a policeman. Then I got hit again and punched around the chest and back as I ran. I turned to an inspector and said that I had not been involved in any aggression towards the police and that I should be free to walk the streets without being attacked by police. He said that anybody who was there was looking for trouble and deserves a good kicking.'

The Death of Blair Peach

2.64 Blair Peach died after being hit near the junction of Beechcroft Road and Orchard Avenue after leaving the Broadway at about 7.45 pm. The circumstances surrounding his death are dealt with in chapter 3.

The Town Centre

2.65 Police pressed another group of demonstrators eastwards along the High Street to the beginning of the Uxbridge Road. The police cordon was eventually established just west of the entrance to Southall Park to the south of the main highway and Park View Road to the north. (Events in Park View Road are related in the following section.) By 5 pm the section of the High Street enclosed by the police cordon included both 46 High Street, the offices of the National Association of Asian Youth and 54 High Street, the Southall Rights Legal Advice Centre, where volunteer lawyers were in attendance from 2 pm. Thus, two key focal points for the organisation of the demonstration were blocked off by the police cordon.

2.66 At about 4.15 pm, a police inspector visited both offices (No.46 and No.54) and demanded that the premises by cleared. That section of the High Street, he declared, was to be a 'sterile area'. Frances Webber, volunteer legal adviser at Southall Rights, stated that when she arrived at the centre it 'was busy but completely peaceful. There were approximately 8-10 volunteers there and 15-20 members of the public seeking help. Almost as soon as I arrived however a large group of police entered (10-12) led by a senior officer. He . . . demanded that everybody leave and close the centre down.' Mohammed Asghar, full-time co-ordinator of Southall Rights, stated: 'I . . . told the police who I was and asked them what they doing in my office. I told them that the office was private property and since they did not have my permission to be there, they were trespassing . . .

'After an argument with one of the officers outside, they agreed to let us out but refused to let anyone in and told us we would be arrested if we attempted to re-enter . . . The officers outside were insolent and aggressive. During this whole period, the street outside was free of demonstrators and there was no conceivable threat to public order.' A dozen police officers were posted in front of the office and others at the rear. People were prevented from entering but not from leaving. V. Garge stated that at what appears to be an earlier time just after 3 pm he was refused entry to Southall Rights. 'When I told them I was working there, the police said: "Sorry — we don't understand English any more!"' As a result of its isolation, Southall Rights despatched one of its lawyers, John Witzenfeld, to the First Aid Centre at 6 Park View Road, towards the eastern end of the High Street, to establish an emergency legal advice centre there.

2.67 An incident witnessed by Stephen Nory, volunteer adviser at Southall Rights, casts light on the way in which Community Liaison Officers are viewed by some other police: 'I noticed Chief Inspector Gosse, Community Liaison Officer, walking from the Police Station . . . I called him over. He came greeting me, cheerily. I told him the problem, he went straight to go in to Southall Rights. The police constable . . . denied Gosse entry. "Who are you?" "Chief Inspector D. Gosse, CLO". At this at least three of the police lined up in front of Southall Rights laughed. Gosse had to show his card to get in. I asked the police constable who laughed loudest if he had no respect for the job of CLO. "Did I say that?" he asked, still grinning.'

2.68 Southall Rights, after considerable difficulty, managed to send one of its representatives to release a press statement on their plight to journalists near the Town Hall. Police guards outside the premises were withdrawn about an hour later.

2.69 An SYM leader claims to have managed to filter back into the central area at about 3.30 pm where he tried to regroup some of the scattered SYM members. People were brought from Avenue Road (leading southwards from High Street), but then the police moved to cordon off Avenue Road and those that had managed to get through were pushed eastwards towards Uxbridge Road. A crowd remained trapped down Avenue Road, many of them, it seems from witness statements, being residents attempting to reach their homes beyond the police cordon (they had filtered through to Avenue Road from the railway station, directed by police away from South Road to cross the railway line by a footbridge which connects Bridge Road to Park Avenue).

2.70 Between 6 and 7 pm, some 30 demonstrators were permitted by the police to line the pavement opposite the Town Hall and others with a loud-speaker manned a first-floor balcony above the Ashoka Tandoori and Sweet Cafe, also on the side of the road opposite the Town Hall. This was the only token demonstration allowed by the police close to the Town Hall. Press and camera crews had by this time gathered in the area. At about 7 pm, a group of about 40* National Front supporters were escorted by the police to the Town Hall, having arrived apparently by coach at Lady Margaret Road. They were accompanied by the shouts of the demonstrators, such as 'No Nazis in Southall' and 'National Front Out'. In response, National Front members gave Nazi salutes on the steps of the Town Hall. NF stewards then checked the entry of press representatives, refusing entry to the *Daily Mirror* representative, Kevin O'Lone, on the grounds that: 'The *Daily Mirror* supports these niggers and is a Labour rag. We are allowing in reporters from decent papers who are not black lovers'. (*Daily Mirror* 24 April 1979.) Councillor Cotter states: 'I was angry that a National Front meeting was taking place in the ward which I represent and where I live and I wanted to test whether it was really public . . . We told the police we were councillors and asked to get through to the Town Hall. A senior officer let us through and detailed someone to escort us. We walked up the Town Hall steps and explained our purpose to the police there . . . An NF steward . . . told us that the meeting was full but that we could take our places in the queue. We stood there for about 15 minutes . . . Two or three NF members

---

*This is the figure given by the *Daily Express* (24 April) and confirmed by other witnesses. However, the *Daily Telegraph* (24 April) put it at 59 and the *Daily Mirror* (24 April) 100; these figures cannot be correct as the Hall only held 60 in all.

arrived and were put in the queue, but when the time came, they were in fact let in first by the steward. We were not let in although we had been told by the steward that there were 14 places and only five had gone in. I spoke to the council official . . . and told him that the NF and press had gone in but we had not been let in. He said that the press was regarded as part of the public, when I pointed out it was not a public meeting. I was gently evicted by NF stewards.'

2.71 During the meeting, according to press reports, the National Front youth organiser, Joe Pearce, promised his audience: 'There is a white minority here being persecuted by a black majority. The National Front will send back every single Asian out there.' (*Daily Express* 24 April 1979.) The *Southall Gazette* reported: 'National Front supporters sat at the front and an air of foreboding seemed to fill the hot, stuffy room. Above the heads of the speakers hung the Front's flag. Portly leader, Martin Webster, fussed around making sure all the seats were filled. Then a council official was called in to count the members of the public. I counted eight including three members of the press, but the number was swelled to 20 by Front supporters who raised their hands. Local Front organiser, Ernest Pendross, chaired the meeting and the three local candidates spoke on various topics.

Clive Wakeley, candidate for Ealing Acton, said members who attended the meeting had "a lot of guts" and went on to criticise the Common Market and Trade Unions. Ealing Southall candidate, John Fairhurst, spoke on his theory for the rebirth of the trolley bus. And Ealing North candidate, James Shaw, went into complicated economic policies. Youth leader, Joe Pearce, hotted things up with a rousing speech calling for all immigrants to be sent home.

But the race bombshell was left to the robust Mr Webster who didn't disappoint his supporters with a fiery speech.'

2.72 The Parliamentary candidate, John Fairhurst, was reported in *The Guardian* on 25 April 1979 as promising that a National Front government would 'bulldoze' Southall to the ground and replace it with an 'English hamlet'.

2.73 The meeting ended at about 9.30 pm, and a group of National Front supporters came to the entrance of the Town Hall to shout at demonstrators, sing 'Rule Britannia' and give Nazi salutes, while Mr Martin Webster, the main speaker at the meeting, was smuggled by the police out of a back door. Those at the front of the Town Hall were then shepherded back into the hall by the police before being allowed to leave for their coaches. The demonstrators in front of the Town Hall then dispersed. No arrests are recorded.

The Eastern Section of High Street, North Road and Uxbridge Road East

2.74 The police cordon to the east of the Town Hall — stationed between North Road and Park View Road on the northern side of Uxbridge Road — closed the entire street except for the passage of police vehicles. In addition to

Southall Rights and the National Association of Asian Youth offices, which were blocked off by the cordon, the police station was also behind the cordon. The cordon was some three to four officers deep, with possibly some 200 officers in line by about 4 pm. Behind the cordon, other units of the police, including SPG and about two dozen mounted police, were marshalled. There were about 400-500 people on the pavements at around 5 pm, and these had increased to around 1,000 by 6.15 pm; they were of all ages, some elderly, and of both sexes. Some had been diverted from the railway station via the footbridge already mentioned and some were residents awaiting permission to reach their homes beyond the police cordon.

2.75 The atmosphere seems to have been good, without any provocation. Public Librarian P.E. Jones, standing at the edge of Southall Park, reports: 'The atmosphere, although somewhat tense, was basically good-humoured and there were even ironic cheers as police vehicles drove along Uxbridge Road and through the cordon. I saw nothing thrown at the police and heard nothing in that part of the crowd around me to suggest that agitators were at work.' Martyn Grubb, prior to the incidents on the Broadway, had approached the eastern sector from the police side. 'I stood behind the police cordon and listened as Clarence Baker (the senior steward on this section) was addressing the crowd beyond with a loud-hailer. He was telling people not to provoke trouble and this must be on all accounts a peaceful demonstration. On no account was anybody to provoke the police or to do anything violent because that would destroy the purpose of the demonstration.'

2.76 At about 6 pm there was an attempt to push forward toward the police line by some people in the crowd. A witness told us: 'We had been standing there in the rain for a long time and were beginning to feel frustrated. So the crowd surged forward to the police line . . . after shouts to go forward but the stewards had managed to keep people back.'

2.77 One witness has told us that some of those involved in trying to organise the demonstration had agreed to break through the police cordon in order to establish the planned sit-down demonstration in front of the Town Hall. An Anti-Nazi League member states: 'The aim was to have a peaceful sit-in outside the Town Hall and the only possible way of achieving this aim was to push through the cordon.' Another ANL member who was present on Uxbridge Road at this time said that there was a 'rumour' going round the crowd to the effect that there was a fixed time when they should try to go through the cordon and carry out the planned sit-down demonstration outside the Town Hall. The question of whether or not senior members of the Anti-Nazi League consciously planned a deliberate attempt to break through the police cordon and get to the Town Hall, is discussed in Chapter 8 (see paragraph 8.23).

2.78 Clarence Baker, steward for the area, was heard addressing the crowd by Martyn Grubb who had approached the area for the police side of the cordon.

'I stood behind the police cordon and listened as Clarence Baker was addressing the crowd beyond with a loud-hailer. I admired what he said. He was giving positive leadership. He was telling people not to provoke trouble and this must on all accounts be a peaceful demonstration. On no account was anybody to provoke the police or to do anything violent because that would destroy the purpose of the demonstration'. The *Daily Mail* of 24 April showed a picture of Clarence Baker with megaphone under the caption 'Organiser urges "Be Peaceful".' The Rev. Roy Smith remembers him urging 'the people to unite in peace and love and to stay together'. Two young men, Mr Khatra and Mr Sharpe, gave evidence in court that they had been near the front of the advance which nonetheless followed soon afterwards. They moved towards the cordon shouting: 'This is a peaceful march'. Paul Seligman said that 'a number of people – perhaps 100 – ran at the police cordon. These were mainly in the 12-16 age range – and I did not see any form of weapon'. There were scuffles and some collisions between the crowd and the cordon.

2.79 BBC news film shown that evening shows the advance, which is contained by the cordon. Then from the south side a flare or firework is thrown at the police line. A police officer is hurt and pulled clear. Another officer picks up the object which is giving off a red or pinkish flame and throws it either into the crowd on the north side or over the billboard under which they are standing. Some of the demonstrators, nearer the back of the crowd, thought that the flare was the signal to advance although the film shows it thrown clearly after the advance had taken place. Others thought that the police were throwing flares into the crowd; one thought that tear gas was being used. As the crowd advanced to the cordon it appears that a group of police officers who had been standing in the road ahead of the cordon were surrounded. A witness told us that she had seen two policemen bent double in the midst of the crowd as if rising from the ground, helmets off, and some people kicking them. The Home Secretary's Memorandum (appendix 2) states that a policeman was stabbed here. Some reports say this occurred at the far end of Park View Road after the police advance; we have only been able to establish the officer's name, PC Lavercock.

2.80 The cordon parted to permit a charge by footpolice, armed with riot shields and truncheons, followed by mounted police carrying long light-coloured batons. The police have since given evidence in court that the formation of the shield-bearing serials was nine officers and one inspector in front with shields, with ten behind not carrying them. Judith Power reports: 'The ordinary police melted away from the front row and were replaced by police with riot shields who advanced towards the crowd . . . The police started chasing people with their batons drawn through the park . . . It seemed to me entirely arbitrary and that those arrested had not done anything and that I too would have been arrested if I had run instead of standing still.

'I went back on the pavement in Uxbridge Road. I saw about a dozen police horses come through the police lines. They were moving extremely fast and the

1. Just after 3 pm. The Town Hall crossroads at the time of the incidents involving Mr Aulak and others (see paragraph 2.48). The Town Hall itself is opposite the Three Horse Shoes public house out of the picture. *(John Sturrock, Report)*.

2. Young Asians being moved on, along the Broadway. *(John Sturrock, Report)*.

3. Probably about 5 pm; Uxbridge Road at the junction with Park View Road. Clarence Baker is holding the megaphone on the right hand side of the picture. Two other stewards are marshalling the crowd; the one on the left is in the act of pushing someone back onto the pavement. (See paragraph 2.78). *(John Sturrock, Report)*.

4. The Broadway, probably about 6 pm. The second cordon is clearly visible carrying riot shields behind the front section of the crowd. (See paragraph 2.53). *(Mark Rusher, IFL)*.

5. Uxbridge Road about 6.30 pm. The mounted police charge. The horsemen to the right are turning into Park View Road. (See paragraph 2.80). *(Mark Rusher, IFL)*.

6. Holy Trinity Churchyard shortly afterwards. (See paragraph 2.85). *(John Sturrock, Report)*.

7. An arrest by officers of G Division and the Special Patrol Group (CO 14, second from right) in Uxbridge Road outside the Park. *(Mark Rusher, IFL).*

8. 6 Park View Road, as the police prepare to raid it. The officer arrowed has his truncheon already drawn. The ground floor windows left and right (where, respectively Clarence Baker was arrested and the first aid room was) are shut. The first-floor windows and two top-floor windows are open. Two flares were thrown at about this time from the left-hand first-floor window. (See paragraphs 2.92-2.115). *(John Sturrock, Report).*

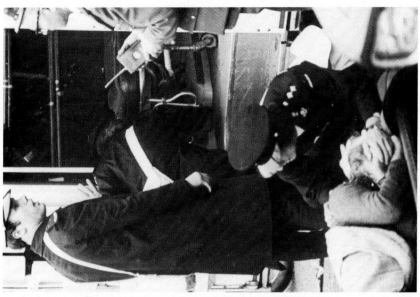

9. Park View Road after the raid on No.6. Richard Bunning, ex-ambulance man is taken to hospital (See paragraph 2.105). *(John Sturrock, Report)*.

10. Police officers end the sitdown on South Road by making arrests. (See paragraph 2.119). *(P.J. McKitrick)*.

11. Town Hall crossroads about 7.15 pm. The National Front arrive. The youth in the combat jacket is a steward and wears an NF armband. (See paragraph 2.70). *(Mark Rusher, IFL)*.

12. The token demonstration opposite the Town

13. The Broadway opposite Beechcroft Avenue about 7.30 pm. (See paragraphs 2.57-2.59). *(John Sturrock, Report).*

14. The Broadway at dusk. *(John Sturrock, Report).*

15. The Blair Peach memorial march on 28 April. (See paragraphs 2.141-2.142). *(John Sturrock, Report).*

mounted police had their batons raised. The idea seemed to be to scatter people and it was extremely effective . . . It was very frightening and uncalled-for. I saw people running and being chased on foot, by police with raised truncheons. I saw people with blood on their faces . . . There must have been dozens of people who I saw chased who did not seem to me to have done anything. There must have been six to twelve people led away holding their heads. There had been a few stones thrown but not enough to really worry the police. The provocative thing was bringing on the riot shields and particularly the horses.'

2.81 Witnesses state that no missiles were thrown until after this charge. Rev. Roy Smith who was standing nearby reports that only after the charge did some of the crowd begin throwing stones at parked police vans and the groups of police officers advancing behind the shields. He saw 'one policeman trip over as he chased someone from the Park into Green Drive. His truncheon fell to the ground and he lay down apparently hurt. As a young man moved in to kick him in the head (his helmet was still intact) I shouted in an effort to restrain him. As I approached, the policeman staggered to his feet, but a young man rushed up and kicked him in the crutch. I pushed the policeman through the narrow gateway to the comparative safety of the park'. The continued charge produced panic. The crowd turned and fled eastwards, along Uxbridge Road, scattered into Southall Park to the south of Uxbridge Road and into Park View Road to the north. John Sharp, social work student, states: 'Seeing the danger of being crushed, people began to run back . . . When we were a little way back and relatively safe we turned back and saw those less fortunate than ourselves who had fallen and been trampled over by the police were being beaten severely with truncheons.'

2.82 In Southall Park, the crowd scattered, hotly pursued by groups of foot-police and mounted police. Mike Pearse said that only a small gate about four feet wide was open. 'There was a mass of people trying to squeeze through. Police horsemen were charging at people so there was a massive crush. Their long batons (2′ 6″) were being used to hit people, as policemen pushed people through the narrow gate . . . Police officers used a lot of racist abuse and hit people with their truncheons and riot shields . . .

'The road was a mass of bricks and stones and some people had tried to vandalise a Ford Transit van in the Uxbridge Road. So the police charged into the park. It seemed to me that they were going specifically for young Asians, because the few whites were ignored. In this attack they did not seem to arrest anyone. They just wanted to give the blacks a kicking. They ran after people indiscriminately and hit them. There was no reason for it − people were just going, there was no noise, no nothing . . .

'There was a big police officer . . . in the park with a riot shield and his truncheon drawn. A group of six or seven Asian youths was nearby and he was taunting them: "Come and take me. Anyone of you. Come and take me and I'll have you". Some of the youths wanted to take him up but singly. He was really big and brandished his riot shield and truncheon saying: "You black bastards. Come on" provocatively . . . I thought he was deliberately inciting the group to attack him because the vans driving up and down gave him protection. It seemed that if he were attacked the vans would have pulled up and nabbed the attackers straightaway. And so no one did attack him . . . The police attack was very violent and unexpected. They were really having a go at people in the park. There seemed little reason why . . .'

2.83 Martin Craxton had been distributing literature in the Park for the Labour Party Young Socialists of which he is a member. 'Everything remained peaceful until some people began to throw stones at the cordon. It was then that the riot shields came out and those of us in the Young Socialists were going around telling people not to throw stones . . .

'I had been reasoning with groups of local people telling them not to shout at the police and get hysterical . . . some groups formed around myself and others to hear our points of view . . . apart from small groups of local youths, everyone was quite calm and not intimidating the police in any way . . . The police began moving forward slowly . . . from their cordon across the Uxbridge Road at the Southall end. At the same time, a cordon was present at the far end of the Uxbridge Road, the Hanwell end. People hurried into the park.

'It was quite quiet apart from one of the black girls still shouting at the police across the other side of the iron gate. I was shouting from the side "calm down" . . . She was at the front of the line inside the park about two feet away from the iron gate. Suddenly one of the police pushed the gate violently into her face. She burst out crying. I went up to see if she was hurt and needed any treatment . . . I heard shouts from the end of the police line "right, now" and the police surged in around the iron gates and over the wall . . . I felt something hit my head and was brought to the ground, either tripped up or pushed over. On the ground I was being pushed and kicked around. I was picked up by two PCs and was briskly frogmarched towards the Uxbridge Road pavement . . . I was shoved to the pavement surrounded by a large number of policemen. The group of them started kicking me again . . .' Mr Craxton was the witness of more violence in the police coach into which he was subsequently put. 'Suddenly PC (deleted) kicked out with his left boot straight for Mr Rehal's face . . . Mr Rehal tilted his head to one side and the boot hit the side of the van and his shoulder instead . . .' At the police station, Mr Craxton was examined by a police surgeon. 'He saw my head wound and saw that the wound had gone through to the bone and was two inches long. He also saw bruises and a scab on my elbow . . . He stitched the wound on my head but it was still bleeding an hour later'. Martin Craxton was charged with threatening behaviour. In December at Barnet court, at which five witnesses were ready to give evidence on his behalf, the police decided to offer no evidence and he accepted a voluntary bindover.

2.84 It was not at all clear what was the purpose of the police charge. P.E. Jones witnessed the confusion: 'My impression was that once the police had made their initial charge, further action was quite unnecessary as the demonstrators had scattered and were making no attempt to re-group. I must emphasise my strong impression that the police pursued and arrested demonstrators quite at random – simply, it appeared, because they were running away'. Many witnesses testified to indiscriminate and unnecessary police violence. Rev. Roy Smith, who had earlier aided the escape of a police officer, saw a young man known to him being taken to a police van: 'He was obviously in great pain as the arresting officer was pulling his head back hard by his Rastafarian locks'. John Hall, a Community Relations worker, said: 'I saw policemen grab a fellow just because of his long hair. He was just running from the horses like everyone else. They pulled him to the ground, jostled him, and were poking his stickers saying, "What's this, what's this?" I saw police run after a black youth, five of them got hold of him, kicked him in the back and chest and then arrested him'. Steward David Greaves recorded: 'I saw policemen charging through the park gates with riot shields and truncheons. I saw the boy going down and then I saw a policeman hit another boy who was watching all this, on the back of the head, and run off'. Another witness argues that the police were, apart from the violence, very abusive: 'The police were very abusive, swearing at us and calling us "communists" and "scum" and saying we had "tunnel vision" . . . I went home in a state of shock at what I had seen. I did not believe British policemen could act in such an abusive, provocative and brutal manner. I would not have believed it if I had not seen it with my own eyes'. A journalist, observing the park, noted: 'It was as if they (police) were let off the leash after a frustrating day for them as much as for the rest and went too far'.

2.85 About eighty people, many of them elderly and very frightened, took refuge in Holy Trinity Churchyard (on the corner of Park View Road and Uxbridge Road). Here they were rounded up and beaten by mounted and foot police. The *Daily Telegraph* (24 April) recorded the scene: 'Within three minutes, mounted police had cornered about 50 demonstrators against the walls of Holy Trinity Churchyard, and moving through the Churchyard, rounded up stragglers. As we watched, several dozen, crying, screaming coloured demonstrators were dragged bodily along Park View Road and along the Uxbridge Road to the police station and waiting coaches. Nearly every demonstrator we saw had blood flowing from some sort of injury; some were doubled up in pain. Women and men were crying'.

2.86 Mrs Prem Bhassi had gone to the demonstration with a friend, Diane Lambert, and two young girls about 13 or 14. Her parents were active in the IWA and she thought that there would be a peaceful demonstration. They were forced off the churchyard wall by the charge of mounted police. 'We sheltered under a holly tree in the churchyard with our arms round each other when police horses came in the churchyard with batons raised and prodded us and shouted at us to get out'. Park View Road was by this time cordonned off and the only way out was over a wall and into a woodyard. They were arrested and charged with being in enclosed purposes for an unlawful purpose. It was alleged that they were throwing pieces of wood at the police from the woodyard. Both were acquitted. Amarjit Khera states: 'At about 6.20 pm the police suddenly pushed at us with their shields hard. Everyone panicked and fell back . . . We could see in the park three or four police standing around in a circle hitting someone with their fists and truncheons – this scene was repeated all over the park. The helicopter seemed to be following groups of people overhead'.

2.87 Others of the crowd attempted to escape into gardens, over walls, and northwards along Park View Road, only to discover it was a cul-de-sac. Police, including SPG and mounted police, gave vigorous pursuit to the end of the road, beating and arresting those they caught. David Burnett said: 'Next to me a girl was pleading with a number of policemen who had hold of a guy who I recognised as Chris, a white guy involved with Misty, the local reggae group. He looked in a pretty bad way, almost in a state of collapse. His face was a horrible colour, his eyes were staring and his tongue was hanging out'. The man was Chris Bolton who was subsequently convicted of assault on the police. He said, however, that he had started to move away from the charging policemen when he was over-taken. '. . . I was aware of someone on my back and four or five officers around me. I had my head down. I was just trying to get away from them . . . I fell down or was forced down onto the ground, just immediately adjacent to 6 Park View Road. I received blows all over my body and face. One officer had me in a stranglehold, I couldn't breathe. Others were trying to break my arms by twisting them as hard as they could round my back . . . I kept blacking out and coming round again. I was dragged to the side of the road in a stranglehold. The stranglehold lasted so long I thought I was going to die. I passed out twice for lack of air'.

2.88 Balraj Purewal states: 'A mounted policeman threatened me with his baton. There was no question of arrest. The horse pushed me against the wall and he shouted, "Move, you black bastard".' Paul Seligman remembers the scene in Park View Road: 'I saw one policeman throw himself on top of a man who crashed forwards onto the street under the policeman (this happened about 20 yards up Park View Road). A group of police then started kicking him and generally roughing him up . . . It was at this stage that people started shouting and throwing missiles . . . I was trying to calm people down if only because nearly all the missiles were falling amongst the demonstrators . . .

'I had a chance to observe that most police were hitting people on the back and other parts of the torso – principally, they seemed to be aiming for the kidney area. However, some were exceeding this – in the garden next to mine one screaming, red-faced burly policeman was mercilessly lashing out, clearly berserk . . .

'I was grabbed and marched some yards down the street – I kept saying "I won't struggle" . . . Then they got me onto the ground . . . The senior officer said "Pull his head back" which one officer did by the hair. He (the senior officer) then kicked me in the face . . . I was quite dazed by this blow and I could taste blood and feel bits of teeth in my mouth.

'The police officers were saying "What were you doing?" and I was saying "nothing". They said: "Just being there's enough", and "You're lucky to have any teeth left". In the police station horrible things were going on all over the crowded lobby. A white lad was brought in doubled over. He collapsed semi-conscious, his face a ghastly green. A policeman and policewoman were shaking him and shouting "Get up. There's nothing wrong with you, you bastard". An Asian boy was holding his hand at a strange angle. His wrist was broken. Another Asian was brought in with a severe head wound, holding a completely blood-soaked piece of clothing to it'. Mr Seligman's injuries were 'three lower front teeth badly chipped, damage to corresponding upper teeth causing great sensitivity, both lips damaged but upper lip badly split and initially very swollen. Sore points on jaw. Pain on one side of throat on swallowing. Nose bleeding on both sides. Nose very painful to touch'.

2.89 After the events, Rev. P.B. Crick was summoned from his vicarage by parishioners and reports: '. . . I found the residents mainly agitated, pointing to damage sustained to their front gardens, obviously by police horses jumping in over the hedgerows and fences. Hoof-prints and broken plants were everywhere. I then went to No.17 when three elderly residents were surveying piles of horse-dung all up the front paths to the very doorstep'. Balwinder Singh Rana reports seeing the police even hitting people who were just standing in their own front gardens looking on.

2.90 Some demonstrators, in order to escape the violence in Park View Road, had run through gardens and into an alleyway leading to North Road. Southall Police Station is situated at the bottom of this road and when these people emerged they found police advancing at them from both ends of North Road. In October the cases were heard at Barnet court of six defendants charged with threatening behaviour in North Road and later while trying to escape down another alley. The threatening behaviour was supposed to consist of waving their fists and shouting at police. All six were acquitted and one, Mr Ungpakorn, records: 'The first officer to reach me punched me in the right temple . . . A second officer punched me in the side and also moved past me. A third officer grabbed me by the head and knocked it against a window, breaking it . . . At no time did I see anybody make the slightest attempt to hit a policeman or even to defend themselves. The people arrested with me in the alley turned out later to have been rather frightened young lads.

'. . . The police were discussing whether or not "to nick this lot" . . . I saw a policeman knee a man from behind between his legs while the man had his arms spread out on the van. "Nigger bastards" was a phrase frequently used by the police.'

2.91 Neither North Road nor Lady Margaret Road (parallel to it) were the scenes of major violence that day. However, Rev. Theo Samuels, Anglican Chaplain at Brunel University, got rough treatment. He was observing in the Uxbridge Road, near the junction with North Road, having helped give out cups of tea to the police cordons. 'I wanted to understand why they were there. Some of them wanted to be there and were not merely obeying orders . . . An inspector came up and told me to move on in an aggressive manner. There was no understanding on his part that I had a right to be there just as much as the National Front whose rights they were purporting to protect. Police were trampling on my rights to be there as an observer. I asked him therefore to explain why I should move on. He told me once again to move. As I still felt that he owed me an explanation, I stayed there and said "Would you please let me know why I should move on? I am within my rights to stand here". He shouted this time "I won't ask you again". Other police officers who had heard their superior officer shouting seemed pleased at the treatment I was receiving and so I replied "I don't intend moving until you give me the reasons for doing so". He refused to do so, turned to the officers behind him and said something to them. Two of them then took hold of each shoulder and dragged me the hundred yards along the pavement. Along the road, police officers both men and women, were making crude remarks to one another about me. Their actions and attitude were undisciplined — discipline had broken down.

'A hundred yards down the road (possibly North Road) the police dumped me with a crowd of white demonstrators standing on the corner. All along the police we passed expressed an exultant feeling of triumph at my treatment. Some police officers in a green coach were laughing . . . Overall there was an atmosphere of fear on the part of the ordinary citizens. They did not dare to venture in the streets by and large, because of the police whose discipline seemed to have completely broken down.

'Most of the violence that I saw was committed by the police both physically and mentally. Another example of this attitude occurred when I was being dragged along the streets. A policeman in a van held up an ace of spades playing card to the window facing the youths. That, to me, is violence in that it was a provocative gesture of contempt.'

6 Park View Road

2.92 This house was to be the scene of some of the most violent police action of the demonstration. It belonged to the London Borough of Ealing and was planned for demolition in 1982-5 to make way for an old people's home. For a time the house stood empty but was then occupied by a collective of young people known as Peoples Unite. This organisation had developed out of a musicians co-operative, People Unite, which was based around a band, 'Misty'. Members were mainly West Indian though Asian and white young people were also involved. It was fiercely independent and rejected any grant aid or outside funding. The idea of creating a self-supporting arts workshop had existed in the minds of the group of musicians for some time. After a period of fruitless searching for premises, they decided to redecorate and refurbish the semi-derelict house at 6 Park View Road and thereby to convince the council that they should have a licence to remain. This they successfully did to the extent that the Social Services Department let it be known, through the mediation of the Ealing CRC, that a blind eye would be turned to the occupation. Clarence Baker, a leading member, described the operation of the house: 'Young people could come in and do anything which was creative. We banned games. There was art, music, discussion groups. Mainly it was young West Indians who came. Also a number of Asians. We were however multi-racial . . . With the help of local kids we did (the house) up. They saw it as something they were doing for themselves. It became very creative. We renovated the house with money from our own pockets. People involved related much better to it that way . . . It was open all day and all evening. It brought them off the streets and they did things which were creative.' In the period up to 23 April, there had been a lot of activity in the house. The middle floor, which was the last to be finished, was being decorated with the intention of providing a photographic darkroom and day nursery. The philosophy behind Peoples Unite had clear links with Rastafarianism. Though not explicitly such, it was non-militant – advocating love, harmony and peaceful co-existence. Rev. Roy Smith of Emmanuel Church gave his verdict on the organisation: 'I have been in touch with this organisation since it was formed by a group of young people seeking to help themselves and the community in general. Amongst the musicians I have noticed a real spirit of co-operation, with the more experienced always willing to give advice and practical help to beginners. Much work went into the repair and decoration of their premises . . . I visited the house on a number of occasions, sometimes for meetings, sometimes purely informally, and was always welcomed with great courtesy.'

2.93 There is some indication that the house was marked out by the police prior to 23 April. A member of Peoples Unite had been told by a policeman previously: 'We know what you are doing round at No.6 and we are going to get you'. On 9 March, it was raided by the police allegedly in search of stolen sound speakers, but nothing was found. On 31 March Peoples Unite jointly with local clergymen and the ECRC had held a small peaceful demonstration against this treatment and 'sus' laws generally outside the local police station. This received prominent coverage in the local paper. On Sunday 22 April, it is said that the police attempted to search the premises and garden. On 23 April, there were police vans parked outside from a relatively early time. John Sharpe noted several things in the police coach going to the station after the police charge down Park View Road which made him think that there was a pre-arranged police plan to arrest the occupants of No.6.

'First, the policeman on the other side of the coach to me told my arresting officer that his squad of 20 policemen had been stationed outside No.6 with orders to go in and arrest all the occupants at a given signal.

'Secondly, a senior police officer came into the coach asking if any officers had prisoners arrested in No.6. When the constable near me said yes, the senior police officer (with two stars on his shoulder) came down to the constable and began to tell him what to charge him with and how to make the charge . . . I caught the phrases "causing an affray" and "send all the details to X division". Later three plain clothes policemen came onto the coach and asked for any police or prisoners with paint on their clothes, or who were arrested in No.6 to come with them.'

2.94 It appears that the local Anti-Nazi League had decided to use No.6 Park View Road as a distribution centre for placards, banners and badges. A lorry containing ANL members arrived about 10 am on 23 April. Paul Holborrow, working in the national ANL office, thought that the house had been agreed as a central organising point, and others who gave evidence also said that they knew that No.6 was the 'centre' for getting placards, information and so on. There is evidence to suggest, however, that this had not been agreed by Peoples Unite. Members of Peoples Unite told us that there was no prior agreement for use by outsiders of the house except as a medical centre. Clarence Baker said that this was agreed only on the day at about 2 pm after a visit by Mohammed Asghar of Southall Rights when it became clear that access elsewhere might be impeded. The first aid centre was established on the ground floor on the right-hand side as seen from the road. A notice was placed on the door indicating this. In attendance were Dr A. Nehmad from Barnet Hospital, Richard Bunning, a former ambulance man from the neighbouring area of Hanwell, and some other people with nursing experience. John Witzenfeld, a solicitor who had been sent over from Southall Rights to give legal advice, was also in this room. The office of Peoples Unite was across the corridor on the left-hand side of the ground floor. Clarence Baker, appointed steward by the Co-ordinating Committee for the local area, only realised at about 3 pm that 'the room on the other side of the hall had been used to store ANL leaflets. It was hard to know who was doing what. I could not understand for a long time how Tariq Ali got arrested in our house. A long time after I realised that the ANL used it as an office. We confined ourselves basically to the top room which we used for reading or quiet discussion and the basement.' The latter was a sound-proofed music studio.

2.95 Another Peoples Unite member, who worked on maintenance at the house, arrived there at about 10 am on 23 April. 'I started doing jobs about the house, and I was surprised when I arrived to see badges and stickers all over the place. I must say that I would not have bothered to do any maintenance on the house if I had envisaged hundreds of demonstrators trampling about. It would have been quite useless. I had no idea that about 100 people would eventually end up in the house . . . I expected it to be a normal day.' Later in the morning, when there were so many people about that work became impossible, he put his tools in the basement and locked it.

2.96 One of the Peoples Unite musicians took a truck used by 'Misty' in the morning to collect musical equipment which they brought back to the house, arriving between 1 and 2 pm. 'Amongst the equipment that we took to No.6 Park View Road was an H and H sound mixer, 16 channels . . . It's not a piece of equipment that one would want lying around if one anticipated that the Peoples Unite house at Park View Road was going to be occupied by hundreds of demonstrators.' This witness told us that the Managing Committee of the house had agreed to have the first aid centre in the house, 'but nothing more'.

2.97 Between 2.30 and 3 pm a number of people left the house, carrying leaflets and banners, planning to march towards the Town Hall. Because Uxbridge Road was cordoned off by the police, the marchers went through Southall Park to South Road. On the way up South Road, they were stopped by another police cordon by the Liberty Cinema. People further back were pushing forward: those at the front were trying to hold them back. Witnesses who were on the march say that the police ran across from the other side of the road and made a number of arrests, including many of the leading members of Peoples Unite. The crowd dispersed, some people returning to No.6. One of these told us that he wanted to go home, fearing that there might be trouble. 'However I discovered that there were no buses, indeed no transport appeared to be running at all.' (He lives in Ealing.)

2.98 During the afternoon the house filled up with people. Clarence Baker said that once the medical centre was established it became impossible to keep a check on the identity of people coming into the house. Paul Holborrow told us that when he visited the house at about 5.30 pm he was concerned that the floors would not support the weight of people on them. Peoples Unite had decided at about 11 am to keep the house open because it would be far from the proposed demonstration. The advance of the cordon to the edge of the Park in the Uxbridge Road brought it within a hundred or so yards of the crowd. People flocked into the house for a number of different reasons. Peoples Unite members used it as usual, keeping mainly to the basement and top floor. ANL and Socialist Unity appear to have used the house as a base and thus a number of their members were inside, mainly on the first floor. People came to shelter from the rainstorms or to dry their clothes. John Bruno had got soaked and changed into decorators' overalls that were in the house. Others came to the medical centre. Balbir Gill brought his cousin, Parmigjit, who had suffered a facial injury. According to Clarence Baker, 'People came into the house because they could not go home . . . We told them that the house would be safe and they could stay and then go home.' While the police cordon remained on the Uxbridge Road the house could not have been the scene of any trouble since it was too far from the police lines for any missiles to be thrown. The danger of a police raid was, however, apparent to members of Peoples Unite aware of the previous trouble; Clarence Baker told us: 'We knew that we had to be careful. I stayed in the house and advised youths not to go on the march.'

2.99 After the attempt was made to break through the police cordon on the Uxbridge Road, the police charge forced many demonstrators to flee up Park

View Road. Most of the demonstrators do not seem to have known that Park View Road was a cul-de-sac. An ANL member who walked down Park View Road away from the police lines states that the police proceeded down Park View Road in a line. 'Suddenly, the lines of police parted and mounted police charged at the crowd. The police proceeding down Park View Road in the cordon stayed in a line, but snatch squads grabbed individual demonstrators.' Rev. Roy Smith, who was running along the Uxbridge Road eastwards, away from the police pursuit, looked back and saw mounted police entering Park View Road with batons drawn. The police regrouped outside No.6 Park View Road, on the pavement opposite.

2.100 Mounted police broke through the line of foot police and chased demonstrators down the cul-de-sac. Sarah Woodin said: '. . . twenty to thirty police on horseback charged into the road and people scattered. They jumped into gardens to get away. They were being chased and beaten up by the police. I saw a few horses jump garden walls . . . Police on foot came and beat people about the heads. Fleeing people flooded into the garden of No.6 because the high wall offered some protection from the horses. I saw people trying to shut the gate behind them but they couldn't because it was constantly pushed open by others trying to escape.'

2.101 Police gave evidence in court cases that as mounted and foot police came within range of the house they became the target of missiles thrown from the garden and house. BBC news film showed the house just as the raid begins. Large numbers of police are massed outside. The windows of the house are shut on the ground floor and also apparently on the top floor. On the middle floor the windows are open. Two flares or fireworks are thrown from the left-hand window as seen from the road. There appears to be no evidence of other missiles being thrown from the house although puffs of dust from the walls of the house appear to suggest that things are being thrown at it. Clarence Baker stood at the top of the steps leading to the front door and ground floor watching. He saw nothing thrown from the garden before he went into the house and shut the door, having realised that a raid was inevitable. He was aware of things thrown from the garden over the wall once he had gone inside. John Witzenfeld, stationed at the window of the first aid centre on the ground floor, saw 'some missiles and I think a fire cracker land in the road near the police' after the charge of the mounted police. Eve Turner ran back from the advancing police cordon and 'got punched in the face by a policeman. It was then there started to be stones thrown from the sides of Park View Road and the roof of No.6. People were terrified . . .'

2.102 The police then entered the grounds of the house. Some officers appear to have climbed the wall and made for the back door; others under the protection of riot shields made for the front. No evidence has emerged from witnesses or court cases of any serious attempt by police on the scene to evacuate the house peacefully. No mention has been made of any loudspeaker appeal. No attempt was made to talk to community leaders in the house and ask them to assist in dealing with the situation. The only warning allegedly given was by Inspector Billing who, in the case of Kharay, said that he was the officer in charge of the detachment of police making for the front door. He shouted at people inside to open the doors. Subsequent court hearings have been given conflicting accounts of whether the decision to clear the house was taken by a senior officer or on the individual initiative of officers on the spot. Sergeant Bunning of the Special Patrol Group, whose officers appear to have composed the majority of those involved, was reported by an observer at the case of Knight and others as saying '. . . there was no overall direction of police forces at this point' and that a 'free for all' would be a fair description of the situation. He had taken the decision that the house had to be completely cleared of people whether or not they had done anything 'to prevent a recurrence of the stone throwing'.

2.103   The total number of people in the house at the time of the police raid is impossible to calculate. It would appear to have been in the region of 100. Of the 37 occupants from whom the enquiry has received statements 31 allege assault in corroborating accounts. Witnesses have repeatedly suggested to us that the number of missiles thrown has been exaggerated in police evidence; that identification of alleged offenders has been based on a random selection and that intimidatory violence was used by police officers in a concerted attempt to administer what they no doubt saw as 'rough justice'.

2.104   The police entered the house first through the back door. Shortly afterwards they advanced through the front. Inside the house, there was confusion, panic and fear. People ran in and out of rooms, not knowing what to do. The basement appears to have been empty. The first rooms entered by the police were those on the ground floor. To the right they kicked in the door to the medical room. John Witzenfeld, the solicitor present in the room, told the Enquiry: 'In this room were an ambulance man whose name I now know to be Richard Bunning and a woman doctor called Annie (Nehmad). They had medical equipment such as bandages and other items on a table. I was seated in a chair by the window in the room, with my briefcase and umbrella. I saw mounted police with long batons drawn charge down the road. Either before or after this a body of police formed up on the pavement or road opposite the house. Two Indian boys came in to bathe their faces and wash the blood away.

'The police advanced on the house with riot shields and truncheons drawn. They kicked in the panel on the door to the medical unit and waving their truncheons told us to get out. Richard protested that people who had been injured were being treated and I told them I was a lawyer. They ignored this and still waving their truncheons shouted at us to get out, so we all went to the door to comply as we were intimidated by their wild manner and behaviour. I was pushed into the hall with others behind me. Suddenly I felt a blow to the back of my head and I managed to half-turn and saw a hand holding a truncheon disappearing downwards.

'I saw Richard holding his head from which blood was pouring. He fainted on the floor . . . then I saw the woman doctor was also bleeding badly from her head . . . The other girl Eve had a bloody bandage on her head and another young boy's head was swathed in bandages. Richard was slumped across the table. Whilst we were waiting for the ambulance, two police stood in the doorway with their backs to us whilst people were brought down from upstairs and I saw truncheons rise and fall and I heard shouts and screams from women.'

2.105 All the occupants of the first aid room appear to have been hit. A boy of 14 attending for medical treatment was beaten. He had suffered a cut on hand from a riot shield. He was acquitted of all charges on appeal (see paragraph 5.23). Richard Bunning, who had dressed the boy's hand before the raid, was himself hit on the head by police truncheons. He said 'The door of the room opened and a boy with a hand wound came in. I dressed it to stop the bleeding. While I was doing this I was hit a glancing blow on the head. I turned round and saw a police sergeant. I said, "I'm not a demonstrator. I'm running a first aid post. Please stop hitting me". He said, "Have you seen what they've done to our blokes?" I said "Are any of them hurt?" He said "Oh. You'll treat them will you?" I said "Yes. I'll get my first aid equipment." I turned to my box and walked towards the table. More policemen came in and a very large one with a riot shield and a truncheon in his hands. He screamed "You – out" and pushed me towards the door. I saw people being propelled downstairs. There were two lines of policemen stretching along the hall, down the steps and into the garden. The people being pushed down the stairs had to run the gauntlet of these policemen and were being kicked and truncheoned on the way. I was in the hall and then I was hit on the back of the head two or three times and perhaps a couple of other glancing blows. I saw an inspector and I said, "For God's sake. I'm only here to give first aid. Tell them to stop hitting me." They stopped . . . and I staggered back into the room. I put my hand to my head and it was covered in blood. I collapsed onto the floor facing the hall . . .' He was taken by stretcher to an ambulance and spent a day in hospital, suffering from severe concussion. No charge was laid against him.

2.106 Dr Nehmad has stated that no one in the medical room resisted when the police ordered them all out. She stated that there was a line of police on each side of the steps leading away from the house and that as people walked out, they were all hit at least once by a truncheon. Dr Nehmad was not arrested and was not charged with any criminal offence. Her account, and that of John Witzenfeld and Richard Bunning, are confirmed by Eve Turner, one of the stewards and a worker for the National Association of Asian Youth, who had to be given four stitches in hospital after being hit on the back of the head by a police truncheon. Like the other three, Eve Turner was not arrested or charged with any offence.

Joan Rudder, a public relations consultant and a member of the Anti-Nazi

League who was also in the medical room, states that she saw several people hit by truncheons and was herself hit as she was forced out of the house between the two rows of police officers holding shields and truncheons. She states: 'There was blood everywhere . . . the police were going for people's heads. I was hit on the crown of the head with a truncheon. I fell and was kicked about like a football . . . I (later) had six stitches put in my head.' Joan Rudder was not arrested nor charged with any criminal offence.

2.107 Clarence Baker went into the room on the left, opposite the medical room. He said that he had previously been threatened by a police officer as he was addressing the crowd, advising moderation. The officer said: 'You black bastard. We are going to get you.' Somebody in the crowd had remarked: 'They have picked you out.' His account of the entry of the police into the room where he was also suggests that he had been singled out. 'I went into the room on the left. There were a load of little kids in there. There were young ladies. With a loud bang a brick came through the window. Other things came through . . . Everyone made a move into the back room which is a kitchen. A crowd of police came in. One policeman said "Get him." I was standing by the kitchen door. About six were hitting me with their truncheons. I felt one blow. I did not really feel anything after that. I was knocked out. I ended up in the kitchen. I remember vaguely things that happened in the police station but not clearly . . . I did not really know where I was. I was conscious but did not know what was happening . . .' At 6 am next morning he could not drink a cup of tea that he was offered. He was taken to hospital, where he remained for 15 days in all, being under hourly examination for one day. The blow he received caused a blood clot on his brain. He still suffered headaches six months later. He was acquitted of all charges against him when the prosecution was dismissed as offering no case to answer. His arresting officer said he had seen him being forced out of the room by other officers, that he would not get up from the ground when requested. The officer saw no trace of injury all the time that Clarence Baker was in his custody.

2.108 Police officers moved upstairs. Sarah Woodin was in the first floor right room. 'They came into the room and everyone was facing the door as they came in. No one was at the window. The door opened and one of them shouted at us "Move you bastards." We were all pushed out of the room towards the stairs and I saw six other officers trying to kick in the door to the loft. There was a long line of police down one side of the staircase on the right hand side as you go down. As we were made to go down the stairs one by one this row of policemen kicked each person's legs. We were waiting in a group to be pushed down the stairs. Some of the people in front of me were taller than I am and my view was obscured. I could hear however screams as they went down the stairs . . . I remember hearing the man in front of me say how scared he was. I still did not realise at this time exactly what was happening . . . I still could not see much. Then the policeman at the top of the row got me by the hair. He pulled my head back. He then brought his truncheon down on my forehead. It was a heavy blow and I was completely stunned. I did not lose consciousness however. My head hurt a lot . . . By this time blood was pouring down my face and was in my eyes. I shut my eyes. I held my head down and tried to protect it with my right arm . . . As I went down the stairs I was being kicked and my hair pulled . . . When I was about half way down the stairs I heard one of them say "Steady on. It's a girl." Then another said "She's a nigger loving cunt" . . . I was kicked in the stomach with someone's knee. This was a hard blow. I received another in the back . . .' She was taken to Ealing Hospital and given 11 stitches to close the wounds. She was not charged with any offence.

2.109 Mak Davies and Vincent Conway hid in the toilet on the first floor when they heard the police coming in. Mak Davies said: 'A policeman kicked in the door to the toilet and hit me with his truncheon on the back of the head, once. He said nothing. He did the same to Vince. He made no attempt to arrest me. I hadn't been throwing stones or anything. He then told us to get up and go down stairs. There were police down one side of the stairs hitting everyone, punching and using their truncheons to people's heads. I got three separate blows on the head on the way down . . .' He had four stitches placed in the front of his head at Ealing Hospital. He was not charged with any offence. Vincent Conway was acquitted of a charge of threatening behaviour. He states that he 'was hit at least six times with truncheons . . . I saw police officers lined up standing on one side of the staircase with riot shields . . . I was flung down the first flight of stairs and I was hit on the head with truncheons . . . Police officers were hitting out all the time . . . There were two lines of police in the hall. I was shoved out of the door and made my way into the garden. There were two lines of policemen with truncheons in the garden punching and threatening people . . . One of the police officers pulled my head forward and jabbed me in my teeth. Another police officer hit me in the face with his fist . . .' His wounds required three stitches.

2.110 Other witnesses confirm the presence of the gauntlet stretching into the front garden until dispersed by the arrival of cameramen and pressmen. Vincent Conway's description is corroborated by that of Belinda Shaw, who was in the garden next door. 'The first people out of the house were women, they were black women. The police were kicking them. The procedure the police used for getting people out of the house was to literally throw them down the steps so that they landed on their heads and then kick them as they tried to get up. I saw people hit in the crotch with truncheons . . . I saw a man I know to be Vincent Conway dragged out of the house and hit on the head. By this time I was crying . . .' Tariq Ali was also pushed through the gauntlet. 'I was pushed down some steps leading to the front door of the house. Outside there was a gauntlet of police officers with their riot shields up and with white truncheons drawn. I crawled through . . . on my knees with my hands round my head trying to protect myself against their blows. I was hit repeatedly. The police were shouting at us "Black Bastards".' He was acquitted of a threatening behaviour charge relating to alleged conduct at a first floor window but, surprisingly, was convicted of obstructing police in the execution of their duty by insisting that he return to the house from which he was being removed. He himself described such an act as one 'of lunacy' in the circumstances. The police surgeon agreed that his injuries were 'compatible with a blow from a truncheon'.

2.111 The police drive through the rest of the house was halted temporarily on the stairs to the top floor. Here John Knight and others erected a hasty barricade of two tables thrust through the banisters to obtain time for a negotiated and peaceful exit. Someone kicked a pot of paint down the stairs. Police officers with their riot shields could not advance past the obstruction. A senior officer eventually did promise a safe exit. They left peacefully, removing the barricade. After they reached the middle floor they were accorded the same treatment as those who had previously left the house. John Knight and three others with him, William Simon, Adrian McKay and Terry Ward were acquitted of all charges against them.

2.112 The police have suggested that there was an 'armoury' of weapons which was built up in 6 Park View Road during the day, for use on the police. But the evidence of the police themselves does not support the allegation of a deliberate attempt to collect weapons for use against the police. In many of the cases of those charged with using an offensive weapon against the police, the police witnesses were unable to produce the object concerned and often were unable to say what the object was. Furthermore, despite the fact that the police closed off the house for 'forensic examination' immediately after clearing it in the evening of 23 April, they have produced no evidence of any weapons found there.

2.113 Immediately after the house was cleared, the police closed it off. A deputation from Southall Rights were refused permission to enter No.6 later that evening, as was an ANL member, Caroline O'Reilly, who had left her handbag at No.6. The police told her that her handbag had been impounded, as had the ANL lorry which had brought some of the demonstrators to No.6 that morning.

2.114 No one other than the police was allowed to enter 6 Park View Road until 3.30 pm on Tuesday 24 April, when Gareth Pearce, a solicitor, was permitted to enter. She has told the Enquiry that she saw in the house a scene of total destruction. Basement rooms, which had been locked during the demonstration itself and which contained valuable musical equipment, had been broken open and the equipment in them vandalised. Clarence Baker estimated that £10,000 worth of equipment was destroyed. Civil proceedings are under consideration.

2.115 Peoples Unite never reoccupied 6 Park View Road. It was demolished within a month by the Council, well in advance of any previous expected date of demolition. Peoples Unite is still looking for premises which this time it intends to purchase or lease.

South Road/Railway Bridge

2.116 Demonstrators who were joined during the afternoon by new arrivals from the south and the railway station assembled for the advertised beginning of the demonstration and were pushed slowly by the police southwards from the upper end of South Road near the Town Hall to the bottom. There were incidents *en route*, one of which has been mentioned as occurring outside the Liberty Cinema (see 2.43). Another clash occurred outside a chemist's shop, Sherry's, and more arrests followed. The police finally established a stable main cordon on the northern end of the railway bridge (on the peak of which, just south of the cordon, is the railway station) permitted the entry and exit of vehicles up to about 5.15 pm but not the admission of pedestrians. Since residents of areas north of the cordon continued to arrive at the railway station, there was much resentment among them at being prevented from reaching their homes. This feeling was exacerbated, according to several witnesses, by the feeling that white people were allowed through the cordon to the north, but Asians were not. Mr Post, a judge's clerk at the Royal Courts of Justice, was let through the cordon as late as 7 pm with a personal escort and the expression of 'courtesy, tolerance and good humour'. Rev. Jim Parkinson, however, '. . . spent an hour arguing to get people through the cordon on South Road, if they lived within the cordoned area. Some I managed to get through, others just had to walk round the outskirts of the area. Police reception was cold.'

2.117 Police established a second cordon at the southernmost point of the railway bridge. Police then directed pedestrians from the railway station southwards. Some of them were permitted to go down Bridge Road, to cross the footbridge to Park Avenue, to reach the crowd held by a police cordon on Avenue Road or go down Boyd Avenue to Southall Park and Uxbridge Road. Witnesses record that many of the people caught at these points were simply residents trying to get home rather than demonstrators.

2.118 At about 5.15 pm, the southern police cordon permitted some people to enter the bridge area from the south, four at a time. Rev. Jim Parkinson reports: 'I broke through the police cordon and went to meet the crowd and tried to help organise a sit-down of four or five hundred people. Though it was hard to stop the progress towards the police, we succeeded and a gap of several yards was maintained between demonstrators and police. No stones or missiles were ever thrown, except for one tin can, that fell short. After half an hour, I saw riot shields and extra police assembling. I approached the three most senior police officers and asked for a common sense and sympathetic approach. The reply was "Control that mob!" After another five minutes I was called by the police to clear the crowd off the road. "You've had long enough now to make your point", he said. We were given an impossible five minutes to clear an angry but peaceful crowd. The police moved in, pressing through the crowd and dragging out what seemed to be previously marked agitators. They were dragged rather than carried and I was yelling for non-violent arrests and humane treatment of our citizens. However, the bridge was cleared and I got my share of cold determined, physical pressure of police.'

2.119 Malcolm Hurwitt, a local solicitor, who was standing in South Road, states that 'Quite suddenly, a large group of police officers started to walk up the bridge from the corner of Beaconsfield Road. At a rough estimate there were 20-30 police officers. They marched briskly and resolutely straight towards the crowd on Southall Bridge. The police went into the crowd and came out again very swiftly, either singly or in twos, with individual demonstrators held by the arms . . . It all happened so quickly that it did not seem at all possible to me that there was enough time to commit any offences . . . The arrests were peacefully carried out and passively accepted. Only the one person appeared to struggle.

'There was no incident that I saw that could have given cause for such a move . . . South Road and Southall Bridge could not be used by its normal north-south traffic . . . In view of these circumstances and the lack of violent incidents to provoke police action, the wave of arrests (which were mainly for obstruction of the highway) seemed to me unjustified.' This view of events is borne out by the many statements of defendants given to us. Thus Councillor Pathak states: 'A police officer asked me to move on and I asked him where he wanted me to go to. He just said "Move". I showed him my councillor's identity card and told him I had to get to a meeting in Ealing, but also that I wanted to attend the public meeting in Southall of the National Front. Then he just arrested me, but did not tell me what he was arresting me for. He started to jostle me and I told him there was no need for that since I would go peacefully.' D.S. Ghiani recalls: 'There was no violence and no serious confrontation. They did not arrest the leaders, but rather the younger people. I myself was in the front line, arms linked with my fellows keeping the crowd back. There were not even anti-police slogans, only anti-Nazi ones. Some cans had been thrown but there was nothing else. I felt that the police violence was intended to provoke the youths and pointed this out to the senior officer. I asked him why the youths were being arrested and beaten even though they were being peaceful. They then arrested me.'

2.120 A quite separate incident took place in the railway station in the evening. The National Front organiser for Wandsworth, Mr Richard de Jongh Wagenwaar, was found lying near the railway line with severe injuries. He was taken to Ealing Hospital for emergency treatment. As far as can be ascertained no one has been charged with assaulting him.

2.121 South Road was the scene of a relatively quiet series of events. Partly this was because it was the only place where the original strategy of a peaceful sit-down could be implemented. There were a number of Indian Workers Association members, councillors and church leaders present, who carried through this plan. Partly, also it was quiet because demonstrators moved to the eastern and western sectors, leaving, in the main, tired working people anxious only to get home from work. Between 80 and 90 people were charged following the events on South Road, mainly for obstruction of the highway. Most of the cases were dealt with at Ealing Magistrates Court by means of a bind-over for £50 to keep the peace for one year.

24-28 April

2.122 On 24 April at 2 pm the Co-ordinating Committee and the IWA called a press conference in the Ballroom of the Dominion Cinema. There was a large attendance of those who had been involved in the events of the previous day. Many had had little or no sleep during the night as they awaited release from police custody or assisted in co-ordinating information and providing transport from distant police stations back to Southall. The conference became in effect an open meeting. The Co-ordinating Committee had always been loosely constituted of representatives of local groups. Members of the Southall Youth Movement, IWA and Ealing CRC attended as did Paul Holborrow of the Anti-Nazi League and Tariq Ali of Socialist Unity. Individuals who had suffered arrest or injury gave their stories emotionally. Feeling about the police was not assisted by the obvious presence of police officers observing all those who attended the meeting from the upper floor of the Manor House opposite. Anger was expressed about the conduct of the police and what appeared to be a bias in the newspapers' coverage of events. Without consultation, Tariq Ali called for a demonstration on the following Saturday, 28 April. Vishnu Sharma told the enquiry: 'When Tariq Ali spoke he said "We will fight in the streets of Southall. We will be carrying on the struggle". He called for the demonstration. No one knew of this. I took Tariq Ali and Paul Holborrow into a corner. I pointed out that the fury of the young people could flare up. We three agreed that we should have a demonstration but rather than just a demonstration we should organise in memory of Blair Peach, as a demonstration of sorrow.' The Co-ordinating Committee issued a press statement giving a brief account of events, announcing a Defence Fund, calling for an independent public enquiry into the actions of the police and stating that 'Southall is shocked, depressed and very sad. There are not many families or friends who have not had someone arrested or injured.'

2.123 Tariq Ali's intervention came as a surprise to the Southall community but does appear immediately to have struck a chord within it. Martyn Grubb, the Community Relations Officer, felt that some commemorative demonstration of the death of Blair Peach would have inevitably occurred. 'If Tariq Ali had not started it there would have been a groundswell wanting a demonstration. There really was a feeling that you could not just ignore the death of Blair Peach. He died for a cause and he could not be ignored. Lots of ordinary Indian people felt that. They said that last time a young Sikh (Gurdip Singh Chaggar, see paragraph 2.2) died in a fight with whites. Now a white had died for them.'

2.124 A further meeting occurred in the Dominion Cinema at about 7 pm that evening, chaired by the secretary of SYM, Balraj Purewal. The attendance was mainly young people who had been involved in the previous day's events. The march of sorrow for Blair Peach was agreed and the SYM decided to set up its own Defence Fund.

2.125 The events of the previous day inevitably drew comment in the press conferences held by the major political parties on 24 April. Merlyn Rees, Home Secretary, called for a review of public order legislation; David Steel proposed a review of the Representation of the People Act under which the council had felt obliged to let the hall to the National Front; and Mrs Margaret Thatcher demanded the 'full weight of the law' to be applied against those involved in assaults against the police. She added: 'The foundation of a civilised society is respect for the law and it is the duty of every citizen to support the police in their difficult and dangerous task.' (*Daily Telegraph* 25 April.) The Prime Minister attacked the National Front as 'pernicious . . . provocative . . . too reminiscent of the Nazis to be comfortable for this country.' He called on the Asian community 'to show patience and forebearance' despite the provocation of the National Front or outside extremists, and went on to say: 'There is some prospect that extremists have been coming in from outside the area in order to begin the violence against the police . . . not because they have primarily sympathy with the residents of that community, but basically because some of them wanted to foment disorder in this country and to provoke attacks on the police and destroy what we have built up in the way of a tolerant society in this country.' The accusation of violence inspired by outsiders was an echo of Sir David McNee's earlier press statement: 'The disturbances were unprovoked acts of violence against police and property by groups of people determined to create an atmosphere of tension and hostility.' (*New Statesman* 4 May.) Enoch Powell, campaigning in Ulster, seized the opportunity to proclaim that without a reduction in the number of New Commonwealth immigrants, 'something which I have described as civil war is inevitable.'

2.126 In stark contrast to events in Southall, a National Front meeting in Plymouth was peacefully abandoned after the hall at which it was to be held was filled by Anti-Nazi League members before the National Front arrived. There was a suggestion that this had been due to oversight on the part of the police at the scene. (*Sun* 25 April.) The Chief Constable concerned, however, had indicated at a press conference that he had severe suspicion of the National Front and recommended that police officers should attend all their meetings with a view to seeing if there were grounds for prosecution on the grounds of incitement to racial hatred. (*Guardian* 25 April.)

2.127 At 9.30 am the next day, 25 April, Commander Thornton, head of Scotland Yard's A7 division came to the office of Dilbagh Chana, chairman of

Ealing CRC. Before his appointment to the Yard, Commander Thornton had been in charge of the police division that included Southall and the two knew each other. Mr Chana said: 'I felt John Thornton wanted me to accept that the police were very concerned and that Sir David (McNee) wanted to do everything possible to put people's minds at rest.'

2.128 Mr Chana was later invited to a meeting at the Yard with Sir David McNee, DAC Helm and Commander Thornton at 4 pm. The meeting took place in the Commissioner's room. 'Sir David expressed concern. I made two or three points. I said that we were let down completely and utterly. ECRC had not hidden information about procedures we were going to use. We had felt there was a complete understanding but the Scotland Yard boys had taken over everything from the hands of local police officers who were left without any effective control. I and the community did not believe that only the police had suffered injury . . . He mentioned provocation . . . My reply I remember was — crowds in emotionally charged moments do things which are wrong. How come a disciplined force does things wrong? He suggested that outsiders were trying to cash in on the weakness of the Asian community.' DAC Helm, who had been in operational command on the day, remained silent. Mr Chana's feeling from the meeting was that he 'was convinced that despite Sir David McNee's constant rebuttal of arguments about police making mistakes he knew that his men had not acted correctly as they should have, even though he could not admit it.'

2.129 That day the Chief Executive of the Commission for Racial Equality, Peter Tucker, wrote to the Home Office calling for a public enquiry and immediate discussion between the CRE, Home Office and Commissioner of Police. Some senior CRE officers had witnessed events on the day and there had been subsequent consultation with local groups. Peter Tucker wrote: 'Everyone we have spoken to has taken the view that one of the main causes of the disturbance was the over-representation of the police and the activities of the Special Patrol Group.' A number of groups including the TUC took up the call for a public enquiry.

2.130 At a joint press conference with Sir David McNee, Merlyn Rees announced that there would be no public enquiry. Commander Cass had already been instructed to investigate the circumstances surrounding the death of Blair Peach; Chief Superintendent Linnett was to be appointed to investigate other complaints concerning police actions. He further said that the review of public order legislation currently taking place between the Home Office and the Police would be widened to include meetings under the Representation of the People Act. Sir David McNee expressed his confidence in the SPG. 'They are good professional officers.' (*Daily Telegraph* 26 April.)

2.131 The *Daily Express* (26 April) reported under the headline 'Hand Over Your Truncheons' that the regulation police truncheons carried by 50 members of the SPG who had been on duty in Southall had been taken for examination in connection with the Blair Peach enquiry. It was not until 5 June that Commander Cass's investigators opened the lockers of some SPG officers on duty to find a gruesome array of non-regulation weapons (see paragraph 3.37).

2.132 At 8 pm on 25 April Ealing CRC called a meeting in the Manor House, Southall. The intention was to ensure the peaceful nature of the march on Saturday. Representatives from the Sikh temples, the mosque, ECRC, Peoples Unite, SYM, the Chamber of Commerce and churches were among those who attended. The younger people were still angry over their treatment on 23 April, and there was concern that the Saturday march would get out of control and end in violence. Rev. Jim Parkinson said: 'I fought hard against the revenge aspect pointed against the police. We had had enough of violence. Another confrontation would have torn the Town apart.' Mr Chana said, 'People like me were trying to find out what the local community could do to pick up the pieces and start building bridges. What I failed perhaps to appreciate fully was the anger of the young people.' Earlier in the day, Socialist Unity had produced a leaflet boldly headed 'AVENGE BLAIR PEACH'. Vishnu Sharma, with the assistance of Paul Holborrow, prevailed on Tariq Ali to change this to 'REMEMBER BLAIR PEACH' although many leaflets had already been distributed and the correction, when made, left unchanged a smaller repetition of the original slogan on the reverse of the leaflet.

2.133 On the next day, 26 April, James Jardine and Joe Martucci of the Police Federation met Merlyn Rees. They called for greater public order powers for the police and more protective gear for police officers at demonstrations. Sir David McNee appealed to people in Southall to 'keep calm and not allow themselves to be exploited by agitators'. (*Daily Mail* 27 April.)

2.134 During the afternoon in Southall there was another meeting in the Ballroom of the Dominion Cinema. It was agreed that there should be no incidents on the Saturday march, that the young people should themselves act as stewards, that the march should be dignified and there be no slogans or provocation.

2.135 At 7.30 pm that evening in Ealing Town Hall, the ECRC held an emergency executive meeting. They discussed the events on the Monday and decided to support a silent march on the 28 April with banners only from the ANL and NUT to which Blair Peach belonged. They mailed their members to that effect the next day.

2.136 On 27 April two meetings took place at Scotland Yard. At 10 am Paul Holborrow, Gerry Fitzpatrick (national organiser for the ANL), Tariq Ali and Balwinder Rana met a group of about six officers headed by Deputy Assistant Commissioner Helm. They agreed a route for the march from the Dominion Cinema to Southall Park via The Green, Beaconsfield Road, Hamborough Road, The Broadway, Beechcroft Park, Orchard Avenue, Herbert Road, Broadway, High Street and past the police station.

2.137 At 11.30 am the same police officers met Rev. Jim Parkinson, Vishnu Sharma, P.S. Khabra, Dilbagh Chana and Habrus Singh Ruprah. Since this group had been in ignorance of the earlier meeting there was some surprise at what was seen as an attempt to split those concerned in organising the march. Vishnu Sharma said: 'Gosse saw us at reception. He told us of another meeting already held to work out a route which I had been supposed to attend. I was furious.' They were prevailed upon to see if they could amend the route to avoid the police station, though in this they were to be unsuccessful. The group pleaded for a 'low profile' policing policy and this was accepted.

2.138 The rest of the day was taken up in a series of meetings to discuss organisation of the march. In the afternoon at the premises of the National Association of Asian Youth, a meeting of, among others, the SYM, ANL and IWA agreed that the SYM would provide its own pickets outside the police station with black armbands. At 5.30 pm in the Dominion Cinema Ballroom there was a larger meeting where feelings rose higher. Dilbagh Chana and Rev. Jim Parkinson in particular were alarmed at the prevailing attitude. Both left the meeting having said that their organisations, the ECRC and the churches, could only support a silent march of mourning, as originally proposed, with limited slogans and placards or none at all. The meeting in effect adjourned to the Ram Garhia Hall in the Broadway where the ECRC planned a discussion of arrangements. Sydney Bidwell, the local MP, attended and spoke. Jim Parkinson said: '. . . there was confusion as to whether this was a continuation of the old meeting or a new one. Tariq Ali and Balwinder Rana came down. There was a conflict of opinion. A chap from Peoples Unite said "I don't trust anyone any more". There was mistrust between the youth and the older people. They had lost confidence in us. There was an unsatisfactory end to the meeting. An attempt was made to calm Saturday down. It was agreed that there would be no political banners, no slogans, only a peaceful quiet march.'

2.139 Dilbagh Chana said: 'In the end to my disquiet the majority accepted the assurances given.' He was still worried that there would be violence on the demonstration the next day. After the meeting he discussed the matter with Martyn Grubb on the phone. Martyn Grubb's view was that there would be no violence if the police could be persuaded to remain largely out of sight and avoid any provocative display.

2.140 Mr Chana then rang Commander Thornton and pleaded again for a police presence with a low profile, making a number of specific recommendations. At about 1 am Commander Thornton rang back to say that they had been agreed. Policing of the march would be done with officers about seven feet apart and the reserves would be well out of sight.

2.141 The march assembled in the Dominion Cinema car park at 2 pm on the 28 April. A lorry became used as an impromptu platform for speeches in Punjabi and English. Banners other than the ANL and NUT were present.

Dilbagh Chana and a group of ECRC members felt that political capital was being made of the procession. They decided that the ECRC should dissociate itself as an organisation. Mr Chana said: 'We were more hurt than anything. Promises had not been kept.' Rev. Jim Parkinson also dissociated the churches from the march. 'We felt we had to pull out to be consistent with what we had been saying.' He had been worried by the possibility of violence, though he subsequently conceded that the decision was made to look rather absurd in the light of how the march actually went. He remained involved in organising the march and helped to ensure that the local people in the SYM and Peoples Unite marched at its head. He followed the march and was in the end impressed: 'Conduct was good'. Press reports stated that between 10,000 and 15,000 people attended the march. No arrests were reported. Vishnu Sharma said: 'The march was quiet. When it reached the Broadway it went absolutely quiet. People stood in groups where Blair Peach had died. They threw flowers and wreaths. Many Indian women were crying. They took off their shoes. There was a prayer in Hindustani by one woman . . . People said that he was white and he died for us. As we moved on, people were shouting in Hindustani "Long live Blair Peach". Outside the police station 25 to 30 members of SYM stood along its wall. They were still bandaged and injured from the Monday demonstration.'

2.142 Martyn Grubb felt that, as Community Relations Officer, he should attend the march even though the ECRC had withdrawn. He too was impressed. 'Above all . . . because of its orderliness. Secondly, because of its size . . . People — ordinary housewives and children, ordinary Southall families — were coming out of their front doors as the march passed and joining. They were not just all Indians though the vast majority were. There were people of every race and colour. It was quiet. Just before it got to the place where Blair Peach died a loudspeaker asked everyone to maintain silence. I left the march for a time at that spot and watched the march go by. That was where I realised it was so big . . . I felt it was a very healing thing — not just neutral but positively good.'

3: The Death of Blair Peach

3.1 The inquest into the death of Blair Peach was adjourned on Friday 12 October when the Divisional Court granted leave for an application to be made for a jury to sit with the coroner. The inquest will not start again until 28 April 1980. For that reason, this chapter is an incomplete account of Blair Peach's death. Members of this Enquiry attended the inquest on 11 and 12 October, when witnesses were heard. We have drawn on that evidence, and other material available to us, for this chapter. But we have not had the benefit of the evidence of other witnesses who will be called at the inquest, including particularly the police officers present in Beechcroft and Orchard Avenues at the time of Blair Peach's death. There are some inconsistencies in the different statements which we quote in this chapter; there may or may not be explanations for these inconsistencies, which will no doubt be explored at the inquest, but we have not sought to reconcile the differences. We will, if we feel it necessary, publish a further report after the inquest is finished.

3.2 Blair Peach was a 33-year-old New Zealander, who worked as a teacher at the Phoenix School for delicate children in East London. He was divorced, but had lived for some years with Ms Celia Stubbs, whose children they both cared for. She was regarded by Blair Peach's friends and family as his wife. Blair Peach was an active member of the Anti-Nazi League and the Socialist Workers Party. He had taken part in anti-racist activity in East London, particularly in countering National Front activities in Brick Lane. He had also taken part in various demonstrations. He seems to have been widely admired as a dedicated teacher and committed anti-racist.

3.3 On 23 April, Blair Peach came to Southall with a number of friends — Josephine Lang, Amanda Leon and Martin Gerald — all of whom were also members of the ANL. They met at Martin Gerald's flat in Pope's Lane in Ealing and drove to Southall in two cars, Blair Peach's and Martin Gerald's. With them was Francoise Ichard, a French woman staying in Martin Gerald's flat. They arrived at about 4.45 pm and parked some way from the town centre. Although they had intended to go to the Town Hall, they found their way blocked by the

72

police cordons and ended up on the Broadway. They remained there until about 7.45 pm. During that period, there were attempts by people in the crowd to break through the police cordon at the end of the Broadway nearest the Town Hall. Confusion, frustration and fear was caused within the crowd by the fact that for much of the time they were hemmed in by two police cordons (see para 2.53). A number of shop-windows were broken and some missiles were thrown at the police.

3.4 From about 7.30 pm onwards, protesters began to leave the Broadway. Many of them went into Beechcroft Avenue, which was not cordoned off and which appeared to offer a means of getting away from the crowd and back to the station. Missiles were being hurled at the police in the Broadway and at the bottom of Northcote Avenue (which runs north from the Broadway, opposite Beechcroft Avenue). The police formed up across Northcote Avenue, moved across the Broadway and charged into Beechcroft Avenue, carrying riot shields and truncheons. They were moving at a fast walk, but, according to some witnesses, broke into a run. Once into Beechcroft Avenue, they made way for two Special Patrol Group vans which drove into the street behind them, went round the junction with Orchard Avenue and stopped inside Orchard Avenue. The police officers moved after them. The vans opened, and now more police officers got out. It was at this time, at the junction of Beechcroft and Orchard Avenues, that Blair Peach was attacked and fatally injured.

3.5 The Home Secretary's memorandum (see appendix 2) refers briefly to these events as follows:

'It was at this time (approximately 8 pm) that an officer at the junction of Northcote Avenue and the Broadway was hit by a brick, which was thrown by someone in a crowd which had gathered in Beechcroft Avenue opposite. His jaw was fractured in three places. Assistance was then summoned to disperse the crowd and Mr Blair Peach was seen at the junction of Beechcroft Avenue and Orchard Avenue having sustained an injury to his head.'

In other words, according to the Home Secretary's memorandum, it was the injury to the police officer in Northcote Avenue which led to the police move down Beechcroft Avenue. Blair Peach's brother, Roy Peach, in a press statement on 28 July 1979, rightly objected to the apparent linking of the injured police officer with the injury on his brother — 'an association could wrongly be drawn adverse to Blair'. The timing is also somewhat confused. The ambulance which took Blair Peach to hospital arrived at about 8.10, having taken, it appears, 10 to 15 minutes to arrive. Blair Peach's injuries must, therefore, have occurred some time before 8 pm. It is very difficult to establish exact times for any of the events on 23 April and there are other discrepancies in the various estimates of time (for instance, J.S. Chana, quoted in para 3.12 says he saw Blair Peach hit at about 8.15 pm). It is possible that the injury to the police officer referred to by the Home Secretary's memorandum took place somewhat earlier than suggested. Alternatively, it is possible that the police charge into Beechcroft Avenue was not a result of the injury to that police officer.

3.6 According to their statements and the evidence given to the inquest, Amanda Leon, Martin Gerald, Blair Peach, Josephine Lang and Francoise Ichard decided to return to their cars at about 7.45 pm. They walked back along the Broadway (away from the police cordon nearest to the Town Hall), until they came to Beechcroft Avenue, which was not blocked by a police cordon and which appeared to offer a route by which they could leave. Amanda Leon and Blair Peach set off down Beechcroft Avenue, some way behind the other three. As they started walking down the road, Amanda Leon heard police sirens sounding and, looking back, saw police vans parked on the opposite side of the Broadway and a row of police standing on the street, with shields and truncheons. When the police started to charge, people ran away from them down Beechcroft Avenue. Fearing she would be hit, Amanda Leon took shelter in a doorway. When the initial charge subsided, she caught up with Blair Peach, who was some way further down Beechcroft Avenue. They were then swept up in a fresh charge of police officers, followed by the two vans. Amanda Leon told the inquest that police officers were hitting out with their truncheons, people were fleeing, there was 'complete chaos'. She was trying to keep up with Blair Peach, since they had agreed not to leave separately.

3.7 It was at this point, when Blair Peach was once again further down the road than Amanda Leon, that she says she saw him hit by a police officer with what she took to be a truncheon. She saw him staggering, although she did not know whether this was because of the blow or because he was trying to protect his head with his hands, as many people were doing for fear of being hit. She could not say how far she was from him when he was hit but said that, although she was not next to him, she was 'quite close'. She described the blow as being an overarm blow, struck by a police officer who was standing sideways to her between where she was and where Blair Peach was standing.

3.8 Amanda Leon then decided to try to return to the Broadway and moved back up Beechcroft Avenue. She leant against a wall and looked around to see what was going on. She saw another man on the ground being attacked by three or four police officers in 'a systematic manner'. She described him as being curled up on the ground, trying to protect his groin. She said to the police officers: 'I think you could stop hitting that man', or words to that effect. One of the police officers looked up, ran towards her and hit her with his truncheon on her head. She ran towards the Broadway, and was hurt on the hand by a riot shield carried by another police officer coming towards her. Mr Tilley, the ambulance attendant who took Blair Peach to the hospital, noticed that she had a head injury. Detective Constable Kensall, who saw her at the hospital, confirmed that she had a lump on one side of her head and a plaster on her hand. As she went to the Broadway, she saw another man who appeared to be badly injured, sitting on a chair, with tissues pressed to a head wound that was bleeding. She then decided she should catch up with the others — Blair Peach, Martin Gerald, Josephine Lang and Francoise Ichard — and went back to Orchard Avenue.

3.9 Meanwhile, Martin Gerald, Josephine Lang and Francoise Ichard left the Broadway at the same time as Blair Peach and Amanda Leon. They had got further down Beechcroft Avenue than the other two when they turned to see police officers heading across the Broadway into Beechcroft Avenue. They saw the two vans come down, and people running in all directions. They ran into Orchard Avenue. Martin Gerald looked back, to see police officers coming out of at least one van and hitting people with what he assumed to be truncheons. They walked further along Orchard Avenue (towards South Road) and were directed by police officers to an alley leading away from Orchard Avenue. They decided to go back to find Blair Peach and Amanda Leon, who would not have known where they had gone.

3.10 Josephine Lang told the inquest that they found Amanda Leon looking very shaken. They asked her whether she was all right, and where Blair Peach was. She told them she did not know where Blair Peach was, but did not mention that she had seen him hit. Josephine Lang then walked towards the junction of Beechcroft and Orchard Avenues and found a number of people standing outside a house (71 Orchard Avenue). She described Blair Peach and was told that he was inside the house. When she went inside, she found him slumped in a chair, and was told that an ambulance had been called. She went back to tell the others that she had found him, and they all went back to No.71.

3.11 Parminder Atwal — a member of the family who live at 71 Orchard Avenue — gave a statement to the *Evening Standard,* quoted on 24 April:

'Demonstrators were at the top of Beechcroft Road. I decided to move my car in case there was trouble. I was in my garden when two police vans came and about 20 police officers got out. The police were carrying shields and black truncheons. They tried to break up the line of people and came running down the road pushing people, pulling them by the hair and hitting them with their sticks.

'This boy was standing on the corner next to the wall, when everybody came running past. He got tangled up in it and was knocked over. Then, when he was lying on the ground, the police came rushing past him as they chased these other blokes down the road.

'As the police rushed past him, one of them hit him on the head with the stick. I was in my garden and saw this quite clearly. When they all rushed past, he was left sitting against the wall. He tried to get up, but he was shivering and looked very strange. He could not stand. Then the police came back and told him like this: "Move! Come on, move!" They were very rough with him and I was shocked because it was clear that he was seriously hurt.

'His tongue seemed to have stuck in the top of his mouth and his eyes were rolled up to the top of his head. But they started pushing him and told him to move; and he managed to get to his feet. He staggered across the road and came to where I was in the garden. I tried to sit him down. He was in a very bad state and could not speak. Then he just dropped down. I got a glass of water for him, but he could not hold it and it dropped out of his hand.'

3.12 This eye-witness account is confirmed by other witnesses, who will be called to the inquest. For instance, J.S. Chana, who lives in Herbert Road (the continuation of Orchard Avenue) said in a statement made on 25 April that at about 8.15 pm he saw a crowd of people running towards Orchard Avenue. He was quite nearby when he saw a man hit on the head by one of a group of police officers. The man fell down and tried to crawl towards No.71. Mr Chana helped move him into the house, called an ambulance and waited until its arrival.

3.13 When Jaswant Atwal got home, he says that Blair Peach was lying on the sofa in the living room. With him were Martin Gerald, Amanda Leon, Josephine Lang and Francoise Ichaud.

3.14 The ambulance arrived at about 8.10 (the Home Secretary's memorandum says that Blair Peach was taken to hospital at 8.12). The ambulance driver, Ivor Poet, told the inquest that Blair Peach was conscious, sitting on a sofa or armchair. One of the women in the room asked Blair Peach for his keys and he indicated that they were in his pocket. (Mr Poet stated under cross-examination that he could not remember whether Blair Peach pointed at his keys, or said so in as many words. But Martin Gerald said that Blair Peach, who was looking extremely dazed, pointed to Amanda Leon to indicate that she should go to the hospital with him. He seemed to be having difficulty speaking.)

3.15 The ambulance attendant, Eric Tilley, said that Blair Peach told him that the pain was in his head, but that he had no pain elsewhere. There was no visible wound, and no bleeding. He and Mr Poet put Blair Peach into a wheelchair to take him out to the ambulance, and transferred him to a stretcher. As they got nearer New Ealing District Hospital, Blair Peach said that the pain was getting more severe. He was starting to get restless, according to Mr Tilley. As they took him in to the hospital, he vomited. Amanda Leon describes him as vomiting 'blood and water' on to the stretcher.

3.16 Dr Richard Bentall, surgical registrar at the hospital, was called urgently to casualty to examine Blair Peach. Dr Bentall observed that Blair's pulse was dropping rapidly, that he was thrashing about and that his left pupil was dilated and unreactive. Dr Bentall said he had been told that Blair Peach had walked into a house, injured and verbally aggressive, but he cannot remember who told him this; it is not borne out by any evidence. Although he had been conscious on arrival at the hospital, he was unconscious when Dr Bentall saw him and was becoming more deeply unconscious. Dr Bentall ordered a transfer to the Intensive Care Unit and the operating theatre. His respiration slowed during the journey in the lift and he was taken straight to the theatre. Dr Bentall told the inquest that Blair's symptoms indicated rapidly developing brain pressure, which would lead to death quickly if not relieved. There was no visible injury to the head, but there was a large extra-dural haematoma (i.e. a swelling from bleeding in the outer membrane covering the brain), on the left side. 200-300 ml of blood were drained off, and arterial bleeding continued. At least three large pieces of bone were removed. A consultant, who took over at Dr Bentall's request, confirmed the diagnosis. Dr Bentall summarised Blair Peach's condition by saying that he was bleeding from a number of veins and arteries inside his skull. Because the skull cannot expand, the bleeding had the effect of compressing the brain. If the bleeding had been allowed to continue, it would eventually have forced the brain through the bottom of the skull. The skull was fractured above the left ear, with the line of the fracture going along the side and back over the top of his head. Blair Peach's condition deteriorated during the operation, and he died at 12.10 am.

3.17 When Amanda Leon arrived at the hospital with Blair Peach, she was taken to have her head wound examined. She was given an injection and had her hand dressed. She was told she could wait for news of Blair. She was joined by Josephine Lang. Martin Gerald also came to the hospital but was not apparently present when the two women were seen by the police. Detective Constable Kensall had gone to the hospital to deal with the case of a police officer who had been stabbed (see para 2.79) and to assist with informing the relatives of injured police officers. He was asked to see the witnesses who had come in with a badly-injured man and went to the room where Amanda Leon and Josephine Lang were waiting. He was joined by Detective Constable Daly, the police liaison officer who had been assigned to the hospital to assist injured police officers. DC Kensall spoke to Amanda Leon and DC Daly to Josephine Lang.

3.18 There is a discrepancy between the evidence of Amanda Leon and that of DC Kensall concerning their conversation in the hospital. According to DC Kensall, Amanda Leon told him that she had been in the Broadway, had seen truncheons being used, and had become separated from Blair Peach and had only seen him again at 71 Orchard Avenue. According to him, she said 'I did not see it (Blair Peach being hurt). We got split up'. Amanda Leon maintains that she told the police officer at the hospital that she had seen Blair Peach hit and, given the general chaos, had assumed he had walked on. If she had said 'I did not see him. We got split up', she was referring to the period after he had been hit.

3.19 Both Amanda Leon and Josephine Lang informed the police officers that they would not make a statement except in the presence of a lawyer. The police officers left the room where they had spoken to the two women in order to obtain further information. When they returned, the women had left.

3.20 After talking to the police officer, Amanda Leon said that someone told her that Blair Peach was being operated on for a fractured skull and that there was no point in waiting, since it would take some time. A nurse asked her to go to the room where Blair Peach had been to collect his clothes. She examined the clothes for signs of blood — there were none — and took them with her. Amanda Leon, Josephine Lang, Martin Gerald and, we assume, Francoise Ichard then returned to 71 Orchard Avenue, where they spent some time talking to the Atwal family about what had happened and making telephone calls.

3.21 After spending some time at 71 Orchard Avenue, the four friends returned to Martin Gerald's flat where they continued to telephone the hospital and tried to contact Celia Stubbs. When they phoned the hospital soon after midnight, they were told that Blair Peach had died.

3.22 Celia Stubbs did not go to Southall with Blair Peach and the others. She arrived at about 6 pm, having made a loose arrangement to meet him there. In fact, she did not see him that evening. By about 6.45, she was in the Broadway, and left at about 7.45. After meeting friends, she went home to Hackney. Amanda Leon, who had been unable to reach her by phone, had contacted a friend who lives in the same road, who telephoned Ms Stubbs with the news of Blair's death. She immediately went by taxi to Ealing Hospital. She was then told to go to Southall Police Station, where a police officer told her to go to Martin Gerald's flat. She was accompanied by police officers and stayed at the flat for a few hours, finally returning to Hackney. She took no part in the discussions that were going on at the flat and spent some time trying to telephone Blair Peach's family in New Zealand.

3.23 During conversations on their way to Martin Gerald's flat, and after they arrived, Amanda Leon, Josephine Lang and Martin Gerald agreed that there was no need to mention that Francoise Ichard had also been present. They were apparently fearful for her position as a foreign worker if she became involved in police enquiries. They admitted that this was a foolish decision, since she might have had evidence relating to Blair Peach's death. In the statements which they gave to the police afterwards, however, they referred to her presence. It appears that Francoise Ichard was not in fact a witness to Blair Peach's being attacked. She has returned to France, but is willing to appear at the inquest as a witness. witness.

3.24 After they arrived at Martin Gerald's flat, Amanda Leon tried to contact a solicitor. When she heard of Blair Peach's death, she contacted Dick North, a friend and fellow-member of the Anti-Nazi League, who had not been present at the demonstration. He gave her the telephone number of Larry Grant, a solicitor at Seifert Sedley, who is the lawyer representing Blair Peach's family at the inquest. Dick North came round to Martin Gerald's flat immediately after receiving Amanda Leon's phone call. A number of other people were also present, including the police officers who arrived with Mrs Stubbs. During the night, Amanda Leon and Martin Gerald went by taxi to Broadcasting House, where they gave a radio interview concerning Blair Peach's death. They also spoke to various press representatives on the phone. Martin Gerald is quoted by the *Daily Telegraph* on 25 April as having said: 'Blair was hit twice on the head with police truncheons and left unconscious'. Questioned on this point at the inquest, Martin Gerald said that he did not know where the press had obtained that quote, but that he might have referred to a witness at 71 Orchard Avenue who said that he saw Blair Peach hit twice and left unconscious. Mr Gerald did not himself see Blair Peach hit.

3.25 Martin Gerald, Amanda Leon and Josephine Lang were asked by the police officers who arrived at the flat to give statements. They said they would do so in the presence of a lawyer. Later on during 24 April, they saw their lawyer, Larry Grant, and gave statements to the police in his presence.

The nature of Blair Peach's injuries

3.26 At the request of the coroner, a post-mortem was carried out by Professor D. Bowen of Charing Cross Hospital. A second post-mortem was carried out, at the request of the family, by Professor Keith Mant, head of the Department of Forensic Medicine at Guy's Hospital and Professor of Forensic Medicine at the University of London. We have not seen Professor Mant's full report, but we have seen his conclusions and extracts from the report. Professor Mant concluded that the cause of death was 'an extradural haemorrhage due to fracture of the skull'. This conclusion bears out the diagnosis of the surgeon who operated on Blair Peach (see para 3.16 above).

3.27 In his report, Professor Mant stated:
'i. Death resulted from a single blow to the left side of the head. There were no other injuries upon the deceased.
ii. The instrument used must have been very weighty and yet at the same time was malleable and without a hard edge as there were no lacerations to the scalp.
iii. A police truncheon is relatively light and when used usually lacerates the scalp unless the head is protected by thick hair or head gear.
iv. Blood was present in the left middle ear having tracked along branches of the middle meningeal artery supplying the area.
v. The deceased had not been bleeding externally as the injury was a closed injury.
vi. The injury was so severe that immediate loss of consciousness would occur and without treatment death within 30 minutes or sooner.
vii. The instrument used could have been a lead weighted rubber "cosh" or hosepipe filled with lead shot, or some like weapon.'
Professor Mant has further stated: 'The surprising feature is the tremendous boney damage without external damage to the skin. This would exclude a police truncheon'. We understand that Professor Bowen's conclusions do not differ significantly from those of Professor Mant.

3.28 It is quite clear that Blair Peach's injuries were not received accidentally.

Had he fallen against a wall, or been thrown against a railing, any head injuries received would have been visible and would – especially if severe enough to cause death – have led to bleeding. Similarly, we find it impossible to believe that he could have been hit on the head by a brick or stone. Professor Mant is quite firm in his conclusion that the instrument could not have been a police truncheon, and could not have had a hard edge of the kind that would cause lacerations.

The investigation of Blair Peach's death

3.29 Commander Cass, head of the Metropolitan Police Complaints Investigation Bureau, was appointed by the Commissioner for the Metropolitan Police to investigate Blair Peach's death. Initially, press reports said that the investigation was being treated as a 'murder enquiry'. But it was not clear precisely what Commander Cass's job was. Both the NCCL and the lawyers acting on behalf of Blair Peach's family requested the Home Secretary to publish the terms of reference of Commander's Cass's investigation. They were not published. In an affidavit read to the Divisional Court on 15 November 1979 – during the hearing of the application for a jury to sit with the coroner – Commander Cass said that he had been appointed 'to investigate the complaint that Blair Peach had been assaulted by a police officer with a truncheon'. But he went on to say that he had also been appointed to investigate other complaints against police officers 'of assaults alleged to have occurred in the same close proximity and time as that alleged in respect of Blair Peach'.

3.30 Soon after Blair Peach's death, at the first hearing of the inquest, Commander Cass said that he wished to trace, in particular, all young Asian boys, aged about 13 to 17, who had been in Beechcroft Avenue at around 8 pm. Since the police were alleging that a crowd of Asian youths had been attacking the police at that time, it is hardly surprising that no such witnesses appear to have come forward to be interviewed by Commander Cass.

3.31 According to the *Leveller* magazine (January 1980), Commander Cass narrowed suspicion down to six officers who were said to be in the van from No.1 Unit of the SPG which went into Beechcroft Avenue: Inspector Murray, the driver PC White, and four other constables, PC Freestone, PC Lake, PC Richardson and PC Scottow. The magazine also stated that all six were suspended from the SPG and then transferred to other duties (one at his own request). We have confirmed that disciplinary action was taken against one inspector and three constables (see para 3.39), but Scotland Yard refuses to confirm or deny whether they were suspected of killing Blair Peach. *The Sunday Times,* 16 March 1980 also named the same six officers.

3.32 Commander Cass's report was submitted to the Director of Public Prosecutions, whose duty it then was to decide whether or not to institute criminal proceedings. The DPP operates a general rule that there should be at least a 50% chance of conviction before he will authorise a prosecution. But in deciding whether or not there is a 50% chance of conviction in a case where the suspect is a police officer, he also takes into account the supposed reluctance of juries to convict police officers. In practice, therefore, the DPP demands a *higher* standard of evidence against a police officer than he does against other suspects.

3.33 The DPP decided that there was insufficient evidence to prosecute any police officer or anyone else for the death of Blair Peach. One difficulty appears to have been identification evidence. Eye-witnesses have sworn to the fact that a police officer assaulted Blair Peach (see paras 3.11 and 3.12 above). We understand that four or five identification parades were held, at which the witnesses were unable to identify the officer or officers who had attacked Blair Peach. The fact that all officers were wearing uniform and helmets would, of course, make identification extremely difficult.

3.34 In November, Commander Cass re-opened his investigation. An anonymous phone caller had told Southall Rights Centre that he had met two former Scotland Yard police officers in Rhodes during his summer holiday in August. He said that the two men made no secret of the fact that they had been police officers, and boasted of having been responsible for Blair Peach's death. They had, he stated, claimed that they had been ordered to disappear for two years. The ex-police officers have been identified as Philip Dyer and Mark Richards, who formerly served with the Willesden Division. But the anonymous phone caller refused to make himself available for interview by Southall Rights or anyone else and it appears that this line of enquiry has proved fruitless. To date, however, no statement has been made by the police or the Home Secretary as to whether or not Commander Cass's new investigation has produced fresh evidence for submission to the Director of Public Prosecutions.

The weapons found in possession of the SPG

3.35 On 5 June 1979, in the course of his investigations, Commander Cass found a number of weapons in the lockers of SPG officers who had been on duty in Southall on 23 April. In an affidavit which was read to the Court of Appeal on 15 December, Commander Cass said that the 3,000 pages of statements given to the coroner contained 'full details of the finding of police weapons'. He further stated that there was 'no evidence that these weapons were carried on 23 April, or that any officers carried anything on 23 April other than regulation truncheons, protective shields and police personal radios'.

3.36 The coroner viewed these weapons before the inquest resumed in October. The family's lawyer, Mr Grant, had heard of the existence of these weapons through unattributed press reports. But he received confirmation of their existence only when he received from the coroner a list of witnesses to be called at the inquest. The list included 'evidence of weapons at the scene and Police'. He applied to the police for permission for himself, a barrister and

Professor Keith Mant, to inspect the weapons. He was informed by Commander Cass that he would be permitted to view the weapons only if he and the barrister signed an undertaking not to disclose publicly any information about the weapons. After objections from the lawyers, Commander Cass withdrew that requirement. After a number of attempts to fix an appointment, the lawyers and Professor Mant finally viewed the weapons on Friday 16 November.

3.37 In an affidavit read to the Court of Appeal on 15 December, Mr Grant describes the weapons which had been taken from police lockers. They were:
'Four police issue truncheons
One brass handle
One leather encased truncheon, approximately one foot long with a knotted thong at the end
One metal truncheon which was encased in leather of about eight inches in length with a very flexible handle and a lead weight in the end
One wooden pickaxe handle
One sledge hammer
One American type beat truncheon which was almost two feet in length
One leather whip which I would describe as a 'Rhino whip'
Two case openers or jemmies
One white bone handled knife with a long blade case
One black plastic handled knife
One crowbar about three feet in length
One piece of wood about three feet in length, two inches in diameter
One further crowbar.'

3.38 With the exception of the four police issue truncheons, this appalling list consists of offensive weapons which it would be illegal for anyone, police officer or not, to carry in public. It remains to be seen whether any of the implements described could have caused the fatal injury to Blair Peach. But any of these weapons, in the hands of a determined assailant, could cause extremely serious or fatal injury.

3.39 In June 1979, three constables and an inspector from the SPG unit at Barnes were transferred to other duties as a disciplinary measure, because of irregularities which had come to light during the investigation into Blair Peach's death and other complaints about police action at Southall. The Metropolitan Police have insisted that the irregularities for which these officers were disciplined had nothing to do with Blair Peach's death or with events on 23 April. Indeed, the Metropolitan Police has stressed that transfer from the SPG back to other police duties is normal, and that most police officers spend no more than two to three years in the SPG. Although the Metropolitan Police never releases the names of officers disciplined, or details of the disciplinary offences concerned, we understand that the 'irregularities' involved were possession of the weapons described above.

3.40 No public statement has ever been made by the police or the Home Secretary — who is the Police Authority for the Metropolitan Police — concerning the discovery of these weapons. The weapons were not found until early June — over a month after Blair Peach had been killed. But police officers who had been on duty in Southall on 23 April apparently felt secure enough to retain potentially lethal weapons in their lockers. The public have not been told what excuse, if any, was proffered by the officers concerned for possessing these weapons, or where they obtained them. No explanation has been offered for the apparently light punishment awarded, and no statement has been made about what measures, if any, have been taken to prevent police officers from possessing or using such weapons in future.

3.41 Commander Cass concluded that 'there was no evidence' that the weapons were carried on 23 April, or that any of the police officers on duty carried anything other than regulation truncheons, protective shields and police personal radios. But there was eye-witness evidence that one or more police officers had beaten Blair Peach outside 62 Orchard Avenue. The pathologist's evidence — the conclusions of which were published on 6 June — made it clear that a regulation police truncheon could not have been the weapon used. In these circumstances, it is puzzling how Commander Cass could have reached so firm a conclusion.

Missiles found in Beechcroft and Orchard Avenues

3.42 During the police investigation, a certain amount of debris was found scattered in Beechcroft and Orchard Avenues. Mr Grant, who inspected these items at the same time as he inspected the weapons found in the possession of certain police officers, described them as being: 'various assorted bricks, milk bottles, four wooden pieces, a butcher's cleaver, a piece of piping, a piece of chain, some castors, four separate pieces of bricks and a piece of pipe'. The police have claimed that missiles were being thrown from 'a hostile crowd' in Beechcroft Avenue towards the police in the Broadway and Northcote Avenue. The evidence found in the road bears out the police claim to the extent of showing that missiles were available.

3.43 Professor Mant was firm in his conclusions concerning the kind of weapon used to assault Blair Peach (see para 3.37). It must have been malleable, weighty and yet without a hard edge. It is therefore impossible to conclude that any of the debris or missiles which the police found in Beechcroft Avenue could have been the weapon which killed Blair Peach.

The inquest

3.44 Because Blair Peach died in West London, the coroner appointed for the inquest was the senior coroner for that district, Mr John Burton. A coroner has extremely wide powers to decide on the procedure which an inquest will follow. He can decide which parties will be represented at the inquest; which witnesses will be called; what questions may be asked of witnesses. Since the Criminal Law Act 1977, he has considerable discretion in deciding whether or not to call a jury. A coroner's task is a restricted one: to decide who died, and when, where and how he died. Since the change in the law in 1977, a coroner no longer has the power to charge any person with murder or manslaughter and no suspect can be named in the verdict. For these reasons, a coroner's inquest differs significantly from a normal court of law, and is no substitute either for a criminal trial or for a full public inquiry.

3.45 Every coroner's court has attached to it a police officer, who acts as full-time coroner's officer. It is the function of this officer to summon a jury where necessary. It is also, in theory, the function of this officer to investigate the circumstances of a death in order to assist the coroner in deciding what witnesses to call. In London and a number of other cities, the investigation function is performed by the police force. As a result, the only police investigation into Blair Peach's death was carried out by Commander Cass, who was not acting on behalf of the coroner, but carrying out an investigation into a complaint against the police under the 1964 Police Act. This situation led to an extremely serious dispute between the coroner and lawyers acting for two parties represented at the inquest – Blair Peach's family and the Anti-Nazi League. (The only other party represented at the inquest is the Metropolitan Police.)

3.46 After the DPP had decided not to prosecute anyone for the death of Blair Peach, Commander Cass gave the coroner copies of the 3,000 pages of statements and interview notes he had obtained during his investigation. It was on the basis of these documents that the coroner decided which witnesses to call. A copy of the same documents has been given to the lawyers representing the Metropolitan Police at the inquest. But the coroner has refused to provide copies of these statements to the lawyers representing the family and the Anti-Nazi League. Commander Cass has backed up this refusal by saying that it was only 'as a matter of courtesy' that he gave the information to the coroner, and that the statements had not been obtained for the coroner's use. Thus, when a witness is called to give evidence, both the coroner and the police lawyer have a copy of what the witness told Commander Cass and can question him or her on the basis of that statement, as well as on what the witness has told the inquest. But the family and the ANL lawyers cannot. When a question arises as to what the witness has told the inquest, both the coroner and the police lawyer can refer back to the previous statement as well as to their notes of what has just been said: the other two lawyers cannot. On the first day of the resumed inquest – 11 October – a discrepancy arose between what Amanda Leon claimed she had told the police at Ealing Hospital, and what the police witness claimed she had said (see para 3.18 above). The lawyer acting for Blair Peach's family objected strongly to being denied a copy of the police witness's statement: the coroner's response was to read out the statement so rapidly that no-one could make a full note of what had been said.

3.47 At the resumed inquest on 11 October, the lawyers acting for the family and for the ANL applied for copies of Commander Cass's statements. They were refused. They also applied to the coroner to have a jury sit with him. That was also refused. The following day, the Divisional Court gave permission for an appeal against the coroner's decisions, and the inquest was therefore adjourned. On 15 November, the Divisional Court dismissed the two applications, made on behalf of Blair's brother, Roy Peach, to have copies of the statements made available, and to have a jury summoned for the inquest. Roy Peach appealed against the Divisional Court's decision, and on 15 December, the Court of Appeal ordered the coroner to call a jury. Because of the difficulty of finding a three-week period when witnesses and lawyers will be available, the inquest has not yet resumed and will not start again until 28 April 1980.

3.48 There have been a number of deficiencies in the proceedings of the inquest so far. The purpose of an inquest is to arrive at the truth. This is not furthered by withholding information from the lawyers acting for parties represented at the inquest. The coroner should make available, in advance, to all parties represented at the inquest copies of the statements obtained by Commander Cass during his investigation. If necessary, the law should be changed as a matter of urgency, to require the coroner to make this information available and to prevent a situation arising again where information can be withheld in this fashion.

3.49 We are also concerned at the suggestion made twice by the coroner that he might withdraw his permission to the Anti-Nazi League to be represented at the inquest. The coroner criticised counsel for the ANL for using the inquest as 'a political medium'. Counsel apologised, but the irritation of the coroner appeared to continue. The Anti-Nazi League has been widely accused of being responsible for the violence of 23 April; they should continue to be represented at the inquest.

3.50 Finally, in view of what is now known about the vetting of juries in criminal cases, we feel strongly that the jury which sits with the coroner when the inquest resumes should be randomly selected from the electoral registers for the coroner's district. In view of the circumstances of this inquest, the process of selection should not be carried out by the police officer attached to the coroner's court but by independent officials under the direct supervision of the Lord Chancellor's Department.

Conclusion

3.51 It is a matter for astonishment that a man has died in suspicious circumstances; that the police investigation into the allegation that he had been killed by a police officer resulted in no criminal or disciplinary proceedings against any officer; and that no other investigation has been undertaken into who was responsible for his death.

3.52 As Lord Justice Bridge said in the Court of Appeal on 15 December 1979:

'There is reason to suspect that Blair Peach died from a blow to the head struck by a police officer with an unauthorised and potentially lethal weapon.'

No evidence has ever been produced to suggest that Blair Peach was assaulted by anyone other than a police officer. But those responsible have not been required to account for their actions.

4: The Response of the Media

4.1 A detailed analysis of the media reporting of the Southall events was not part of the Enquiry Committee's brief. But no comprehensive analysis of those events could fail to pay some attention to the role of the media. The question of how the events in Southall were understood and interpreted cannot be separated from how Southall was reported and interpreted by the media. Many of those who subsequently commented on those events, and the vast majority of the general public, were not present at Southall and had no other access to what occurred apart from the accounts which were made available through the media. Questions of accuracy and detail are of the utmost importance here, because erroneous or incomplete accounts, if repeated often enough and with sufficient force and emphasis, acquire the status of 'the facts of the case'. They become part of what thereafter is taken for granted about the events and, in that way, powerfully shape how the controversial issues are subsequently judged and assessed.

4.2 Analysis must, however, go beyond strict questions of fact and accuracy. Media reports, however conscientiously constructed, are inevitably selective. Some aspects, which seem relevant, will be given prominence. Necessarily, other aspects, which seem less relevant to journalists and editors, will be omitted. In this process of inclusion and exclusion, different factors will be operative: the constraints on journalists securing an overall or comprehensive view of what everyone agrees to have been a highly confused and confusing situation; reliance on particular sources for authoritative accounts; the hierarchy of credibility, which gives greater weight to some versions of those events over others; and (by no means least) the imperatives of news values, which provide newsmen and editors with their criteria of selection and emphasis. The pattern of stresses, emphases and exclusions which emerge from this process influences not only what comes to be known about a particular sequence of events, but more significantly, what that knowledge adds up to — what, ultimately, Southall 'meant'.

4.3 Traditionally, journalists attempt to maintain a sharp distinction between 'fact' and 'interpretation'. In practice, the distinction is inevitably a blurred and indistinct one. Inevitably, descriptive accounts include or, more often, imply and assume some sort of explanation as to the causes of events, especially when they assume a violent and controversial character, even if more extensive speculation on causes is reserved for editorial comment or news feature analysis. Apart from strict questions of accuracy, then, analysis must also take into account the overall *impression* which vivid news reporting conveys. It must also deal with the implied explanations which descriptive accounts often entail. This is especially the case on occasions such as the Southall events which are highly newsworthy (e.g. involving physical violence and injuries); which break the framework of public expectations as to the even and normally peaceful tenor of civil life; which give clear evidence of strong, passionate but polarised feelings on all sides; and which lead to direct confrontation with the authorities, unmediated by the normal processes of negotiation and compromise which the general public has come to expect of the everyday conduct of political affairs. The links between Southall and controversial issues which were already exercising public concern — questions concerning race, political confrontation, law and order, in the context of a forthcoming General Election — heightened the newsworthiness of Southall, and placed a more than usual weight on conflicting, and emotionally charged, interpretations of what happened and to whom responsibility should be attributed.

4.4 These questions relate especially to the immediate reporting of Southall. But, again, analysis cannot be limited to this period. A story of this kind does not die after the first day's news-break. As the immediate violence of the day receded in importance, public attention was directed towards the wider issues. The event itself was mapped into a framework of more inclusive concerns, of which Southall itself became only one, symptomatic, example. This necessarily involved the media in more extensive background exploration of the causes and the consequences of the particular events. It provided the means by which the event could be reinterpreted in the light of these larger issues. Southall was bound to be seen against the general background of the rise of the National Front and of organised opposition to its policies; more immediately, it was bound to be defined in terms of other, similar events preceding or likely to follow Southall. The interpretation of Southall naturally drew on a whole previous history of concern and of reporting of such events. The Front's decision to hold such a meeting in an area like Southall naturally raised more general questions concerning the law covering election meetings, the rights of 'free speech' against the case for a ban on potentially disturbing meetings likely to cause offence to one section of the population. The violence of the day was linked to wider questions concerning political demonstrations and law and order. The confrontations between demonstrators and the police helped to highlight the issue of political violence and the role and conduct of the police. These were lively and contentious issues which were focused, from the outset, even by the apparently descriptive and factual accounts of what happened on the day. And since many of the set themes were already politically charged as a result of the General Election campaign, the event was inevitably raised to the level of issues of a broader political nature.

4.5 Much of the early coverage of Southall — though, as we go on to show, not as much as we might have expected — was given over to a descriptive account of 'what happened'. But, in the last resort, events do not describe or speak for themselves. They have to be made to mean something. Which 'facts' are relevant often depends on which explanations are accepted as relevant and on prior assumptions and expectations. To give an example (its precise relevance to the case in point will be demonstrated further below): if what occurred at Southall is interpreted as primarily attributable to the intervention of outside 'extremist' political elements, with a concerted plan to incite violence and attack the police, then the incontrovertible fact that some supporters of the Anti-Nazi League were present at the demonstration will, from some points of view, become a highly salient and relevant one. This is so, however, *only* if we make some further premises: that the ANL is committed to a policy of violence and disruption of this kind; that they had a concerted plan to exploit the conditions in Southall on 23 April in this way; and that, in fact, they succeeded in putting such a plan into effect. As we have tried to show, in chapter 8, none of these premises has in fact been established, and no supporting evidence for them has been offered. Nevertheless, this was indeed one of the principal ways in which Southall was explained by senior police spokesmen and responsible political commentators; and — perhaps not surprisingly — it was also the preferred explanation on which the majority of news descriptions rested sometimes implicitly, and even more often explicitly, by way of direct quotation.

4.6 The media, however, do not always trace through the full implications or logic of the premises on which their descriptions are based. More often, the link is assumed, without evidence or inspection. Sometimes the link is forged simply by the strategic quotation of an authoritative witness who takes this point of view. These 'definitions' then become part of what is known about a particular sequence of events. Often, the assumption is based on what appears to have been established *before* the actual event is reported, drawn from previous reports and interpretations of similar events. The most authoritative analysis of the news reporting of a political demonstration — the Leicester University Centre for Mass Communications Research study of the 1968 Vietnam demonstration, *Demonstrations and Communication* — provide clear evidence of how a prior framework of definitions and assumptions can enter into and shape the apparently factual media account of an event. The *Daily Mail* editorial on Southall ('A Battle Both Extremist Sides Wanted', 25 April), which predicated its commentary on the supposedly established political character of the ANL — allowing the *Daily Mail* to refer unproblematically to the ANL as 'Fascists of the Left' — is a good example of how prior premises — and prejudices — are mobilised into the analysis of a current event.

4.7 If, on the other hand, the principal provocation for Southall is laid at the door of the National Front, and the events are understood as flowing from the natural and indeed just and wholly explicable reaction of anger in the community, then the presence of a small number of ANL supporters — though still, incontrovertibly, a fact — becomes a largely irrelevant one, compared with other facts. That this is not a far-fetched example can be seen by comparing the *Daily Mail* editorial referred to above with that of the same day by the *Daily Mirror* ('An Affront To Freedom', 25 April). The *Daily Mirror* did lay the blame primarily on the Front's decision to hold an election meeting in the heart of Southall — and, consequently, made no mention of the ANL.

4.8 An event like Southall was bound to arouse fears and anxieties amongst the general public. The seriousness of the occasion demanded and demands public concern. But if these fears and anxieties are not simply to be worked on, spuriously and sensationally exacerbated, it is necessary for the general public to be accurately and comprehensively informed. Discussion and debate about consequences and responsibility — which is bound to be divided and contentious — should be rationally conducted. The media have a heavy responsibility to discharge in this respect. The pressures and constraints on their performance, in the conditions which prevailed at Southall, must have and do appear to have limited the capacity of the media to provide such an accurate, comprehensive, balanced and rational account. But in the committee's view, these mitigating circumstances do not adequately account for the many serious lapses which a close analysis of the coverage clearly suggests. A full assessment of that performance is beyond the scope of this report, but we have tried to isolate those features which give the greatest scope for concern. The commentary is therefore, of necessity, selective and critical.

Southall In The Press: 24 April

4.9 All the national dailies featured the Southall story on the front page on 24 April. All, except the *Sun* and the *Daily Star,* made it the lead front-page story. The story was headlined in the following ways:

BATTLE OF HATE
Election Riot: Police hurt, 300 arrested.
'There were unprovoked attacks by groups against police and property just to create tension' — SIR DAVID McNEE LAST NIGHT
(Daily Express)

RACE RIOTERS BATTLE WITH POLICE ARMY
(Daily Mail)

300 HELD IN RIOT AT NF DEMO
(Daily Mirror)

300 ARRESTED AT POLL RIOT
Asian fury at election meeting
40 police hurt in protest over National Front
(Daily Telegraph)

ANTI-FRONT MOB FURY
(Daily Star)

TEACHER DIES IN FRONT CLASHES
(Guardian)

OUTRAGE EXPLODES OVER NF MEETING
TOWN STRIKE HITS RACISTS
(Morning Star)

300 HELD AS MOBS STONE POLICE
(Sun)

The language of these headlines stresses violence, confrontation, arrest and injury. The dominant image is that of a riotous rampage by a mob against the police. One edition of the *Daily Mail* took this battle imagery to its logical extreme: 'RACE RIOTERS BATTLE WITH POLICE ARMY'. 'Riot' occurs in four of the eight headlines. Three of the remaining four describe the demonstrators as a 'mob'. Several refer to the 'fury of the mob'. The exception is the *Morning Star*. This difference may be explained in terms of that paper's political orientation. But it is not necessary to accept the *Morning Star's* interpretation in order to see that what it demonstrates is that the same event can be seen in more than one way. The contrast therefore helps to establish the otherwise self-evident uniformity of angle adopted by the rest of the press. The *Morning Star* headline is no less accurate than the others; and its report leaves the reader in no doubt of the extent of the violence involved. But, whereas the other headlines emphasise the riotous assault on the police by the demonstrating mob, the *Morning Star* chooses to highlight what is *also* part of the story, but an aspect which the others neglect.

4.10 Of the national dailies, only the *Daily Telegraph's* subheading makes a similar concession in this direction: 'Asian fury at election meeting'. In fact, the *Daily Telegraph's* headlines are the most comprehensive of all (as its reporting is the most detailed and accurate), because they include *four* different aspects of the day's events: the numbers arrested; the anger of the Asian community; the numbers of policemen injured; the fact that it was a protest against the National Front. Measured against this example, the other headlines are not so much inaccurate as highly selective. This selectivity works in a more or less uniform direction, stressing the violence, physical confrontation, the mob versus the police. They point the finger at the rioting demonstrators. It would be difficult to read the headlines as signalling anything other than the malicious and provocative actions of the demonstrators. The overall effect is to present the day's events as very largely an exercise in mindless and irrational violence. The *Guardian* and the *Daily Mirror* also set up their headlines from this angle, though they treat the sensational elements of the story in relatively unsensational language.

4.11 Many of the details which follow these headlines in the lead stories, and the sequence of events which emerges from them, are reported in a strikingly similar way. Given the great confusion which reigned on the day, this uniformity of presentation is, to say the least, surprising. All the newspapers report that there were 300 arrests. All adopt the figure of 40 serious injuries (though there is some variation as to how many of these were policemen). The nature and extent of police injuries is very detailed. The very extensive injuries to demonstrators get little coverage. Most of the papers state that the attacks on the police were unprovoked. Only the *Daily Telegraph* gives any *detailed* account of the violence of the police response. The *Daily Mirror* was under the impression that there were no serious injuries to demonstrators. Only the *Guardian* leads on or gives very extended coverage to the death of Blair Peach.

4.12 There are significant discrepancies. The *Daily Mirror* describes the passage of events around the grounds of Holy Trinity Church as follows: 'At one point mounted police were racing around the grounds of the Holy Trinity Church, rounding up pockets of protestors'. The *Telegraph* report, which is much fuller, describes the same events as follows: 'Within three minutes, mounted policemen had cornered about 50 demonstrators against the walls of Holy Trinity Church and moving through the churchyard rounded up stragglers.

'As we watched, several dozen crying, screaming, coloured demonstrators were dragged bodily along Park View Road and along the Uxbridge Road to the police station and waiting coaches.

'Nearly every demonstrator we saw had blood flowing from some sort of injury. Some were doubled up in pain. Women and men were crying.'

It is hard to read both these as eye-witness accounts of the same set of events. In fact, the more detailed and graphic *Telegraph* report squares with the many reports given by witnesses to this Committee and supports its findings about the behaviour of the police on that occasion. The *Mirror* report is, by contrast, heavily and misleadingly glossed. Inaccuracy here involves more than a question of professional competence or journalistic credibility. Readers whose view of the Southall events was formed exclusively from the *Daily Mirror* report would be likely to view questions raised about police conduct as highly contentious and unsupported. Those who know Southall from the *Daily Telegraph* report would find the factual basis on which those complaints are raised fully corroborated — especially since the report is far more obviously based on eye-witness evidence and comes from a newspaper not widely known for its sympathies with civil liberties or with criticisms of the police.

4.13 Not only are the general accounts very similar; they are also similar as to both irrelevant detail and inaccuracies. Several papers, for example, report the arrest of Tariq Ali — 'Asian militant' (*Daily Express*), 'noted student protestor of the 1960s' (*Daily Telegraph*). Nothing further is made of this detail — though the *Sun* thought it worth supporting with a photograph. There is a suggestion of guilt by association. Several papers describe 6 Park View Road as occupied by

'Indian squatters'. No one seemed to have discovered that it was the non-residential centre for Peoples Unite, or what transpired there on the evening of 23 April. The *Express* gives a very detailed account (given the length of its report), exclusively from the viewpoint of PC Dennis Childs, 'aged 25, married with two children'. The violent nature of the police assault on 6 Park View Road and the injuries sustained by innocent occupants is not mentioned anywhere. Some editions of other papers report that 'Anti Front rioters' besieged 'Injured Officers in Ward', picketting the infirmary and screaming abuse at officers in the casualty department'. The provenance of this story — which puts the demonstrators in a particularly unfavourable light — is, to say the least, dubious. The *Sun,* which used it, attributed the story to Scotland Yard. The Yard press office, however, have denied issuing a story about the 'siege'; it acknowledged only telling the *Sun* that a peaceful demonstration had taken place outside the hospital. A hospital spokesman, however, told *New Statesman* reporters that hospital staff saw no demonstrators (*New Statesman,* 'The Not-So-Thin Blue Line', 4 May).

4.14 Deliberate intention to mis-report or mislead cannot be attributed to the press simply on the basis of these and other inaccuracies. However, the point must be made that, in controversial events of this kind, a great deal turns on the impression of the event formed on the basis of the first news reports — especially those on the immediately succeeding day. Inaccuracies are of the greatest importance, since an impression, even if formed on a not very reliable factual basis, is difficult to displace, and subsequent corrections of fact or emphasis are extremely difficult to establish with anything like equal weight of credibility (even if the press can be pressured to make them — which is extremely rare). In such cases, it is particularly important that second-hand accounts should be attributed to their source, and not presented as if based on first-hand or eye-witnessed accounts. Otherwise this may lead them to acquire a factual status and credibility which they do not deserve and should not claim.

4.15 We make this point for two reasons: first, because — given the confusion which reigned throughout the day, the difficulty of movement in and around the area and the limits imposed on coming to an overall assessment of what was happening — the striking similarity observed in most of the front-page reports in the national press leaves a question in our mind as to how much was first-hand, witnessed reporting, and how much was based on subsequent statements and press briefings. Second, there is a good deal of evidence that a very substantial and efficient police press and publicity operation was mounted on the day. It is clear that several newspapers availed themselves of this service in detail throughout the day, and undoubtedly several embodied many of the details provided by police press statements into their final stories — though how much and in what parts remains largely undisclosed.

4.16 As to the first point, it appears in fact that many journalists, perhaps attracted elsewhere by other General Election news, did not arrive in the Southall area at all until between 5 and 6 pm, several hours after the first incidents had occurred. By then, movement in the area was severely restricted. Mr Bell of the *Daily Express* is said to have arrived at about 5 pm. The *Daily Mirror* reporter, Mr O'Lone, did not apparently get there until about 7.30 pm and was then, by his own account, confined to a vantage point behind the police lines near the Town Hall, to which he was subsequently refused entry by a National Front steward on the grounds that 'The *Mirror* supports these niggers and is a Labour rag' (*Daily Mirror* 24 April). Mr Bell's statement to the *New Statesman* supports our impression of very limited movement for journalists around the Southall area: 'It was a hard situation for one person to cover. There were four separate fronts . . . I was going from one to another checking with police press officers' (*New Statesman*, 4 May).

4.17 As to the second point, Mr Peter Burden, who helped to put together the *Daily Mail* story, followed events in Southall actually from inside Scotland Yard. Other members of Southall press teams seem to have monitored events there through Scotland Yard handouts and reports. Mr Burden described the Scotland Yard operation as 'a remarkable system of public flow of information . . . very low-key and factual'. Special Branch and the uniformed branch, he said, worked as one — though, when questioned on this aspect, he suggested, 'Forget the Special Branch. Talk of official records'. (*New Statesman*, 4 May.) In his opinion, the view on Southall obtained by these means was 'very impartial. I thought we might get a pro-police view but it was supported by the facts from the ground'. Whether impartial or not, the question for us must be whether an account of the Southall events based exclusively on such a source can be used as evidence either way as to the conduct of the police themselves. Mr Burden's view is that 'Facts are facts. They tell themselves'. This represents a touching journalistic faith. It is also, in our view, hopelessly naive.

4.18 There is certainly a good deal of 'positive police focusing' in these reports, regardless of the question of which second-hand sources of information were used. The police behaviour comes through as uniformly admirable and courageous: 'one constable, blood streaming from a gash on the head, told colleagues, "I'm OK. Let me go back".' (*Daily Express*.) Policemen are extensively quoted describing themselves as the object of unprovoked attacks. Five of the papers use supporting photographs; all of them are of demonstrators being arrested. This may seem self-evident, until it is recognised that, even in very restricted conditions, some TV cameramen and some independent photographers also obtained close pictures of aggressive police contact against the demonstrators. The demonstrators — or 'mob' as they were widely referred to — get, as might be expected, a near-universal hostile press. The *Daily Star* report, for example, which is otherwise perfunctory, described 'roaming hordes of coloured youth' and claims to have seen 'one turban-clad youth . . . chasing young whites with a carving knife'. Though not representative of the day's events (the story is uncorroborated), it does show how a small and inconsequential report can be embellished by a lurid touch of detail. The other detail in the *Daily Star* report — the barricading of doors by surrounding street residents 'against the 5,000 strong mob' — is also dubious. We have found no corroborating source for it. The evidence we have is against it; even in the heat of the worst violence between police and demonstrators, local residents were willing to give shelter to fleeing or injured protesters, as they did to Blair Peach.

4.19 The coverage of 24 April was the first occasion available to the press to describe what happened. Since the day immediately following the events is normally the 'hard news' day, concentrating on descriptive and factual material, it is worth drawing attention to the substantial proportion of stories on 24 April which weave into apparently factual accounts statements about the events which provide a very distinctive interpretation. In particular, Sir David McNee's statement, issued early in the evening of 23 April, is widely quoted and strategically placed, with the effect of giving the main definition to the day's confused events. Several of the stories are shaped by this interpretation which, given its source, was bound to be authoritative. This is only the most significant example of the widespread practice in these stories of using material from a police source as *the* authoritative account. Alternative accounts either do not appear, or come later in the story. We stress this point because, first, it demonstrates that the line between 'facts' and 'interpretation' is often blurred in practice; second, because Sir David McNee's statement is, in crucial respects, partial and in some respects misleading (as we have argued in chapters 8 and 9); and third, because stories which are based on interpretations provided by the police cannot provide the evidence for an impartial judgement about the conduct of the police themselves — although, undoubtedly, they were taken to provide just that by many unsuspecting readers.

4.20 We can demonstrate this point in detail by looking at one entire story, that of the *Daily Express*. Sir David McNee's quotation is part of the headline itself (see paragraph 4.9 above); it 'frames' the whole of the story. In the body of the story itself, after two brief paragraphs describing 'pitched battles', police injuries and arrests, a second quotation from Sir David McNee is again given prominence and followed by quotations from the Home Secretary and Mr Whitelaw. The next part of the story, after the subheading 'Siege', leads off with a quotation from the police officer, Dennis Childs (see paragraph 4.13 above), whose squad entered and cleared 6 Park View Road, erroneously described as occupied by 'Indian squatters' who 'locked themselves in a house and refused to come out'. (As we explain in paragraph 2.102, although the door was locked, the occupants of the house were not asked to come out or given an opportunity to do so.) The eviction is described solely through the eyes and words of a police constable: 'We went in and got them'. (For an account of what 'going in and getting them' meant, see paragraphs 2.102 to 2.112.) The events in Holy Trinity Churchyard are described as 'a cavalry round-up'. Other 'minor scuffles' (which, unaccountably, are said to have left 'casualties' reeling for help) once more capped by a courageous statement from a 'young constable, blood streaming from a gash on his head "I'm OK. Let me go back".'

4.21 Although the *Express* describes police injuries in some detail, they do not refer to any casualty among the demonstrators. The death of Blair Peach passes unnoticed. The report ends with a short quote from 'one of the protest leaders' from Socialist Unity, and a description of the National Front meeting, in which an NF supporter, described as 'wearing a long, black leather coat with an NF armband and heavy boots' is quoted, followed by two further quotes from Martin Webster, the NF's National Organiser and Joe Pearce, the National Youth organiser: 'The National Front will send back every single Asian out there'.

4.22 It is not hard to see that this is a highly partial, selective and sometimes downright misleading account of what happened at Southall. Moreover, it is glossed at every critical point by a police view or statement about the events. These inevitably give the entire story a distinctive 'law and order' perspective.

Southall On Television: 23 April

4.23 The first reports on Southall occured in television and radio news broadcasts in the late afternoon of 23 April. This coverage, as might be expected, was almost exclusively concerned with the outbreaks of violence. Violence is traditionally the most important of the 'news values': not only do violent events rate stories a higher place, but the violent aspect will tend to be over-emphasised as against other aspects. This is especially the case with television news, which is geared to the most immediate, visible aspect of news, with a heavy investment in striking news pictures. Accordingly, the first news reports of Southall on television carried graphic pictures of confrontations between the demonstrators and the police, a focus which dominated the successive news bulletins throughout the day and evening.

4.24 While this is so well established a feature of television news reports of these kinds of events as almost to appear natural, it is worth remarking that the inevitable concentration on violence. to the exclusion of any other aspect, has certain unintended consequences. The very specific nature of Southall does *not* appear as a salient fact in these reports. The particular nature of the demonstration, the prior preparation for it by organisations in the local community, the ethnic composition of the community, the differences in policing tactics which may have contributed to how events developed are all absent. The coverage moves, with an inevitable 'logic', from one violent high-point to another — Leicester to Southall — obliterating the important distinctions between them. For example, no television report seemed to have been made of the largely peaceful demonstration in Southall on the previous day. Indeed, taking television and the press together, only the *Morning Star* appears to have thought the *peaceful* demonstration worthy of any report at all ('3,000 March Against NF', *Morning Star,* 23 April). Non-violent demonstrations are not, apparently, news.

In short, though the concentration on violence was only to be expected, and constitutes one, perfectly proper, news angle on Southall, the concentration on this angle exclusively tended to reinforce the interpretation of Southall as newsworthy principally because of its law and order aspect, down-grading its political context.

4.25 In the early television reports, the disturbances are clearly identified as attributable to the protesters. Their protest is unambiguously presented as directed against the police. In these reports, the initiating move – the decision of the National Front to move into Southall, with the possible consequences of violent confrontation – does not figure as a significant cause. The earliest film show police arriving and taking up positions, against a commentary that police vans were stoned as they drove into the area. The source of the trouble is further identified as due to several large groups of Asian youths 'roaming the streets'. The problem surrounding the establishing of an early picket is never clearly established or investigated, though it was mentioned in the late BBC2 news bulletin. Both channels featured Sir David McNee's statement that the police had been victims of unprovoked violence. The BBC supported this view with the comments of Jim Jardine of the Police Federation, complaining of the extremes of left and right and saying that the violence could cost some of his men their livelihoods. This was followed by a balancing comment from the Indian Workers Association, condemning 'police repression' in Southall. The structure of conflicting interpretations was thus established from the very outset – the official interpretation necessarily carrying the stamp of authenticity.

4.26 Independent Television News structured its reports rather differently, relating the Southall events to the wider issues of public order, and including comments from the Home Secretary, Merlyn Rees, and the Shadow Home Secretary, William Whitelaw, on the workings of the Public Order Act. It is here that, for the first time, Mr Rees draws a distinction between Southall and Leicester, showing that the provisions of the Act covered the Leicester march but did not give the police power to act over legitimate election meetings. This distinction did not, however, figure prominently in subsequent reporting. For example, despite it, Mr Whitelaw is still asked whether, as a possible future Home Secretary, he would like the powers to ban marches which could end in violence. The concentration by ITN on the public order aspect of Southall fits squarely with their immediately preceding emphasis. Its coverage of the Leicester demonstration, a few days earlier, had also concentrated on this aspect. On that occasion, both Jim Jardine and the Chief Constable were interviewed as to whether or not the march should have been banned. Though obviously an important and newsworthy angle, this concentration on the public order aspect may also have helped to direct public attention away from the principal cause behind both events – the challenge posed by, and the nature of the electoral appeal of, the National Front.

4.27 In terms of actuality coverage of Southall, the ITN coverage is markedly superior to that of the BBC. The ITN reporters seemed to have managed to get closer to the frontline of the protest. The sequences showing the police warning to demonstrators are striking, well-shot examples of televised journalism. More conventional are the shots of the massing of forces, the alternating lines of policemen and demonstrators, the riot shields and police horses which dominate the visual reports. Shots from above are increasingly used in such reports. These gave visual reinforcement to the idea of a confrontation between two immovable lines of opposed forces, which are clearly visible, and the scale of the demonstration, which comes through strikingly.

4.28 There is, however, in the ITN coverage — perhaps because it is more comprehensive and closer to the action — a marked discrepancy between what is *shown* and what is *said*. The spoken commentary principally concentrates on 'unprovoked attacks against the police'. The visual actuality reports, however, actually present a significantly different picture. They show both violence on the part of the demonstrators and police aggression. For example, some of the arrests look unnecessarily rough, involving both young people — on whom the reports concentrate verbally — and old. These are counterposed to the film of police on the Uxbridge Road being assailed by some sort of flare. The actuality soundtrack which accompanies these images consists of the shouts of people in fear and pain. We do not see the gangs of youth who are said to be running wild, nor the lootings or running battles, though the scenes of crowd *melée* provide a general suggestive grounding for these observations. The overall visual impression is much closer to our reconstruction of the events: an impression, that is, of largely static confrontation, with some mobilisation of police reserves. Subsequent television programmes (such as the London Weekend Television *London Programme* report and the BBC *Open Door* film produced by the Southall Defence Committee) strongly suggest that much more of this side of Southall was available on film than was used in the news bulletins.

4.29 The discrepancy between what is said and what was shown is only to be expected. Though visuals and commentary are combined together in a news broadcast and thus appear to be mutually self-reinforcing, they are each in fact put together in the technical process of news construction at two quite different moments. There is no natural or inevitable correspondence between them. But discrepancies between what is shown as happening, though subject to editorial selection, and what is said in accompanying commentary to have happened, can and do, occur. They occur in the ITN coverage we have examined — and they are telling and significant.

4.30 The most important, immediate reconstruction of Southall occurred in the current affairs *Nationwide* programme on BBC1 on the following day. Here we can see a very distinctive interpretation of Southall beginning to emerge.

4.31 The programme began by establishing Southall as an area of high immigrant population and stating that 'both sides' were set, from early on, on a collision course. But the principal framework for the programme is established by a confrontation between the two protagonists, which are assumed to be the National Front and the Anti-Nazi League. Martin Webster of the NF appeared on the screen, saying: 'As far as provocation is concerned, there are certain people in the body politic — not people who I would say are putting up candidates, Communists . . .' At this point, the interviewer interjected: 'You mean the Anti-Nazi League?' Webster took this up: 'Well, who are the Anti-Nazi League? Let's talk about Trotskyists, extreme Communists of various sorts, raving Marxists and other assorted left-wing cranks. They find the very fact that we live and breathe a provocation. Indeed the Communist Party has actually got in its manifesto for this election that while they want to have a charter to preserve the right to demonstrate and freedom of speech for everybody, in another section they contradict that by saying they want the National Front banned by law'. This generalised smear against the left — which includes the Communist Party, though so far as we know no suggestion has ever been made that it was involved in the Southall events — is not contradicted, but is immediately followed, with no linking commentary, by an opposing statement from Paul Holborrow of the ANL: 'The National Front are a Nazi party. They want to destroy democracy, they want to destroy the Representation of the People Act. And it seems to me that if the people in Germany in the 1930s had stood up to Hitler instead of hiding behind laws and so forth, then the world would be a much better place today'.

4.32 The next part of the programme does not directly follow this constructed opposition between the obvious protagonists. It rehearses the events of the day — 'excitement and tension', 'young Asian youths', 'police with no protection', 'looting and smashed shop windows'. The commentator notes, without drawing any conclusions, that the violence began before the ANL arrived in Southall. This is followed by a 'day after' report by Diane Carron, with actuality footage of boarded windows being cleared, glass being swept up. A youth is quoted, arguing that all the IWA do is 'sit up there on their backsides and do nothing'. Vishnu Sharma of the IWA replies with the announcement of the establishment of a defence committee and the call for an independent inquiry.

4.33 The studio discussion which follows returns to the earlier structure of opposing forces. The participants here are Peter Hetherington (local councillor), Martyn Grubb (Community Relations Officer), Jim Jardine (Police Federation) and Peter Hain (ANL). There is, however, an important difference. Whereas the first part of the programme assumed that the violence could be attributed to the confrontation between the two protagonists — the NF and the ANL — this part of the programme is predicated on the assumption that the violence is attributable to the confrontation between the extreme left and the police. Jim Jardine is the first person on the BBC to refer to the events as a 'riot'; Peter Hain is repeatedly asked if he accepts responsibility for the violence. Jim Jardine wholly repudiates all charges of police brutality, and denies all suggestion that they may have helped to provoke the violence: 'I watched television as well last night and I certainly didn't see any police throwing bricks and certainly no police threw bombs. So don't start making those arguments'. Peter Hain tried to repeat the point that the violence preceded the arrival of ANL supporters, and that the worrying point should be, instead, the manifest alienation and sense of threat amongst Asian youth which made them 'decide to fight back'. This does not break the established framework in which the discussion is pitched. The discussion, instead, pivots on another set of counter-accusations: Peter Hetherington accusing Martyn Grubb of helping to organise local opposition to the meeting, Martyn Grubb saying that the council should not have allowed the meeting to take place. *Nationwide* provides a good example of how, despite the difference in format and approach between news and current affairs, the framework of interpretation established in the first, in the immediate aftermath of the events, provides the groundwork for the amplifications which follow in the second. Unwittingly, this programme seems to play directly into the already well-established theme that, if only political extremism would go away, problems would disappear and the even tenor of life would return. The Southall events are forced into the comforting stance of 'a plague on both their houses' and the implication that common sense always lies in the 'middle ground', producing once again the trite, familiar televised oppositions.

Southall in the Press after 24 April

4.34 The subsequent coverage of Southall in the press can be treated more summarily. The story continued to echo through the national press for weeks afterwards; indeed, if one includes the later reports on the court proceedings against those arrested, the lengthy saga of the Blair Peach inquest, the results of the inconclusive investigation into the SPG and the implications of the review of public order legislation, it still continues to figure in the media more than a year later. This coverage, as we have noted, tended to widen the field of reference in which Southall was placed. Consequently, in addition to follow-up news stories, we also find more background feature articles on particular aspects, editorial comments and 'opinion', and correspondence. The main themes in this subsequent coverage can be roughly grouped under the following headings: success or failure to keep the peace at subsequent National Front meetings; police powers over marches and demonstrations and reviews of public order laws; charges concerning the improper police conduct at Southall, including the death of Blair Peach; background features on the National Front and the Anti-Nazi League; editorial comment on the 'lessons' of Southall.

4.35 The events at Southall set up a series of expectations about subsequent NF Election meetings. Just as the reports of events at the Leicester meeting established an expectation of violence in the reporting of Southall, so Southall tended to set the agenda of expectations about subsequent meetings. They were thus reported in terms of whether they fulfilled or thwarted the ancipations of violent confrontation. This is a good example of how, though particular news stories appear as separate and discrete, the contexts in which they are reported and interpreted in the press depend on a longer, cumulative news-construction process. The heavy concentration in the news stories on violence, to the exclusion of other factors, does suggest that a particular set of assumptions influenced the press presentation. The constant references to the influence of troublemakers from outside and to the role of the Anti-Nazi League even more clearly indicate that prior expectations, based on how the ANL had *previously* been reported in the press, helped shape how the event itself was reported, even when this evidence was contradicted by the facts of the case. Headlines such as the *Daily Telegraph's* 'POLICE FOIL VIOLENCE AT NF RALLY' and the *Daily Mail's* 'POLICE COOL DEMO TEMPERS', referring to the Newham meeting on 25 April, indicate how subsequent news stories were predicated on anticipations of violence based on a knowledge of what had happened at Southall.

4.36 Several papers reported the Prime Minister's announcement of a review of the 1936 Public Order Act in the light of Southall. These stories helped to link Southall with wider, controversial issues relating to police concerns about police powers and political demonstrations, industrial unrest, picketting and so on. These themes were already well established as part of the 'law and order' aspect of the General Election campaign, and Southall thus became an element in the election. This focusing, while in no way attributable to deliberate bias, nevertheless had the effect of stressing the 'law and order' side of Southall, and playing down the aspect of racial incitement. The Home Secretary, Merlyn Rees, was quoted as saying: 'We have looked at it in terms of race relations and now we need to look at in terms of law and order'. The debates about the public order consequences of Southall are dominated by prominent 'law and order' spokesmen: Mrs Thatcher, Mr Rees, Mr Whitelaw, Sir David McNee, James Jardine of the Police Federation. Several papers gave prominence to the representations made to the Home Secretary by the Police Federation that 'senior police officers should be given the right to ban marches which could be a threat to public safety' (*Daily Telegraph,* 27 April).

4.37 A very specific, but unsubstantiated, interpretation of the causes of the violence at Southall appears to have entered directly into the representations made by the Police Federation spokesmen. Jim Jardine, for example, supported his call for increased police powers by apparently generalising from the 'known' facts of the case at Southall: 'Many people are now going to meetings not to fight the National Front but to attack the police. We now appear to be seeing a concerted attack on the police with National Front meetings used as an excuse'. This assumption of a concerted plan to attack the police and the use of Southall as an excuse by outside elements is, as we have shown from our analysis of the evidence, unsubstantiated. Nevertheless, it became the basic framework into which the vast majority of subsequent reports and comments on Southall in the press were cast. This demonstrates again how a *prior* set of expectations or beliefs can serve, despite the evidence, to provide the principal framework of interpretation, which then becomes widely invoked as if it were an established fact — thereby performing the role of a self-fulfilling prophecy.

4.38 Thus, the *Daily Telegraph,* reporting the Prime Minister's announcement of the Public Order Act review, gave prominence to an almost exactly similar interpretation: 'The Prime Minister, who announced that the Public Order Act was to be reviewed, said that there was some evidence that extremists had gone to Southall from outside to foment violence against the police'. Deputy Conservative leader Mr Whitelaw, who 'issued a "cool-it" plea to Southall Asians' said 'they were being "exploited" by extremists from both sides' (*Daily Express,* 25 April). The principle source for this view, insofar as it can be traced, was the authoritative and influential press statement issued by the Metropolitan Police Commissioner while the Southall events were still in progress. This statement, which gave public voice to the view of the events as attributable to certain groups deliberately intent on attacking the police, was enshrined in the Report which the Commissioner made and which formed the basis of the Home Secretary's statement to the House of Commons (appendix 1). It appears to have either been taken over or independently arrived at by the most influential police spokesmen, and then built back into their reasons for recommending increased police powers. At the same time, it was massively quoted, as the authoritative interpretation, in most of the news reports of the actual day, and was then constantly referred to, repeated, expanded on and embroidered in subsequent accounts. Yet it was then and remains now an unsubstantiated interpretation; and the run of the police evidence itself (e.g. the overwhelming proportion of those arrested who were *not* 'extremist outsiders', not members of the ANL and who were neither accused nor convicted of a conspiracy to assault the police) is right against it. It is thus an excellent example of how an interpretation *becomes* a 'fact'. Its unquestioned acceptance by the press did much to speed it on its way to factual credibility. It is as good an example as one is likely to find in the literature of the 'self-fulfilling prophecy'.

4.39 It was only after the first day's reporting that questions concerning the conduct of the police at Southall gained any visibility in the press. The detailed report in the *Daily Telegraph* of 24 April is an outstanding exception to the general rule that the press on that day gave police conduct a near-universal vote of approval. The *Guardian,* also, was exceptional in giving, from the outset, public prominence to the death, in suspicious circumstances, of Blair Peach. When the salience of these questions did, finally, become established, the newspapers were by no means universally sympathetic to the charges and complaints being publicly aired. The *Daily Mirror* opened its report on 25 April with the tendentious observation that 'Teacher's leader Blair Peach was a Left-wing activist stereotype who lived — and died — hotly pursuing his own brand of political agitation. The *Daily Mail,* likewise, observed that Blair Peach was 'not an innocent abroad. He was an active member of the Socialist Workers Party and the Anti-Nazi League, and he was a seasoned demonstrator'. The clear implication is that he got his just come-uppance. The *Daily Star's* report on the call for an investigation of the role of the SPG is centred, not on that substantive issue, but on the defence of the SPG by senior policemen, prior to the results of the investigation: 'TOP COPS BACK SQUAD IN RIOT ROW'. 'Sir David McNee – known as "the Hammer" – praised officers of the SPG'. The *Sun,* with an even more blatant display of partisanship, simply headlined its story: 'TROTS ACCUSE POLICE OF MURDER'. There is not a great deal of commitment to the 'independence of the Fourth Estate' in evidence in these stories.

4.40 Questions concerning the National Front and its policies – and, inevitably, as a required complement to that, about the Anti-Nazi League – were pursued in subsequent feature articles in the press. The *Guardian* did the public some service in giving a first-hand, and chilling, report of what actually happened and was said inside National Front election meetings ('The Front's Rough and Tough Poultice', 25 April). The article also helped to refocus the Southall story towards some of its neglected aspects, including the fact that National Front election meetings have been 'public' in largely a formal sense only.

4.41 The *Daily Telegraph's* piece on the ANL was headed 'Anti-Nazi League Members see themselves as new Crusaders', 26 April. 'Leaders of the Anti-Nazi League project see themselves as latter-day crusaders fighting a determined, relentless and sometimes bloody battle to stop the "pernicious, insidious and odious" activities of the National Front'. It commented on the 'almost fanatical fervour' with which opposition to racialist policies was pursued. It then added that 'for all its avowed commitment a large part of the public regards the organisation as little more than "a bunch of strident Left-wing trouble-makers"'. Others go further and claim that it is a front organisation behind which extremists like the Socialist Workers Party are working to undermine democracy'.

4.42 The occasion for this renewed press attention to the Anti-Nazi League was, of course, Southall. But this clearly shows how Southall itself, for all its sigularity, was gradually related to a longer-running set of themes and issues essentially concerning the question of political extremism. Though the *Daily Telegraph* article is an excellent example of the perfectly balanced 'factual' report – it quotes, even-handedly, the League and its detractors – it was difficult for the paper's hostility to the ANL to be altogether excluded. However, whenever the negative judgement has to be made, it is always done as if through the voice or comments of someone else. Thus, in a key paragraph: 'People from every stratum of society say the League and the National Front they oppose are equally enigmatic and hideous and that, if the League want to do something constructive they should ignore the Front'. The spokesperson for 'People from every stratum of society', who expresses himself or herself in such elegant terms ('enigmatic'?), and who so unambiguously knows what people think, is not identified.

4.43 Two points should be stressed here. The first is to note how frequently in the press an apparent neutrality and impartiality is formally preserved by invoking and speaking on behalf of a popular commonsense even when no actual sector of the public is identified. 'People from every stratum of society' is a very large claim indeed. What this approach appears to do is to construct a popular consensus out of what it assumes is majority opinion and then present it as if it is a universal viewpoint, which it uses to support its own more limited and partial judgements. In effect, the need for the press to take responsibility for its own editorial political judgements (which it makes and is in our system perfectly entitled to make in its own name, unlike television) is here concealed behind a purely rhetorical but legitimating construction — 'the people', 'from every stratum of society'. Who would be bold to stand out against such universally-established truths, so universally validated a consensus? 'Latter-day crusaders' do not stand much of a chance when set up against such a comprehensive rhetorical figure, no matter how much the formal protocols of balance and the separation of comment from fact have been — in letter, but not in spirit — observed.

4.44 The second point links the comments on this section to that which follows in the next section on editorials. It is simply to note how easily Southall fell into the rhetorical figure which has come to dominate much of the reporting of race for the last two or three years: namely, the figure of the National Front and the Anti-Nazi League as absolute equivalents — 'Fascists of the Left and Right', as the *Daily Express* put it — with nothing to choose between them; extremist trouble-makers — 'equally enigmatic and hideous' — who, when constantly counterposed to one another in this way, leave the whole body of the rest of 'us' — good, reasonable, middle-of-the-road, 'constructive', people-from-every-stratum-of-life — in the safe, inactive middle ground. 'People' are both distinguished from, and can feel fairminded in being *equally* hostile to, the extremists. One thing which is always taken as marking off the sensible 'moderates' from the wild 'extremists' is the lack, in the former, of that 'almost fanatical fervour' which the *Telegraph* believed 'led to the death of one of their foremost supporters in Southall on Monday'. It is worth pointing out that it was not Blair Peach's feelings — fanatical or otherwise — which laid him low.

4.45 The most striking editorial, and the significant exception, is the courageous *Daily Mirror* editorial of 25 April, 'AN AFFONT TO FREEDOM'. This argues that the rioting was primarily provoked by the National Front's decision to hold a meeting in an area densely populated by Asians. This was bound, it says, to cause trouble; trouble was what the NF wanted. 'The National Front got the result it wanted. Now let it take the blame'. The other notable exception is the *Morning Star,* which takes a different line, supporting the TUC call for firmer action against the National Front, and calling for wider, mass trade union support. The *Guardian* carried a carefully balanced editorial comment on 25 April, recognising that the police reaction went, on some occasions, beyond justifiable limits, and arguing that allegations about police conduct should be investigated and the findings made public. It ends with the important point – a legal aspect not very extensively commented on – contrasting the eagerness to revise the Public Order legislation against the reluctance to press and apply the regulations of the Race Relations Act. In its liberal thrust, the *Guardian* leader distinguishes itself from most of the other newspapers. But in one crucial respect, it takes exactly the same position as they do: 'Explanations of exactly how all this happened still await a full report . . . But it seems that the trouble started with the arrival of a large number of people from outside the constituency, for whom the police were not initially prepared and some of whom were more interested in battle than in peaceful protest against the National Front'. Here the self-fulfilling prophecy once again makes its appearance.

4.46 The accusation against outside extremists is either repeated explicitly or is assumed as an implicit premise in all the other editorial comments. The *Telegraph* editorial, which speaks of a 'vicious spiral of provocation' holds to this thesis by implication: 'Doubtless the demonstrators too had come to be provoked . . . as provoked they were, and also in turn to provoke. They provoked the police; and as a result, so it seems, one of their number is dead'. Nevertheless, the editorial argued, the police, though 'not exempt from human fallibility' do 'deserve . . . the benefit of reasonable doubt'. The editorial, however, also ends with the ritual invocation of 'extremists on both sides'. The law 'should be vigorously and impartially enforced against fanatics of all sorts, Left and Right alike'.

4.47 In a very similar way, the *Daily Express* editorial ('Politics Of The Gutter', 25 April) opens with a reaction of 'horror and disgust', but moves inexorably towards the same proposition: 'The demonstrator is there because he wants to be. What is their game? In the Anti-Nazi League there are no doubt sincere opponents of what they fear to be a Nazi revival in Britain. But the hard Marxists are using this fear for their own purposes. Their game is to undermine the law and respect for the police, to get the coloured minorities on their side, the side of left-wing revolution. In this sense race and racial tension, is a weapon and the coloured immigrants have been type-cast as cannon fodder'.

4.48 The *Daily Mail* ran no less than three 'editorial comments' over the two days, 24 and 25 April. Its focus is not only – like the others – more or less exclusively reduced to the ritual alternation, between the National Front and the Anti-Nazi League. It took the assumed, 'proven' presence of outside agitators and their 'deliberate and violent attempt to step up tension and hostility' to its logical conclusion. They end up with a full-blown conspiracy thesis, which is offered as only the tip of the general iceberg of the 'anarchy' which threatens to engulf us.

4.49 In one of its comments ('A battle both extremist sides wanted', 25 April), the *Daily Mail* says: 'But the League and its supporters had been busy on the ground a good deal earlier than that. Ignoring the counsel of those who argue that the best way of dealing with the NF and consigning it to political oblivion is to ignore it, a small group of activists attended a meeting in Southall's dilapidated Dominion cinema just 10 yards from the highly active Indian Workers Association on 11 April. The IWA with 8,000 members is headed by bespectacled grey-haired Mr Vishnu Sharma . . . By his side sat another deeply-respected immigrant leader, Mr Dilbagh Chana . . . And with them in the dimly lit hall were leaders of Asian temples, local churches, the Southall Youth Movement — and organisers of the Anti-Nazi League and their allies, the Socialist Workers Party'. The meeting it purports to describe is the critical one in which the community's response to the proposed NF meeting was first discussed. The attempt to suggest that this meeting was unduly influenced by the conspiratorial presence of ANL and SWP 'organisers' is without foundation in fact. The editorial does not say — it cannot — that the proceedings actually *were* influenced by the presence, in the 'dimly lit hall' of ANL and SWP organisers. It cannot because it would then be required to show how it came about that the meeting carried a motion 'to stage a mass peaceful sit-down outside the town hall if the Front were allowed to go ahead', which the *Daily Mail*, contradictorily, also reports. No conspiracy, therefore, can be explicitly traced. But the hint, the implication of conspiracy is allowed to hang in the air. This allows the *Mail* to proceed on its predictable way to its predictable end: 'Fascists of the Right' . . . and of the Left.

Southall And The Press: An Overview

4.50 In order to establish the angle of presentation in press commentary and reports it is sometimes useful to ask 'what is *not* here?' Bearing in mind the range of possible themes and angles to draw out from the Southall story, what impresses itself on our attention is the exceedingly selective and repetitive nature of the limited themes which are highlighted, as the Southall story developed. The role of the National Front, its purpose in holding election meetings in a heavily immigrant area, its commitment to the politics of street violence, the racism of its whole electoral programme — these issues struggle to win any serious attention in the press at all. The fact of an organised community response by, overwhelmingly, local community organisations and leaders is almost entirely obliterated in the subsequent reporting. It is a day or two before the enormity of the clubbing to death of a protester on his way home, in circumstances apparently directly involving the SPG, is admitted to public consciousness as a matter of importance. The questionable nature of policing tactics and strategies on the day is not once commented on in the initial coverage. Though the scene was apparently fully covered by professional journalists, monitoring what happened on and at a distance from the scene, little or no accurate analysis of the day's events ever emerges. Indeed, hardly a salient new fact of any kind is disclosed.

4.51 Instead, stories move, in their apparently 'factual', often brutally sensational way, through what can only be described as a tissue of quotation, unsupported assertion, attribution of causes based not on knowledge or observation but on assumption and prior prejudice. The conduct of the police has to be forced on to the attention of the press by concerned people outside, despite the wealth of evidence to be discovered by anyone interested. But when it does, it is immediately assumed by many that those who raise such questions – issues of the very first importance in a democratic society – must by definition be 'anti-police' subversives, mischief-makers and 'Trots'. Before complaints are investigated, senior spokesmen are eagerly reported as giving the SPG a clean bill of health. Before investigations are even initiated, newspapers opine that the police must under all circumstances be given 'the benefit of the doubt'. In sum, what is there, in the Southall reporting, squeezing and reshaping and reducing everything else to minimal proportions, is first the incorporation of Southall into a wider campaign in which the press has taken a lead, to strengthen police powers, to limit demonstrations and to libel all demonstrators; and secondly, a set of unsupported fantasies about 'left wing conspiracies'. To these prevailing pre-occupations almost everything else of consequence in the Southall story is reduced. In the end, as far as the majority of the press is concerned (we have tried to identify the outstanding exceptions), this ramshackle editorial construction is all that Southall meant.

5: The Response of the Courts

5.1 According to the Home Secretary's memorandum, 345 people were charged with offences as a result of incidents in Southall on 23 April connected with the demonstration. Slightly confusingly, the Southall Defence Committee have used the figure of 342 people charged. We have preferred the Home Secretary's figure. The overwhelming majority of defendants appear to have been local residents and of Asian origin. Of the 260 who appeared at Barnet Magistrates Court, which was set aside to deal with the majority of cases, 205 were identified by the Defence Committee as living or working in Southall and a further 39 as living in neighbouring areas. Thus, 94% had a substantial local connection. This high percentage was substantiated by analysis of information on 139 defendants supplied to us by their solicitors, which showed 98 with Southall addresses and 23 with neighbouring addresses. The percentage living locally was thus 87%. Of the defendants appearing at Barnet, 203 (78%) had Asian names. The picture of a minimal role played by outsiders to the area is thus confirmed (see Chapter 8).

5.2 There is a widespread feeling in Southall that the court system has operated unfairly against the defendants, first by sending many of them to distant Barnet Magistrates Court to be tried en bloc in a 'riot court' and secondly through what has been seen as the hostile conduct of the magistrates chosen to try them. In particular it has been alleged that stipendiary full-time magistrates were initially selected to sit at Barnet who were known to have harsh views on conviction and sentence. It is further alleged that only when publicity was given to conviction rates of 80% and higher were such magistrates replaced by those of a more lenient mind. Two in particular, of the early magistrates, Mr Canham and Mr MacDermott, have been singled out for criticism on the ground of bias against the accused. Typical of such general comment is the headline of the October 1979 issue of *Southall 342*, the bulletin of the Southall Defence Committee. This ran:

'Whilst the police have refused to charge any SPG officer in connection with Blair Peach's murder they have reserved special treatment for the 342 defendants charged on 23 April. We are tried daily at a special court at Barnet, North London, 20 odd miles from Southall, to receive 'justice' from hand picked professional magistrates.'

5.3 Quite remarkably, this hostility to the working of the court system has been shared by a much wider group than the Defence Committee, who might, after all, have been expected to hold such views. On 24 November 1979, a barrister who had appeared in many of the Southall cases wrote to the Lord Chancellor on behalf of 38 lawyers involved, in exceptionally strong terms:

'We are concerned that the number of arrests, the decision to remove cases to Barnet, some great distance from the defendants' and witnesses' homes, and the apparent ability of magistrates there to consistently and unconditionally accept evidence of police officers in the face of credible defence evidence have combined to intimidate and discourage the Asian community in this country and have done irreparable damage to race relations.'

These observations have been picked up by the press and publicised. The *Sunday Times* of 18 November ran an article on the petition and quoted a complaint from another barrister already made to the Bar Council which stated that:

'The atmosphere in the court is rather unfortunate. Justice is not being seen to be done.'

5.4 In the light of these and more detailed criticism made to us concerning the handling of the court cases, we have tried first to establish the statistical facts of what has happened in the court cases and secondly to look in detail at the particular allegations made. We have spoken to officials in both the Lord Chancellor's Office and the Barnet Magistrates Court as well as members of the Defence Committee, solicitors and barristers involved in the cases and defendants. A member of our staff observed a large number of the trials. We have taken as our standard of judgement the aphorism alluded to above, that justice must not only be done but must be seen to be done. This is an oft repeated maxim of the English legal system and is of course crucial to the legitimacy which it is accorded by its subjects. A representative judicial expression comes from Lord Hewart CJ:

'It is not merely of some importance, it is of fundamental importance, that justice should not only be done but should manifestly and undoubtedly be seen to be done.' (*R.v. Sussex JJs*, 1924 1 KB 256)

5.5 Barnet Magistrates Court supplied us with the following information concerning defendants:

Number of defendants appearing in Barnet	260
Number of defendants bound over; charges dropped	52
Number of charges with guilty pleas	21
Contested charges	227

Convictions	136
Overall conviction rate	60%
Appeals lodged	21
Successful appeals against conviction	0
Sentences varied on appeal	3
Appeals outstanding (as at 14 February 1980)	2

In addition we know of one case where, after an unsuccessful appeal, proceedings for judicial review of the decision in the light of new evidence have been commenced. The court told our enquirer that the variation in acquittal between magistrates was between 75% for the highest (16 cases) and 18% (22 cases) for the lowest. These figures do not tally with those produced by the Defence Committee and widely publicised in the Press. These purported to show conviction rate for the first four magistrates who sat for a fortnight each of 93% (Mr Canham), 84% (Mr Cook) 80% (Mr MacDermott) and 78% (Mr Badge).

5.6 It is perhaps not surprising that lay people observing court cases have not noted the result of every charge. The main difficulty to have arisen is that the press quoted figures relating to the number of *defendants* convicted; the court figures (and national statistics) are based on *charges*. We prefer the Court's figures as more accurate, although we find no reason to disagree with the Defence Committee's statistics as giving an indication of the relative conviction rates as between magistrates. Defence Committee details of sentencing, which we accept as likely to be correct, did appear to show a markedly different pattern of sentencing between the first four magistrates to take a fortnightly session — Messrs Cooke, Badge, Canham and MacDermott — and the last five, Messrs Burke, Johnson, Meir, Saunders and Fingleton. Mr MacDermott, for instance, gave seven of the 16 prison sentences administered altogether. The last group only gave six between the five of them. Mr Badge gave 18 of the 73 sentences of fines of £50 or more; Mr Canham a further 15 of such fines and 19 of the 90 awards of costs against the defendants.

The decision to hold the trials at Barnet

5.7 The decision to hold the trials of the majority of defendants in Barnet has been mainly justified on the grounds of administrative expediency. Ealing and the surrounding magistrates' courts were said not to have the capacity to cope with a sudden influx of new cases of this magnitude. Part of their court business would have had to be removed elsewhere and it was logical to transfer the bulk of the demonstration cases rather than other work. Barnet number 3 court, which is physically apart from the main Barnet court rooms, was free and again it was logical to site the special court there and to bring in outside stipendiary magistrates to staff it. Lay benches would have found the commitment of time difficult.

5.8 The Lord Chancellor in his reply of 18 December to the letter of complaint from the lawyers referred to above gave a further reason for the siting of the court at Barnet:

'I can understand many reasons why a series of cases running into some hundreds in which local feeling was obviously high should have been transferred to the quieter atmosphere of another borough. Obviously this involves some inconvenience to witnesses and parties. But of course the interests of justice and judicial independence come first.'

The Lord Chancellor was concerned over the issue of judicial independence and had earlier stated in the context of explaining that he had no responsibility for the siting of the court:

'Since this is not a political function I do not wish to see this position disturbed and the fact that you appear willing to bring political pressure on me as an Executive Minister only underlines the danger to judicial independence were this position interfered with.'

5.9 The defendants saw the matter differently. The removal of the cases from the Southall area operated in fact to enhance political tension and unease rather than to defuse it. The Defence Committee organised transport during the trials for those who needed or wished to attend and the notice which was placed in issues of the Committee's Bulletin tells its own story:

'We have had problems getting defendants to court in time. In fact there have been cases where warrants have been issued when the defendants arrived late.

Of course the real problem is to get to Barnet which is more than twenty miles from Southall.

The Defence Committee organises transport every day to Barnet. So anyone with a car or anyone requiring transport should come to Southall Rights office between 7.15 am and 7.45 am.

It would be helpful if you rang us a day before your hearing date so that transport to Barnet can be arranged efficiently.'

5.10 We consider the decision to hold the court hearings in Barnet to have been at best inept and insensitive. If space could not have been found in local courts, other accommodation of a temporary nature should have been found. This could have been done quite simply. Court No.3 at Barnet, where the trials were held, did not appear to possess any particular court facilities. There was no specially constructed dock with direct access to the cells. Indeed one good point about that court was that the defendant sat by the side of his legal adviser. Any large room could thus have been adapted to perform the same function. We are aware that the decision over the location of the trials was not made by the Lord Chancellor's Office. We feel, however, that advice should have been given, and should generally be given, that trials of this kind be held locally. This, we feel sure, could be done without compromising the independent role of the clerks to the court.

Legal Aid

5.11 The Legal Aid Act 1974 gives a magistrates' court the power to grant legal aid, 'where it appears to the court desirable', to a defendant when 'it appears to the court that his means are such that he requires assistance in meeting . . . costs' (section 29). Since the Act leaves the grant and refusal of criminal legal aid to the discretion of the individual magistrate, it is a common criticism that courts vary widely throughout the country as to the extent to which they will grant legal aid and on what criteria.

5.12 Defendants to charges arising out of the Southall incidents were mainly represented by six firms of solicitors experienced in this kind of work. These firms and some of the barristers whom they instructed were prepared to act for clients without knowing whether they would be paid. This was just as well. On 12 July the six firms took the unusual step of writing in complaint to the Lord Chancellor. They pointed out that the prosecution were taking the view that they needed legal representation in every single case:

> 'It is quite clear that the police are treating this series of cases as abnormal in that they have instructed their solicitors to appear on their behalf in every case, including those in which the *prima facie* evidence of the charge reveals the most trivial examples of highway obstruction; extensive resources appear to have been deployed by the prosecution in mounting an operation room.'

Nevertheless by the time of the letter, some two and a half months after the incidents, the solicitors said that only about 60 defendants had been granted legal aid.

5.13 The pattern appears to have been that most applications originally made to Ealing Court were refused. Fresh applications were made to Barnet Court which gradually became more prepared to grant legal aid. In the majority of cases where legal aid was still not available until the date of the hearing, the magistrate then granted it. One firm which handled about sixty cases found that the average delay between application and grant was 47 days. This would be unthinkable in the ordinary criminal case.

5.14 We consider that in contested demonstration cases, the problems of identity, evidence and the inevitably political atmosphere of such cases (if only arising from the political context of the arrests) require that legal aid should, as a rule, be refused only on financial grounds. Applications in these cases should be considered with the usual degree of expedition. Legal aid orders cannot be backdated to cover work done before the date on which they are granted. Considerable preparation was necessary by the solicitors before the cases came to court and legal aid should not have been restricted in so many cases to the hearing itself. We have no evidence to suppose, as is widely believed, that the dilatory administration of legal aid was a deliberate act of policy. We consider that it is more likely that the legal aid office of Ealing Magistrates Court was overloaded by the unexpected inflow of applications. We consider that it was highly regrettable that, if extra resources were needed to process the applications, these were not made available.

The conduct of the prosecution

5.15 It is accepted practice in contested cases for the prosecution to tell the defence prior to the hearing the broad outlines of their case. Where the matter is to be heard by a judge and jury statements of the prosecution witnesses are served on the defence before the case is committed to the Crown Court from the magistrates' court. The Criminal Law Act 1977 gives power for rules to be made, by the rule committee for magistrates' courts:

'. . . requiring the prosecutor to do such things as may be prescribed for the purpose of securing that the accused or a person representing him is furnished with, or can obtain, advance information concerning all, or any prescribed class of, the facts and matters of which the prosecutor proposes to adduce evidence' (section 48).

No rules have yet been made under this section. Metropolitan Police practice is currently governed by a Memorandum of 21 October 1974 from the Metropolitan Solicitor to his department. This states that it is the Solicitor's view that disclosure of statements to the defence should not be required in all summary cases because of the burden on prosecution authorities which would be caused thereby. But, he says:

'. . . prosecuting authorities should provide statements in summary cases to the defence on request if the cases are difficult or complicated or where the interests of justice require it . . .'

The Solicitor gives the following directions to his own staff:

'As stated in earlier directives all solicitors preparing cases must disclose at the request of defending solicitors statements which fall within the above definition . . . It will be for the solicitor preparing the case in this Department to decide whether the case is difficult or complicated or one where it is essential in the interests of justice for the defence to know the details of the statements. It is important that solicitors exercise their discretion with regard to this carefully and when in doubt give the benefit to the defence.'

5.16 The main defence solicitors felt that this memorandum was not being complied with. Their letter of 12 July to the Lord Chancellor deals with this question as well as that of legal aid:

'. . . the Metropolitan Police Solicitor's office has consistently refused to provide defence solicitors with statements of the prosecution witnesses to enable them to prepare their cases.'

We are told that there were cases where due to lack of knowledge of the details of the charges witnesses were not sought who would otherwise have been. From a defence solicitor's point of view demonstration cases can be very difficult. The charge may often have been drafted hurriedly under pressure of a large number of arrests and may be in the most general terms e.g. 'threatening behaviour on 23 April on the Uxbridge Road.' To prepare the case properly a solicitor needs to know when and where exactly the alleged offence took place. His client may be saying that he was just picked at random from a crowd. He has to know if the allegation of threatening behaviour involves for instance, a shout, a threat or a brick. In many cases solicitors have said that they did not know proper details before the date of the hearing. We understand the pressures that there must be on a prosecution authority's department during a long series of trials such as those at Barnet. Nevertheless, proper attention must be given to adequate briefings of the defence.

5.17 We consider that section 48 of the Criminal Law Act 1977 should be implemented, so that prosecution statements are available in all contested cases if requested by the defence. The prosecution should be particularly willing to provide statements in demonstration cases because of their sensitivity. We feel that the nature of demonstration cases is such that the police and their solicitors should be particularly careful to serve statements in such cases where requested. We recommend that the Memorandum of the Metropolitan Police Solicitor be amended in this regard and hope that note will be taken of the shortcomings in the use of this Memorandum by the Royal Commission on Criminal Procedure to whom it was submitted in evidence by the Metropolitan Police. We would consider in any event that demonstration cases came within the terms of the document as 'difficult or complicated' or at least within the area of doubt in which officials are required to give benefit to the defence. We hope that this will be made clear within the Solicitor's department.

Selection of charges

5.18 There is some evidence to suggest that the police deliberately chose charges which carried no right for the defendant to elect trial by jury and which would therefore be dealt with in the magistrates' court. The advantage to the prosecution of such action is that it avoids the preparation necessary for a Crown Court trial. Furthermore, juries show a lower conviction rate than stipendiary magistrates. We understand that in at least one case which is now awaiting trial at the Crown Court, attempts were made to drop a charge justified by the *prima facie* evidence where the right to elect trial allowed the defendant to take to trial all the other charges which he faced. Furthermore, a consistent policy was adopted, according to defence solicitors, in offensive weapon charges of substituting a charge initially preferred under the Prevention of Crimes Act

1973 for an identical charge under the Public Order Act 1936. Since the wording of the two charges was essentially the same, the only point of such a move was to avoid the right of jury trial present for the former offence but not the latter. We regret in general the increasing removal of the right of defendants to elect trial by jury as evidenced by the Criminal Law Act 1977 which removed the right from a number of serious offences, including the offensive weapon charge under the Public Order Act 1936. Serious offences involving the allegation of violence, particularly violence against police officers, should provide the defendant, who must in any such case face the possibility of loss of liberty with a right to elect trial by jury.

Conduct of the magistrates

5.19 The official figures referred to earlier (paragraph 5.5) show a low number of appeals from those who appeared in Barnet Court and were convicted. We do not, however, draw the conclusion that the court cases have therefore been handled by the magistrates without giving cause for concern. Three factors at least appeared to have mitigated against appeal by aggrieved parties. First, on appeal against a conviction an appeal court can vary sentence as well. It was well known to advisers that this had occurred in the case of an appeal relating to alleged offences at the Grunwick demonstrations where a harsher sentence was substituted for the original one when an appeal against conviction was dismissed. Secondly, many of the Barnet defendants had lost confidence in the impartiality of British justice. Thirdly, a large number just wanted to forget the whole matter and get on with their lives. There is some evidence from the solicitors involved that the defendants were, as a group, of better character than the average defendant in criminal matters. There was widespread distaste for being involved in the criminal process at all.

5.20 We do, however, have criticisms of certain of the magistrates which do not rely on the high alleged conviction rates of the Defence Committee or the low statistics for appeals. We rely largely on the notes of our own observer sitting at the court and the experience of some of the lawyers who were involved. We accept that with any group of nine magistrates variations of approach will be found. Past research for instance on the patterns of sentencing in magistrates' courts would have led us to expect that. Further, certain of the magistrates who sat at Barnet have reputations among those appearing in their own courts as taking robust views of defence evidence and strong views on sentencing. Such variation has been seen as indicating some deliberate policy. We discount this. We, consider, however, that the problems perceived at Barnet magistrates' court by the Southall Defence Committee and others reflect problems inherent in the system of magistrates amd magistrates' courts in general.

5.21 Many of the cases depended crucially on identification evidence. These present two particular difficulties: how much credence can be placed on police evidence rather than that of fellow demonstrators, and how good must the surrounding circumstances of the identification be? The first question is a matter of the subjective judgement of the facts of each case. As to any predeliction to believe police evidence rather than defence evidence, Mr Burke made in the case of Aulakh and others what must be regarded as an exemplary statement:

'To believe that the evidence of a police officer by definition to be more readily accepted than that of any other evidence is quite absurd and an idea unworthy of discussion. There is no such predisposition and no court could conceivably be moved by such an idea. This is a court in which both sides weigh in an equal scale.'

Unfortunately, earlier magistrates did not appear to consider their words so carefully. Mr Canham in judgement in the case of Khatra and Sharpe is reported to have said:

'A police officer is trained and disciplined. A police officer like a military officer is trained to note a situation . . . it falls upon the shoulders of a responsible man to note responsibly . . . as opposed to people who come along to shout and demonstrate.'

This is clearly open to interpretation quite contrary to the spirit of the previous quotation.

5.22 The standard of identification evidence is not such a subjective matter. The leading case is that of Turnbull (*R.v. Turnbull and others* 1976 ER 549). This case dealt with the problems of satisfactory identification evidence which, for the general public, was well publicised by the case of Peter Hain, who was positively identified doing something which it was highly unlikely he would have done. The judgement requires a court to be satisfied on a number of criteria: the length of time of the sighting; was the defendant near enough to be seen clearly; the adequacy of the lighting conditions; any impediment to the view; had the accused been seen before; was there corroboration; was there any discrepancy between the original description of the accused and his actual appearance. In the last case to be heard at Barnet, that of Clarence Baker, identification was based on a momentary glimpse, a lapse of four to five minutes and then positive identification by one police officer. The magistrate, Mr Fingleton, did not let the case proceed beyond the prosecution case, and ruled there was no case to answer.

5.23 A number of the prosecution cases depended, like that of Clarence Baker, upon uncorroborated identification by one police officer. In any case where such evidence is challenged by a number of defence witnesses giving an alternative description of events it clearly behoves a court to tread with care in returning a finding of guilt. A very clear illustration of the dangers of conviction in such circumstances was the case of a 14 year old juvenile with no previous convictions whose case was heard in Hanwell Juvenile Court in August and later in December at Kingston Crown Court. Representatives of the Enquiry attended both hearings. Evidence against the juvenile was given by only one police officer who said that he arrested him at about 6.20pm as he advanced with others on the police cordon in Uxbridge Road (described in para 2.78). He was holding a stick in his bandaged hand with which the officer feared he would be hit. He therefore struck a pre-empting blow on the juvenile's arm and arrested him. The defence evidence was that the boy had in fact been arrested about 20 minutes later in 6 Park View Road. He had attended the medical room there because of a previous injury to his hand. This had been examined by both the doctor in attendance, Dr Nehmad, and also Richard Bunning the ex-ambulanceman, who said that he had actually bandaged it so tightly that the boy 'would have been able to move the top joints of his fingers, but he could not have gripped anything with his right hand, because the thumb was bound to the forefinger by the bandage.' This evidence was supported by the solicitor also in the room, John Witzenfeld. Three other witnesses said that the boy had been in that room when the police had entered the house. The defence evidence could really only be discounted on the ground of a conspiracy to give perjured evidence in which both a doctor and solicitor had actively participated. The magistrates convicted. Counsel for the boy had to remonstrate in relation to sentence with a magistrate who had remarked that the boy should get a job. A full-time job would have been illegal until the boy was 16. On appeal, the Crown Court acquitted. It is widely felt that this case is exceptional only for the strength of the defence evidence available because the boy was arrested in the presence of so many people who were not themselves charged and had some sort of professional standing. Even so, credence was only given to this evidence on appeal.

5.24 A disturbing pattern emerged in a number of cases where police officers opted to give evidence without reference to their notebooks which could not therefore be examined by the defence. This is lawful but is somewhat unusual. It means that there is no check on what the officer wrote at the time and what he is now saying. Given that the officer can only believe that the accused is guilty or he would have recommended that charges be dropped, this gives disturbing leeway for the critical shifting of emphasis and the hardening of identification evidence. The problem was exposed in Clarence Baker's case where the officer originally opted to give evidence without his notebook but where the notebook was subsequently examined. The notebook described the missile allegedly thrown as a 'stone' whereas in evidence the officer had said 'brick'. It contained no description of the accused as the officer saw him allegedly throw a missile and therefore no explanation of how he recognised him again. In evidence in chief the officer had misdescribed what the accused was wearing on the day (as proved by press photographs).

5.25 The evaluation of the merit of defence witnesses is, like that of prosecution witnesses, a matter of judgement for the magistrate in each case. Cause for concern arises, however, if magistrates give any indication that they are hostile to such witnesses as a class rather than individually. Some magistrates, particularly Mr Canham, have been accused of showing such a bias. Notes taken by our observer during cases in which he was sitting seem to show that he made remarks which are open to this unfortunate interpretation. On 21 September, in the case of Owen Earlington, our observer recorded Mr Canham as saying: 'these cases fall into a pattern . . . the defendant brings a witness saying that he was not involved . . . I keep wondering why these witnesses did not get arrested.' A witness selected by the defence, whose evidence is not intended to show that the defendant was not involved in the alleged offence, must indeed be rare. On 24 September in the case of Bhrambrah, counsel's note records Mr Canham as saying:

> 'An unmolested bystander is witness for the defence. Such a witness has become a matter [which is becoming common in these cases] and has increased the credibility of the prosecution case, it is tactically a mistake on the part of the defence. The witness for the defence has been a person who drew attention to himself and it then immediately throws into relief the roles of the witness and the defendant. Mr Singh [the witness] left the demonstration without any police attention; that reinforces in my view PC Parker's evidence as being reliable.'

These comments, which are a little difficult to understand, seem to imply that the defendant's guilt is reinforced by the fact that a person standing near to him was not arrested and that this gives substance to the allegation that the defendant must have done something to merit arrest.

5.26 On 26 and 27 September Mr Canham bound over defence witnesses to be of good behaviour. Our observer saw two occasions where this occurred although we understand that there were a total of four. Binding over in such circumstances depends upon a discretion granted under an Act of 1361. It allows a magistrate to bind a person over without proof of any criminal act on his part. The power has long been the subject of criticism. In 1969 it received considerable criticism in a case where a number of respectable citizens including a magistrate were dealt with under the Act. The *New Law Journal* (13 July 1969) called for repeal:

> 'Binding over is a punitive measure imposed in circumstances which usually render it contrary to every principle of which the fairness of our system of justice is said to be founded.'

Among those who have protested at such action by the courts is Sir David Napley, past president of the Law Society, who said in a television broadcast on 26 October 1970:

> 'It's vitally important in this sort of case where you are depending largely on the police evidence, that those who are charged should feel free to call any evidence that they can from other people who were present. Anything that discourages people from coming forward and presenting evidence I would have thought, was to be, in itself, discouraged.'

5.27 In conclusion, we do not consider that the high standards expected of

English justice have been upheld in cases concerning events in Southall on 23 April. We do not feel that justice has 'manifestly and undoubtedly' been seen to be done. Indeed we think it likely that substantial injustice may have occurred. The combination of such doubts over the judicial process, with severe criticisms we have expressed on the role of the police at the demonstration itself, cause us redoubled concern. A witness to the enquiry, who was in fact acquitted at Barnet, told us more in sorrow than in anger that he had lost all faith in the British system of justice as a result of what he had seen at the court. There can be no doubt that a substantial section of opinion in Southall, particularly among the young Asians, has lost its trust in British institutions for the preservation of law and order. With the intention of preventing any repetition of this unfortunate situation we recommend that:

1. Trials relating to incidents at demonstrations be heard within the locality of the alleged offence as is normal with other criminal cases.

2. Legal aid be as a rule available in such cases to all defendants facing contested charges except where it is refused on financial grounds.

3. Legal aid applications be processed with expedition.

4. Rules be made under section 48 of the Criminal Law Act 1977 so that statements of prosecution witnesses are available in all contested matters if requested by the defence solicitor. In the meantime this should be current practice among prosecuting authorities.

5. Magistrates sitting in demonstration cases should take particular care to avoid charges of bias through injudicious comment and should pay particular heed to the standard of proof required in matters of identification. The Lord Chancellor's Office should issue a circular to this effect.

6. Mr Canham's alleged conduct in Barnet Magistrates Court should be investigated by the Lord Chancellor's Office.

6: The National Front meeting and the Representation of the People Act

6.1 The events in Southall on 23 April stemmed directly from the decision of the National Front to hold an election meeting in Southall Town Hall and the decision of Ealing Borough Council to let them do so. In chapter 2, we have set out the facts relating to the National Front's application to the Council to hold this meeting and the decision of the Council to make the Town Hall available. In this chapter, we consider a number of issues relating to the Representation of the People Act and to other provisions for public election meetings. In particular, we will consider:

— whether or not, as the law now stands, the Council could have refused to allow the National Front candidate to hold his meeting;
— whether or not the Council should have refused to allow the National Front candidate to hold his meeting;
— whether or not the Representation of the People Act should be amended;
— whether or not the enforcement of the present law relating to incitement to racial hatred is adequate and whether any amendments to that law are required;
— what provisions should be made for stewarding public election meetings.

The present law on election meetings

6.2 It has been argued that Ealing Council was under no obligation to allow the National Front to use Southall Town Hall for an election meeting on 23 April 1979. The Council, however, rejected this view and maintained they were required by law to allow the National Front to hold their meeting.

6.3 Sections 82 and 83 of the Representation of the People Act 1949 give candidates the right to use certain schools and public halls for public meetings 'in furtherance of their candidature' during Parliamentary and local government elections. The aim is to ensure that candidates of all parties, however impecunious, have a public platform for their views. The Act makes it clear that two conditions must be fulfilled before a candidate can exercise his or her rights to hold a meeting in public property during an election campaign. First, the purpose of the meeting must be to further the candidature of the person holding the meeting. Secondly, the meeting must be public. It is possible for a local council to refuse permission for council-owned property to be used for a meeting during an election campaign on the grounds that the meeting is not in fact designed to further the candidature of the person holding the meeting. In practice, however, no council has attempted to refuse permission for a meeting on these grounds.

6.4 The council is required by the 1949 Act (Schedule 7) to maintain a list of council-owned meetings in the constituency, together with a list of school premises available for meetings in the constituency itself and neighbouring constituencies. All candidates in the election are entitled to inspect that list. It is up to the candidate to decide which hall he wants to book. He can be refused a particular hall if it is already booked and can also be refused permission to use school premises in a neighbouring constituency if there are suitable and accessible school premises in the constituency where he is a candidate. Other than that, the council does not have a discretion in the matter. It is, therefore, wrong to suggest, as some people have done, that Ealing Council could have required the National Front candidate to hold his meeting somewhere else in the borough, or in a different meeting-room within Southall constituency.

6.5 There have been a number of occasions when local councils have refused an application by a National Front candidate to hold an election meeting. The decisions have been based wholly or partly on the Council's belief that the meeting would not in fact be public. In June 1978, Greater Manchester Council refused to grant a series of applications made by the National Front candidate under section 82 of the 1949 Act for the use of school premises for election meetings in connection with the Manchester Moss Side Parliamentary by-election. Two grounds were given for this refusal: first, that NUPE and NALGO employees had refused to co-operate in making council premises available for such meetings; and secondly, that the Council was not satisfied that the election meeting would be public as required by the 1949 Act. The National Front commenced proceedings in the High Court to challenge the Council's decision. Although the Divisional Court granted the Front's application for leave to commence proceedings, it was not prepared to hear the case before the date of the by-election. The National Front has not pursued the case.

6.6 In April 1979, Brent Borough Council in North London refused an application from a National Front candidate to use a school hall for an election meeting during the election campaign. The refusal was based on the Council's view that, despite assurances by the National Front election agent that all members of the public would be admitted until the hall was full, the National Front could not in fact be trusted not to exclude members of the public as had happened at previous election meetings. The National Front challenged the Council's decision in a legal action which was rejected by the court on technical grounds.

6.7 The ILEA requires candidates applying to use school premises for an election meeting to complete a questionnaire which includes details of how entry to the meeting is to be controlled. When a National Front candidate has applied to use school premises, the ILEA has decided, on the basis of answers to the questionnaire and of experience of two National Front election meetings held previously in the area, that the meeting would not in fact be public and has therefore turned down the applications. The National Front challenged one such refusal by an application to the High Court, but left the application so late that it could not be heard in time for the election campaign. They have not pursued the application.

6.8 The general policy of Ealing Council over many years has been to refuse the National Front permission to hire public halls for meetings. But the Council took the view, in relation to election meetings, that they would be obliged under the Act to allow any candidates facilities for an election meeting — providing that the meeting would be a *bona fide* public meeting. The Council sought and obtained an assurance from the National Front candidate that one-third of the seating in Southall Town Hall (i.e. 20 out of the 60 seats) was to be allocated in a block for members of the public other than the candidate's supporters. The Council went on, however, to say that not all members of the public who presented themselves while seats were available would necessarily be admitted. The Council stated in correspondence that 'members of the public who it cannot reasonably be considered would themselves disrupt the meeting will be entitled to be admitted subject to seats being available'. The Council did not state whether it was to be a National Front steward, a council official or the police who would decide whether or not a member of the public was to be admitted. In the event (see paragraph 2.70), it was the stewards and the police who made the decision.

6.9 The Representation of the People Act 1949 does not contain a definition of a 'public meeting'. Since no case involving a refusal to allow the National Front or any other party to hold an election meeting has been fully heard by the courts, there is no judicial ruling on the definition of a public meeting for the purposes of this Act.

6.10 The rights given by the Act to election candidates to hold public meetings are designed to ensure that a candidate can make him or herself known to constituents and that any constituent who wishes to establish or challenge a candidate's views has an opportunity to do so. Commonsense tells us that the definition of a 'public meeting' for electoral purposes is, therefore, a meeting to which members of the public are admitted on a 'first come, first served' basis, subject only to the availability of tickets or seats. (Obviously, seats on the platform and some others, for instance the front row of the meeting-hall, should be reserved for the chairperson, the candidate, the agent, the speakers and prominent members of the local party.) Ealing Council's requirements — that 40 seats be allocated to the candidate's supporters and only 20 to members of the public and the press — showed that the meeting would *not* be a genuine public meeting. As events turned out, of the 20 seats available to people other than the candidate's supporters, 15 were occupied by journalists and only five were available to people who would be described as genuinely members of the public and who were voters in the constituency. Although the police claimed that they were defending the electoral rights of the National Front candidate, the meeting they were defending was not a public meeting and was not therefore protected by the Representation of the People Act. We believe that the Act should be amended to clarify the definition of a public meeting for electoral purposes, as suggested above.

6.11 As the law now stands, Ealing Council should have taken steps to ensure that the meeting was genuinely open to the public. If they were unable to obtain a satisfactory guarantee to that effect, they could and should have refused permission for the meeting.

Should the Representation of the People Act be amended?

6.12 Proposals have been made in several quarters for bans on the National Front and similar organisations, or on their activities. The measures proposed range from the complete outlawing of such organisations, through prohibiting them from putting up election candidates, to denying such candidates the privileges normally accorded under the Representation of the People Act.

6.13 The main argument in favour of a complete ban on racist organisations is that such bodies directly attack the existence of racial minorities in this country and set out to foment hatred and contempt for them. An attack on someone because of his or her racial, ethnic, linguistic, cultural or religious attributes is particularly obnoxious. Such criteria concern the most personal characteristics by which an individual defines his own identity. Any attack on a group of people defined by these criteria is an attack on their right to be who they are: the National Front does not merely question the rights which racial minorities have within this society, but would deny them membership of this society completely. Such attacks, therefore, cause far deeper affront and provoke far deeper resentments than, for instance, an attack on trades unionists as such, or on members of some other group. The banning of terrorist organisations provides a precedent for banning organisations like the National Front.

6.14 It is also argued that the views of the National Front and other racist organisations are outside the bounds of legitimate political debate and activity and that it is therefore proper for Parliament to curtail their activities. The fact remains that racist views continue to be held by many people in this country, by no means confined to the members or supporters of the National Front. The problem of combating racist ideology goes far beyond attempts to curtail the activities of the National Front. Leaders of the two major political parties in Britain are unequivocally committed to racist immigration policies, the defence of which has strengthened the assumptions which lie behind the overt racism of the National Front. A ban on National Front election meetings is unlikely to diminish support for their policies. It might, however, have the undesirable effect of suggesting that only the racism of the National Front is to be disapproved of and that other, more insidious and arguably more damaging, forms of racism are therefore respectable.

6.15 We have come to the conclusion that no attempt should be made to outlaw the National Front and similar groups. The basic argument against banning an organisation is that no government or other authority should be allowed to curtail the rights of their opponents to enjoy freedom of association and of expression. These freedoms, which are fundamental to political activity in a democracy, involve the right to make one's views known and to organise with others of similar convictions. Views expressed in a democracy will often be objectionable to other people, and to those in authority, who are inevitably tempted to deny to people holding such views the opportunity to associate or to express themselves.

6.16 The experience of bans on organisations in this country shows that the law cannot, in practice, prevent an organisation from existing or prevent people from supporting its views. In Northern Ireland, the Irish Republican Army and four other organisations are banned under the Emergency Provisions Act. In the rest of the United Kingdom, the IRA is banned. But the organisations continue to exist; their leaders are well known; and support for their views has not been diminished by the ban. In 1967, the Northern Ireland authorities made an attempt to ban the Republican Clubs. The banning notice referred to '"republican clubs" or any like organisation howsoever described'. Although the ban was upheld by the House of Lords, it was widely criticised for being unconstitutionally vague. The ban was not, in fact, seriously enforced and its wording indicates a major practical difficulty — the members of a banned organisation can regroup under another name, or with slightly different objectives, in order to evade the ban on technical grounds.

6.17 A further ground for objecting to bans on organisations is that whenever the authorities have been granted the power to discriminate between those organisations allowed to exercise political freedom and those not permitted to do so, that power has been abused. For instance, whenever the police and the Home Secretary have decided that it is necessary, for public order reasons, to ban a National Front march from taking place, they have used their powers under the Public Order Act 1936 to ban *all* political processions. If Parliament were to pass a law banning organisations or activities designed to promote hostility to or contempt for racial, ethnic, religious or other groups, there is little doubt that the powers would be used extremely widely by those who wish to outlaw 'totalitarians of the right and the left'.

6.18 The arguments set out above apply to proposals to ban racist candidates or racist meetings, as well as to the proposal to ban racist organisations altogether. But there is a further argument used to support the proposal to ban National Front election meetings — that they should be banned because of the public disorder which results from them. It is not, in fact, the case that National Front meetings inevitably lead to violent disruption. Shortly after the disastrous events in Southall, the National Front held an election meeting in Plymouth. The Chief Constable took the view that, since this was a public meeting under the Representation of the People Act, the duty of the police was to ensure that the public were admitted. The public were duly admitted until the hall was full. When the National Front candidate and his supporters arrived, they decided they did not wish to face the public and cancelled the meeting.

6.19 There is an important reason of principle for rejecting the view that, because National Front meetings often lead to violence, they should be banned. The right of individuals to express their views is destroyed if a hostile audience can impose a veto. If the reception of the audience were to be the criterion for permitting or denying a speaker the right to speak, Martin Luther King would never have been able to organise civil rights marches or meetings in the southern states of the USA. It is for this reason that the Supreme Court of the USA, in deciding free speech issues, has never upheld a ban on a meeting on the grounds that the audience would be provoked to violence. Unfortunately, the British courts have been all too willing to allow the threat of public disorder, however remote, to be the overriding criterion for deciding whether or not a speaker should be permitted to speak.

6.20 It has also been suggested to us that Sections 82 and 83 of the Representation of the People Act should be repealed, removing the requirement on local councils to make premises available to candidates. This would enable local councils to use their discretion in deciding which candidates would be able to hire publicly-owned halls. Outside election campaigns, local councils have such a discretion, and have shown themselves willing to ban, not only organisations like the National Front, but also left-wing political groups to whose views they object. Because the right of candidates to hold public meetings is an important democratic safeguard, its abolition would be too high a price to pay for an end to election meetings of racist candidates. The repeal of the law relating to election meetings would lead to a number of councils banning all except the major political parties from holding election meetings.

6.21 The Representation of the People Act requires each candidate to put up a deposit of £150. The deposit was intended to discourage frivolous candidatures — an aim which, never having been increased, it no longer fulfils. The deposit is now by far the cheapest means of distributing political propaganda, by virtue of the right given under the Representation of the People Act to a free delivery of election addresses to all households in the constituency. When the deposit was introduced, it met a large part of the cost of the delivery — an exercise which would now cost at least £3,000. A steep increase in the amount of the deposit

125

(perhaps accompanied by a lowering of the proportion of the total vote needed to save it) would restore the original function of the deposit and, by discouraging small parties from putting up a large number of hopeless candidates, would significantly diminish the motive for any other means of preventing the exploitation of the electoral process for the fomentation of hatred. We are for this reason in favour of bringing the amount of the electoral deposit into line with current value of money.

The law concerning incitement to racial hatred

6.22 Under the Public Order Act 1936, amended by the 1976 Race Relations Act, it is a criminal offence to use threatening, abusive or insulting words in a public place or at any public meeting in circumstances where racial hatred is likely to be stirred up. The speeches at the National Front meeting in Southall appear to have been in breach of that law. We do not know if the Director of Public Prosecutions has examined them with a view to bringing a prosecution: if he has not, he should now do so.

6.23 If the incitement to racial hatred law had been enforced as, presumably, Parliament intended, the activities of parties such as the National Front and the offensiveness of its spoken and written propaganda would have been significantly curbed. As it is, despite some convictions, the law has been largely a dead letter. When originally introduced in 1965, it was used mainly to prosecute black speakers, the only prosecution against a white person being for anti-Semitic activity. By the early 1970s, the law had fallen into disuse. When the Race Relations Bill 1976 was introduced, the then Attorney General argued that the reason for the failure of the law was that the prosecution had to prove that the speaker *intended* to stir up racial hatred. The difficulty of proving intent was, it was claimed, the reason why so few prosecutions had been sanctioned by the Attorney General. (No private prosecutions can be brought for incitement to racial hatred and the Commission for Racial Equality, like anyone else, can only refer offensive material to the Director of Public Prosecutions for his consideration.) The 1976 Act therefore removed the requirement to prove intent.

6.24 This change in the law has not, however, made much difference..We are disturbed that although at least 70 cases had been referred to the DPP by the end of 1978, only nine cases had been authorised. The Attorney General offered two explanations: firstly, that 'hatred' was a very strong concept and it was difficult to prove that offensive words or material would be likely to stir up hatred; and secondly, that 'the consequences of prosecution might be so unfair or so harmful as heavily to outweigh the harm done by the breach itself'. There have been a number of cases where apparently gross violations of the law have gone unprosecuted or unpunished, the last straw being the acquittal of Kingsley Read in 1977 for his 'one down, one million to go' speech. (The 'one down' referred to was the murder of Gurdip Singh Chaggar in Southall in 1976.) Kingsley Read was prosecuted under the pre-1976 law. On the first trial, the jury was unable to agree a verdict. On the re-trial, he was acquitted after a controversial direction by the judge.

6.25 Various proposals have been made to strengthen the present law, for instance by outlawing incitement to racial prejudice or racial hostility, rather than incitement to racial hatred. Ealing CRC proposed in evidence to us that the law should be amended to made advocacy of repatriation a criminal offence. We are extremely sceptical about the value of such proposals. A law against incitement to racial prejudice might not be different in effect from the present law, but would be more open to the criticism that it was dangerously vague. Outlawing the advocacy of a particular policy would not alter the fundamental problem that many people support that policy. The use of the criminal law to ban advocacy of a particular policy — however obnoxious the policy — is a dangerous extension of state powers of censorship and would no doubt be seen as a precedent to be used against other policies which a particular government found objectionable.

6.26 It may be argued that there is a practical problem in enforcing the present law, since the police do not have the power to arrest or demand the name and address of someone whom they reasonably suspect to be committing an offence of incitement to racial hatred. The police do, however, have the power to arrest without warrant someone who is using threatening, abusive or insulting words likely to cause a breach of the peace. The police have not used that power of arrest in cases of incitement to racial hatred, even though a speech that would constitute incitement would usually also involve threatening, insulting or abusive words likely to cause a breach of the peace. Consideration should be given to extending the power to demand the speaker's name and address, or to arrest him, to cases of incitement. But what is really needed is not additional police powers, but a strong directive to the police to enforce the law. Mr John Alderson, Chief Constable of Devon and Cornwall, has, for instance, instructed police officers to attend public meetings and to obtain evidence where they suspect that incitement to racial hatred laws are being broken.

6.27 Furthermore, we believe that consideration should be given to removing the necessity to obtain the Attorney General's consent before a prosecution can be brought, and allowing the police and possibly a body such as the Commission for Racial Equality to bring prosecutions for incitement to racial hatred.

6.28 In conclusion, it is thoroughly objectionable that racism can be preached with impunity. We do not, for the reasons explained earlier, favour a ban on the National Front or its activities. But we deplore the apparent unwillingness of the Attorney General to bring cases of incitement to racial hatred before the courts. If the problem is the unwillingness of magistrates and juries to convict, then this reflects the absence of a real commitment by political leaders and government to combatting racism at every level and underlines the need for a fundamental change in the attitudes of the authorities.

Stewarding election meetings

6.29 A number of people have complained about the way in which National Front stewards at election meetings vet those trying to attend. At the meeting in Southall, for instance, the *Daily Mirror* reporter was refused entry on the grounds that his paper 'loved niggers', and only five members of the public other than journalists were admitted. Ealing Council had specifically stated that 'trouble-makers' would be turned away.

6.30 The legal powers of the organisers of a meeting depend on whether the meeting is being held on public property or not. Although a town hall and other rooms owned by the local council are often thought of as being 'public property' in the sense that they are owned by a public body, they are in law *private* property. The organisers of any meeting held on such property are therefore entitled to appoint stewards to regulate admission and generally keep order. The organiser of the meeting is entitled to admit people to the meeting on whatever conditions he chooses — for instance, entry may be made conditional upon consenting to being searched. He can refuse admission to people he does not want to admit, and (except where payment has been made on admission) can order anyone to leave during the meeting. If someone refuses to leave after being asked to do so, the stewards may use 'reasonable force' to eject that person as a trespasser.

6.31 Because an election meeting in a town hall is held on private property, the powers of the police to enter the meeting are limited. The police are entitled to enter at the request or with the permission of the organiser of the meeting, or when they have reason to believe that an arrestable offence or a breach of the peace has been or is likely to be committed. Under the Representation of the People Act 1949, it is an offence for anyone to act in a disorderly manner for the purpose of preventing the business of an election meeting. If someone is behaving in such a way, the chairman may request a police officer to ask the person to state his name and address to the police officer; if the person refuses to give the information, or if the police officer has reason to believe that the name and address given are false, the person may be arrested without a warrant.

6.32 The organiser, the stewards and the chairman of a public meeting held on private property do, therefore, have the right to control attendance at such a meeting. Their power to do so is entirely appropriate for most public meetings, and indeed enables the vast majority of meetings to be conducted without any need for police interference. But election meetings are in a different category from other public meetings held on private property. Local authorities are under no general duty to make facilities available for meetings. But the Representation of the People Act does require them to make premises available for public election meetings. As we have argued above, this important provision allows candidates of all parties to make themselves known to constituents, and, in turn, allows constituents to take the opportunity to hear and question candidates. We believe that such meetings should be genuinely open to the public, and have suggested a change in the law to ensure that this should be the case (see paragraph 6.10). But a further change will be required, to remove the power of the organisers of an election meeting to refuse admission to someone to whom they object. The function of stewards at an election meeting would then simply to be ensure that people queued in an orderly way, and that people were admitted until the seats were all taken. If there were reason to fear that some people might bring weapons to the meeting, the police should be requested to be present, rather than asking stewards to search people wishing to attend.

7: The Response of the Community and Law relating to Demonstrations

7.1 As we have described in chapter 2, local community organisations responded quickly to the news that the National Front were to hold an election meeting in Southall. The meeting of community organisations on 11 April agreed that if, despite their protests, the National Front meeting was allowed to go ahead, they would organise a shut-down of business in Southall from the middle of the day and would hold a peaceful sit-down demonstration outside the Town Hall from 5 pm. Both the shut-down of businesses and the sit-down demonstration were clearly felt to be within the Gandhian tradition of non-violent protest.

7.2 The Home Secretary told the House of Commons on 27 June that 'there were two reasons for expecting violence on this occasion'. The first was the decision of the National Front to hold a meeting in Southall. The second, he said, was 'divisions within the Asian community in Southall', which exploited the decision of the National Front to hold a meeting in Southall and the decision of the council to permit the meeting. In chapter 8, we consider the allegations that 'extremist outsiders' were responsible for the violence. In this chapter, we consider the way in which the community decided to organise its protest and the law governing such protests.

7.3 It may be argued that the community should not have organised any protest demonstration at all. It is, of course, true that if no-one had attempted to demonstrate, there would have been no public disorder. But the community was responding to the National Front's decision to hold a meeting which could only be seen as an insult to the community. Had there been no National Front meeting, there would have been no need for a demonstration, no police presence and no violence. But once the National Front had decided to hold its meeting, and the council had taken the view that they were entitled to use Southall Town Hall for the purpose, local community organisations were entitled to respond to the situation. There is no constitutional guarantee of the right to assemble in this country. Nonetheless, freedom of expression, in the form of a peaceful demonstration of one's views, by means of assembling in a march or public gathering, is recognised as fundamental to a democratic community. In 1934, for instance, the then Home Secretary, Sir John Gilmour, told the House of Commons that 'the right of holding peaceful meetings and processions is one of the most cherished rights'. The European Human Rights Convention, ratified by the United Kingdom in 1953, states that 'everyone has the right to freedom of peaceful assembly and to freedom of association with others'. We think that it would have required quite extraordinary forbearance for people in Southall to have ignored the National Front and the insult which was being offered them. We therefore reject the view that the community should not have tried to organise a peaceful protest.

Divisions within the community

7.4 It is already apparent from our account of what happened before and on 23 April that there were divisions within the community over what kind of protest should be staged. First, there was the argument over whether the National Front should be met by contemptuous silence or by a demonstration. The IWA Executive Committee proposed that there should be no demonstration but, when it became clear that the majority of those present at the meeting on 11 April wanted to show their anger about the National Front's presence by means of a demonstration, the IWA agreed to play a full part in its organisation. Vishnu Sharma, then President of the IWA, was appointed convenor of the Co-ordinating Committee which was set up to organise the protest. Secondly, there was disagreement between the Southall Youth Movement and the Co-ordinating Committee, which is presumably what Mr Whitelaw had in mind when he referred to the difference between the young Asians and their elders. Southall Youth Movement did not join the Co-ordinating Committee and, as we explain in paragraph 2.35, had their own plans for a picket outside the Town Hall.

7.5 Mr Whitelaw's assertion that these differences helped to precipitate the violence which took place on 23 April appears entirely without foundation. The initial difference between the IWA and other present at the meeting on 11 April does not seem to have affected the work of the Co-ordinating Committee. There is no suggestion that the IWA, once it had committed itself to supporting the demonstration, tried in any way to undermine plans for the demonstration. The Southall Youth Movement took the view that the Co-ordinating Committee's call for businesses, public transport and workplaces to close on 23 April would produce a demonstration too large to be consistent with the proposal for a sit-down. They decided instead to concentrate on the Town Hall and to organise a picket outside. But the only point at which the 'difference of view between the young Asians and their elders' had a bearing on what actually occurred was the decision of a small group of SYM supporters to move towards the Town Hall at about 1 pm, somewhat earlier than the planned time of 3 pm. Both the Co-ordinating Committee and the SYM had, however, discussed their plans in detail with the local police (see chapter 9) and, according to the Home Secretary's memorandum, the police knew on the morning of 23 April that SYM members were likely to try and establish their picket earlier than originally intended.

The legal position

7.6 A crucial question in what happened is whether the community organisations had a legal right to make their protest in the forms they chose – by a picket and a sit-down demonstration – and whether the police were lawfully entitled to prevent that protest by cordoning-off the central area of Southall.

7.7 As the law stands, the community who wished to protest in Southall on 23 April were not on an equal footing with the National Front against whom they were protesting. In the view of the council and the police, the right of the National Front to assemble in Southall Town Hall was protected by the Representation of the People Act 1949. (For our own analysis of the Act, see chapter 6.) But the right of the community to assemble outside that meeting in a peaceful protest was *not* protected by the law nor recognised by the authorities.

7.8 The law covering demonstrations on the street is extremely complex. There is a public right of passage along the highway – a right 'to pass and repass without let or hindrance'. Processions and marches are, generally speaking, included within this definition. Someone who uses the highway for purposes other than passing and repassing along it may be, technically, a trespasser (a matter which involves civil, not criminal law). In practice, many activities other than merely passing and repassing along the highway occur every day, without necessarily attracting the intervention of the civil or criminal law: for instance, distributing leaflets, selling flags, conducting market research, playing musical instruments, meeting other people and so on.

7.9 Brownlie, a leading authority on the law relating to public order, argues that there is a *liberty* for people to meet lawfully on the highway and quotes Dicey* to the effect that 'a number of persons may, as a general rule, meet together in any place where otherwise they have a right to be for a lawful purpose and in a lawful manner.' There are two crucial difficulties facing anyone who tries to exercise this freedom to meet on the public street. First, although there may be a liberty, there is no *right* recognised by law to hold a meeting on a highway, and, correspondingly, there is no duty on the police or other authorities to allow such a meeting to take place. Secondly, anyone who does become involved in a meeting or stationary demonstration on the highway is at risk of falling foul of the laws relating to public nuisance, obstruction of the highway and so on.

7.10 The Co-ordinating Committee recognised that people participating in the sit-down demonstration would be obstructing the highway and would there-

The Law Relating to Public Order, Brownlie, 1978. (p.144).

fore be liable to arrest. Under common law, an obstruction of the highway by 'an unreasonable and excessive' use of the highway is a public nuisance. According to Brownlie, a public meeting on the highway is not a public nuisance simply by virtue of being a trespass; but it will be a public nuisance if the use of the highway is unreasonable and other people are prevented from going about their business.

7.11 Obstructing the highway is also a statutory offence under the Highways Act 1959 which provides a maximum fine of £50 for anyone who 'without lawful authority or excuse wilfully obstructs the free passage along a highway'. In some cases, people have been convicted for this offence even though no-one was actually obstructed. The police have a power to arrest without warrant anyone reasonably suspected of committing this offence, and often use it to arrest people distributing leaflets or selling literature in the street, as well as against demonstrators.

7.12 The police would, therefore, have been able to arrest without warrant people taking part in a sit-down demonstration or picket outside the Town Hall which would have impeded the movement of pedestrians and, presumably, vehicles.

7.13 The only sit-down demonstration which took place on 23 April, other than brief attempts by small numbers of people on the Broadway, occurred on the bridge at the bottom of South Road by the railway station. In paragraph 2.119, we describe how the police broke up this demonstration by arresting many of those present and ordering others to disperse. It is essential to remember that the police had themselves cordoned off the bridge at both ends. The demonstrators were contained within the two lines of police officers, and anyone trying to cross the bridge to get into South Road would have been barred by the police cordon. Thus, although the demonstrators were technically obstructing the highway, the police had themselves decided to prevent the public from using the bridge for access to South Road and any additional obstruction presented by the demonstrators was quite irrelevant. Although the demonstrators were shouting slogans, there is no suggestion from the Home Secretary's memorandum or elsewhere that the demonstrators would have attacked the police cordon or caused any breach of the peace. Many of the demonstrators, who were almost entirely Asian, were older people, carrying out the original plan of a peaceful, sit-down protest. We deplore the fact that this protest was not allowed to continue. We recommend that the offence of obstructing the highway under the 1959 Highways Act should be amended to ensure that an arrest can only take place when there is an *actual* obstruction caused which makes it impossible or very difficult for other users of the highway to go about their business.

7.14 No sit-down demonstration was ever allowed to take place, as planned, outside the Town Hall. SYM's attempt to arrange a picket, for which they believed they had obtained Chief Inspector Gosse's permission, was broken up by officers from Scotland Yard (see paragraphs 2.39 and 9.26). The next question is whether the police were entitiled to take the steps they did – forming police cordons to bar access to the area around the Town Hall – in order to prevent the demonstration from happening. The area cordoned-off was extremely extensive, reaching along Uxbridge Road beyond the police station to Park View Road to the west, along the Broadway to the east, and involving police cordons on the South Road bridge over half a mile to the south of the Town Hall.

7.15 Because there is no legal right to hold a demonstration on the street, the police were not infringing any such right in refusing to allow people to demonstrate. But the decision to cordon off the entire central area meant that it was impossible for other residents, as well as protesters, to use the main roads of Southall. In effect, the police themselves were causing a massive obstruction of the highway. (The police were not, however, committing a criminal offence as long as they had 'lawful authority or excuse' to obstruct the highway.) Were the police justified in this action?

7.16 The police are under a duty to disperse an unlawful assembly – which is defined as 'three or more people, assembled together with a common purpose to commit a crime of violence or to achieve some other object, whether lawful or not, in such a way as to cause reasonable men to apprehend a breach of the peace'. The demonstration planned had been widely advertised as a *peaceful* protest, and, although some arrests had taken place, there would have been no reason for 'a person of ordinary firmness in the neighbourhood' – the definition of a 'reasonable man' – to fear a breach of the peace. If the planned demonstration had been allowed to take place, it is our view that it would not have been an unlawful assembly.

7.17 But quite regardless of whether the demonstration would have involved an unlawful assembly, the police also have a duty to prohibit or disperse *lawful* meetings on the street if they reasonably believe, in the light of the information available to them that a breach of the peace might occur. In the case of *Duncan v Jones* (1936) 1 KB 218, DC, a woman who was about to speak at a meeting held near the entrance to an unemployed training centre was told by the police that she could not hold her meeting there. She nonetheless started to address the meeting and was arrested. Her conviction for obstructing a police officer in the execution of his duty was upheld by the Divisional Court, which decided that, because another meeting at the same place had been followed by a disturbance, the police had reason to fear a breach of the peace. The police were therefore under a duty to prevent the meeting from being held and the speaker, by trying to continue with the meeting, obstructed the police officer in the execution of his duty. This case has been widely criticised, since it gives the police extensive powers to act, even where no criminal offence has been committed and no breach of the peace is about to take place. Once the police have decided that they have reason to anticipate a breach of the peace – however remote –

they can order people to disperse and refusal to obey that order constitutes obstruction of the officer in the execution of his duty. (Obstructing an officer is *not* in fact an arrestable offence, although the police widely believe that it is. But in practice, the police can arrest for obstruction of the highway even if they later charge the person with obstructing a police officer.)

7.18 The lawfulness of the police action in Southall has not been challenged in the courts. A court would probably decide that the police reasonably believed that a breach of the peace might occur if the sit-down demonstration were allowed to go ahead, and that they were entitled to cordon off the area in order to prevent any demonstration even though this involved denying protesters and other residents the right to use the highway.

Conclusion

7.19 It is our view that the police plan for cordoning off the centre of Southall was unreasonable and unjustified. First, the cordons prevented the community from expressing their opposition to the National Front and thus completely denied the community their right to assemble and make their views known. Secondly, the police gave neither the Co-ordinating Committee nor the SYM any indication that their demonstrations would be prevented and made no attempt to discuss with them any other way in which they could organise a demonstration which would not, in the eyes of the police, lead to a possible breach of the peace. Thirdly, and most importantly, the police operation, far from reducing the risk of a breach of the peace, actually increased the likelihood of violent confrontation. The result of the police cordons was to throw into utter chaos the Co-ordinating Committee's plans for the demonstration; to make planning, co-ordination or leadership from the stewards or community leaders impossible; and to confuse and frustrate the protesters. The use of double cordons, as on the Broadway where protesters were confined between two police lines, often unable to leave at all, exacerbated these problems and was undoubtedly a factor in the attempts to break through the police cordon and the missile-throwing which took place. Although the Home Secretary's memorandum claims that the police intended to allow a limited number of demonstrators to stand in pre-arranged positions, no such arrangements were ever made with the organisations concerned who were not even informed of these plans. Only about 30 people were allowed to mount a picket on the pavements opposite the Town Hall between about 6 and 7 pm (see paragraph 2.70).

7.20 It is our view that the police should have allowed a picket and a sit-down demonstration to take place, either diverting traffic along other routes, or agreeing with the organisers that the demonstrations would be contained within a space that would have permitted vehicles and pedestrians to use the rest of the highway. If the police had remained unwilling to allow the demonstrations, they should have advised the community organisations of their view and discussed alternative forms which the protest could have taken.

7.21 Detailed criticisms of the police action are contained in chapter 9. At this point, we would stress our concern with the state of the law regarding demonstrations in public places. We consider it highly objectionable that whereas a political candidate is entitled during an election campaign to exercise freedom of speech rights in publicly-owned property, members of the local community wanting to express their opposition to the candidate have no entitlement to assemble peacefully on the public highway. Furthermore, we consider that the courts have generally taken too wide a view of the powers of the police to deal with a breach of the peace which they consider might take place. In particular, we recommend that the law relating to public order and freedom of assembly should be substantially reformed as follows:

— There should be a statutory right of demonstration, which would protect the right of people to take part in peaceful gatherings in public places. Such a right would, of course, need to be balanced (as the right to hold processions is now) against the right of other people to walk or drive along the highway. But in Southall neither right was protected.

— The power of the police to take action when they reasonably apprehend a breach of the peace should be restricted to circumstances when a breach of the peace has already taken place or is imminent. It should not extend to a breach of the peace which *might* occur at some later time.

— The offence of obstruction of the highway under the Highways Act 1959 should be redefined to make it clear that the offence is only committed when the highway is actually obstructed in a way which makes it impossible or very difficult for others to use the highway.

8: The Role of 'Outsiders'

8.1 It has been widely alleged that the violence at Southall was caused by 'outsiders' — usually referred to as 'extremist outsiders' — who came to the demonstration determined to have a fight with the police. The *Daily Mail* (24 April) referred to the Anti-Nazi League as 'a clandestine anti-police league . . . whose main aim now is to sabotage the peace of our cities and to savage policemen struggling to do their duty'. The *Guardian* (25 April) stated that 'the trouble started with the arrival of a large number of people from outside the constituency . . . some of whom were more interested in battle than peaceful protest against the National Front'. George Gale (*Daily Express,* 25 April) spoke luridly of 'Red Fascism' rampaging through the streets of Southall. Sir David McNee, in a television broadcast spoke of the arrival of extremists 'hell-bent on violence'. The *Daily Telegraph* (29 April) said that: 'Anti-Nazi League members are known to have been gathering in the Southall, Middlesex area for three days before last Saturday's *(sic)* riots . . . The demonstrators arrived in private cars and hired coaches from all parts of the country'. (There is no evidence at all for this remarkable statement.) Finally, the Home Secretary, in his statement to the House of Commons on 27 June 1979 referred to 'extremist elements, not all of them from Southall, some of whom seemed determined to bring about a confrontation with the police'.

8.2 This Enquiry has sought evidence to establish the truth or otherwise of the allegations that 'outsiders' were responsible. At the outset, it is important to stress that allegations such as those just quoted show an extraordinary contempt for the ability of local community groups in Southall to organise their own protest against the National Front. As the evidence presented in chapter 2 and later in this chapter shows, people in Southall did not need to be told by outside organisations what to do. The media references to the Anti-Nazi League also distort the nature of a nation-wide, loose grouping of individuals and local groups. The ANL has a group in Southall, as in many other parts of the country, membership of which overlaps with other community organisations.

8.3 It is also essential to stress at this point that, although some of the protesters were not local people, they were not the only 'outsiders' present in

Southall on 23 April. The National Front candidate, and the supporters attending his meeting, were outsiders. The evidence we received made it clear that there is no National Front branch or activity in Southall; that the constituency was chosen by the National Front, not because they had a branch and a candidate there, but because Southall is nationally known as a large Asian community and a National Front candidate there would attract maximum publicity; and that the National Front supporters attending the meeting at the Town Hall arrived by bus from other parts of London. Those who seek to blame 'outsiders' should, therefore, direct their attention to the outsiders whose decision to use Southall as a target for electoral activity sparked off the tragic events of the day.

8.4 Furthermore, the majority of the 2,750 police present in Southall on 23 April did not come from the Ealing and Hillingdon division. The Special Patrol Group — which appears to have been responsible for some of the worst violence of the day and which has attracted particular criticism — is a mobile unit of police officers, drawn from throughout the Metropolitan Police area and used throughout that area on special operations. Most importantly, the command of the police in Southall on that day was placed in the hands not of the local police but of Scotland Yard's public order division. As we explain in chapter 9, the failure of Deputy Assistant Commissioner Helm — the senior officer in charge on the day — and his colleagues at Scotland Yard to involve the local police, and especially the police liaison officer, in their planning was at least partly responsible for the disastrous nature of the policing operation.

The planning of the protests on 22 and 23 April

8.5 The planning and organisation of the response to the National Front meeting was in the hands of local community organisations. On 7 April, the Indian Workers Association (Southall) issued an invitation to local organisations to attend a planning meeting on 11 April. On the same day, Vishnu Sharma, then President of the IWA (Southall), and Paul Holborrow, national secretary of the ANL, spoke on the phone about the news that the National Front were to meet in Southall. They disagreed about the form which the protest against the National Front should take. Vishnu Sharma took the view — as the Executive Committee of the IWA later did — that the National Front should be met by a shut-down of businesses, but that their meeting should be contemptuously ignored, with no demonstration taking place. Paul Holborrow argued that, whatever decision the IWA took, the strength of feeling within the community would make a demonstration inevitable. It was not clear from his evidence to us whether he told Vishnu Sharma that the ANL would organise a demonstration, or whether he believed that other groups (such as the Southall Youth Movement) would do so. Paul Holborrow was clearly concerned to make sure that the meeting of community organisations on 11 April decided to hold a demonstration, and he telephoned Balwinder Singh Rana, secretary of the local ANL branch, over the weekend to discuss the matter.

8.6 Paul Holborrow was unable to attend the meeting on 11 April, and the ANL was represented instead by Balwinder Singh Rana. At that meeting, the IWA explained its proposal for ignoring the National Front. In the discussion which followed, it appears that one speaker referred to a broadcast in which, he claimed, an Anti-Nazi League spokesman (possibly Peter Hain) had said that there would be an anti-racist demonstration in Southall to protest against the National Front meeting. The position of those who argued that the National Front should be ignored was, therefore, undermined by the fact that people at the meeting believed that a demonstration would take place anyway. Accounts vary as to how much effect the report of the broadcast had: one witness said he believed the meeting would have decided to organise a demonstration anyway, because the anger and resentment against the National Front was so strong. Another said that he left the meeting early, believing that the IWA's plan for a shut-down and no demonstration had been virtually agreed.

8.7 We have been unable to establish whether or not the broadcast mentioned at the meeting actually took place, or what was said on it. Peter Hain has told us that he made no broadcast specifically in relation to Southall. He believes it is possible, although unlikely, that during an interview on the ANL's planned demonstration against the National Front in Leicester, he might have been asked about what would happen in Southall on 23 April. It is also possible that he or another ANL spokesman, used a phrase such as 'Wherever the National Front is, the anti-racist movement will be present', referring to the ANL's general view that any National Front march or meeting should be met with an anti-racist demonstration. The fact remains that people present at the community meeting on 11 April believed that the Anti-Nazi League had already broadcast its intentions and that a demonstration would be taking place anyway on 23 April. It seems likely that the meeting would have decided to hold a demonstration in any case, but their decision was clearly influenced by what was said about the broadcast and the ANL's plans. To that extent, the ANL influenced the decision made by local people.

8.8 The meeting on 11 April finally decided on a petition to the Council, a march to Ealing Town Hall on 22 April, a shut-down of businesses at 1 pm on 23 April and a sit-down demonstration outside the Town Hall later in the day. The ANL was one of the organisations involved in the Co-ordinating Committee which was established to carry out these plans, its representative being the local ANL secretary, Balwinder Singh Rana, who was later appointed chief steward for the demonstration on 23 April. No-one from outside Southall was a member of the Co-ordinating Committee, and the ANL was the only nationally-affiliated organisation represented.

8.9 The Co-ordinating Committee and its members were not the only organisations to mobilise support for the proposed sit-down demonstration. The ANL nationally circulated leaflets to its members in and around London. The Socialist Workers Party called on SWP branches in London and the Home Counties West to support the 'picket and mass demonstration to stop the Nazi meeting'. The front page of *Socialist Worker* on 21 April was devoted to publicity for the demonstration in an article written by Balwinder Singh Rana and Peter Alexander (who was temporarily appointed chief steward because of Balwinder Singh Rana's late arrival at the stewards' meeting on 23 April). A special Punjabi issue of *Socialist Worker* was also published to publicise the demonstration.

8.10 Socialist Unity (an organisation established by the International Marxist Group) also had a candidate, Tariq Ali, standing in the Southall constituency. Tariq Ali was a member of the ANL at that time and has since become a member of the ANL executive committee. Socialist Unity published their own leaflet advertising the demonstration on 23 April. One leaflet — Vote Tariq Ali 3 May — called for support for the picket at the Town Hall. It appears that there was some resentment within local organisations at Socialist Unity's use of the proposed demonstration — a non-party event — to publicise a particular candidate.

The number of demonstrators who came from outside Southall

8.11 It is, of course, impossible to obtain a precise figure for the number of people who came to Southall on 23 April from outside the Ealing and Southall area. It is common, at a major demonstration against the National Front or on some other issue of national importance, for organisers and supporters of the demonstration to arrange coaches or trains to ensure a large turn-out. For instance, at the demonstration on immigration laws held in London on 25 November 1979, demonstrators came in large numbers from the West Midlands and other parts of the country. It is not, of course, unlawful to travel from one part of the country to another to take part in a demonstration. But there is no evidence whatsoever that coach-loads of demonstrators were brought to Southall or any other meeting-point for the protest on 23 April.

8.12 The Home Secretary's memorandum (see appendix 2) refers to a crowd of about 2,000 people who had assembled by about 4 pm at the police cordons in the Broadway, South Road and the High Street. According to the memorandum: 'The vast majority were of Asian ethnic origin'. This is borne out by photographic and eyewitness evidence. Furthermore, the Home Secretary's memorandum refers to a police estimate that, by the end of the day, 'some 3,000 demonstrators' had been present. Those who arrived later in the afternoon included people coming from other parts of London to attend the demonstration advertised for 5 pm. But the later arrivals also included local residents who were, willingly or not, caught up in the crowds. The police evidence, therefore, gives no ground for believing that there was a substantial proportion of non-local protestors, and, furthermore, makes it clear that 'outsiders' were not involved in the clashes with the police which took place between about 1 pm and 4 pm.

8.13 The absence of an organised body of demonstrators from outside the area is not surprising. The National Front meeting was held on a Monday when many people would be unable to leave work in time for the proposed demonstration. General Election campaigning would have kept away many who would otherwise have wished to show their opposition to the National Front. (Peter Hain, for instance, was electioneering in Putney and for this reason did not go to Southall.) Anti-Nazi League activities and publicity efforts had concentrated on the demonstration against the National Front in Leicester on the Saturday two days previously. Other leading black organisations, particularly the two other Indian Workers Associations, which are based in the West Midlands, seem to have regarded it as the business of local community organisations to organise their own forms of protest against the National Front in Southall, just as they had done in their own areas.

8.14 The Anti-Nazi League and the Socialist Workers Party are clearly the 'extremist outsiders' which the police and politicians had in mind in their statements. We have therefore tried to establish as much as we could about the activities of ANL and SWP members on 23 April. A number of ANL members — including Blair Peach — came to Southall for the proposed demonstration from the East End of London. Others came from Ealing, other parts of London, Oxford and Kingston. Most came by car, although Kingston ANL hired a minibus and other ANL members from Ealing brought a lorry (see 8.17 below).

8.15 Amongst the ANL members present were Paul Holborrow, Mike Pearse, full-time organiser of Schoolkids Against the Nazis, and Tariq Ali. Peter Hain was not present. Paul Holborrow has told us, in written and oral evidence, that he arrived at about 1 pm, failed to meet up with Balwinder Singh Rana outside the Town Hall as planned, and spent the afternoon wandering about trying to find out what was happening. He claims to have seen little of the day's events. He went into 6 Park View Road on at least one occasion, but was not present when the house was raided by the police at about 6.30 pm. He was not arrested. Mike Pearse arrived in Southall about 5 pm, having driven from East London with friends. He was part of the crowd in Uxbridge Road when the police charged into the crowd after a surge forward towards the police cordon, and fled into Southall Park away from the mounted police. Tariq Ali was in 6 Park View Road when the police entered the house. He was arrested and charged with threatening behaviour and obstruction of the police; the outcome of his trial is described in paragraph 2.110.

8.16 We are disturbed by evidence we have received of the attitude of some ANL members towards the local community organisation, Peoples Unite. Although Peoples Unite had been involved in planning the protest, it appears that their members did not all intend to take an active part. Nor did they intend their premises — 6 Park View Road — to be used as a focal point for the demonstration. Clarence Baker, one of the founding members of Peoples Unite, was away in Scandinavia on a tour with the band in which he plays for the week before the demonstration, only returning on the Friday. He told the enquiry:

'When I came road to the house about 11 (on 23 April) it was already opened. Some musicians came round. We knew of the demonstration. We had to decide whether to close or not. We decided to keep open. The house was quite far from where we thought the demonstration would be. About 2 pm or earlier, Asghar (Mohammed Asghar) and some people from Southall Rights came round and asked if they could use our house as a medical centre. We considered it and did not see anything wrong. We agreed and gave them the use of a front room on the right on the ground floor. Also they asked if a number of lawyers could come and be there. We agreed. They set up the room as a first aid centre and put a First Aid sign on the door. Because it was a first aid centre people came in and out that we did not know.'

8.17 Unknown to Clarence Baker, it had already been decided to use 6 Park View Road as a centre for some people attending the demonstration. One ANL member told us that she and some friends arrived at about 10 in the morning, in a lorry carrying ANL posters and banners, and went to 6 Park View Road which it was planned to use as a distribution point. Clarence Baker told us that during the afternoon, he came upstairs from the basement in which he and other Peoples Unite members had been working and found that the room on the other side of the hall from the first aid centre had been used to store ANL leaflets. He said: 'A long time after I realised that the ANL used it as an office'. Clarence Baker also told us that Peoples Unite had mainly used the basement (for the music groups) and the top floor rooms, and that their members had been in the basement and top floors on the day of the demonstration. He also told us that Tariq Ali and 'a lot of the white people' were on the first floor, which had recently been decorated. 'It was hard to know who was doing what. I could not understand how Tariq Ali got arrested in our house.'

8.18 We have been unable to establish how the ANL came to use 6 Park View Road as an office and distribution centre for their material, or whether this was done with the full knowledge and consent of Peoples Unite. If it was not, then it suggests discourtesy and a lack of respect towards the local community organisation on the part of at least some ANL members. But it is not evidence of any intention to create a violent confrontation with the police, or to incite the local community to do so.

Attacks on police cordons

8.19 The Home Secretary's memorandum refers to a number of attacks on police lines, the worst being 'a concerted and unprovoked attack on the police cordon in the High Street' at about 6.30 pm. The evidence we have received makes it clear that there were a number of occasions when protestors surged towards a police cordon, or when a police cordon moved to clear back a group of protestors. Such episodes are common when a crowd of people is confined by a line of police. People trying to see what is going on or, as in this case, trying to get near to the place where a demonstration is planned, become frustrated by the presence of the police line. Those at the back may try to push forward; the police may have received orders (of which the protestors are not aware) to push the crowd further back down the street. For the police facing a frustrated, angry crowd, including people who are throwing missiles at them, such episodes will amount to an attack. But they do not necessarily involve any concerted plan or intention to use violence against the police.

8.20 It was the attempt to break the police cordon in the Uxbridge Road at about 6.30 pm which led to the violent dispersal of the crowd into the park and up Park View Road. Rumours had spread amongst part of the crowd that an attempt would be made to push through police lines and establish the sit-in as planned outside the Town Hall. A surge towards the police lines did take place at about 6 pm, but was contained by stewards and the police. At about 6.20, a group of Asian youths marched towards the police lines from the crowd next to the junction with Park View Road (see paragraph 2.78). Some police officers became separated from the police cordon, were isolated in the crowd of pro-testers and were attacked. The police cordon parted to let through officers equipped with riot shields and others on horse-back who proceeded to 'disperse' the crowd.

8.21 It must have been apparent to many of the protesters, who had come to attend a sit-down outside the Town Hall at 5.30 pm and who knew that the National Front meeting was planned for 7 pm, that since the police would not permit them anywhere near the Town Hall, the only way to carry out their original plan was to break through the police cordon. Some witnesses have said that, as the Asian youths moved towards the police cordon, one or more of the leaders said 'This is a peaceful march'. But any attempt to challenge the police was, of course, bound to lead to violent clashes and was, therefore, seriously misguided.

8.22 The question which arises at this point is whether 'outsiders' were involved in planning or leading the attempt to break through police cordons. One witness told us that such a proposal was discussed by people present earlier in the afternoon at 6 Park View Road. The people in the house included members of Peoples Unite, as well as ANL members who had come from outside Southall. Clarence Baker, a Peoples Unite member, told us that, during the afternoon, 'we knew that there were a lot of police. We knew that we had to be careful. I stayed in the house and advised youths not to go on the march. People came into the house because they could not go home'. At about 5.30 pm, Clarence Baker was seen by a number of witnesses with a megaphone, urging the crowd in Uxbridge Road to remain peaceful. 'I called on people to calm down. It worked. People cleared the street'. One witness claims to have seen a West Indian with a megaphone leading the group of Asian youths towards the police cordon at about 6.20 pm. But very shortly after, Clarence Baker was in 6 Park View Road where he was injured and arrested during the police raid on the house. We think it extremely improbable either that Clarence Baker would have taken part in a

143

move which would inevitably end in violence, or that he could have got away from Uxbridge Road quickly enough to be injured and arrested back in the house.

8.23 It is possible that ANL members participated in discussions that took place about how to break through the police cordon. Paul Holborrow, ANL national secretary, was in Southall throughout the afternoon and had been into 6 Park View Road. Contrary to Paul Holborrow's own evidence, Balwinder Singh Rana says that he met Paul Holborrow, Peter Alexander, some people from the Southall Youth Movement and Clarence Baker in 6 Park View Road some time in the late afternoon. Paul Holborrow told us that he knew of no proposal to break through the police cordon, and that he was involved in no discussions on this or any similar proposal. We are puzzled by Paul Holborrow's account of what he did during the afternoon. As we said in paragraph 8.15, Paul Holborrow told us that he spent the afternoon wandering about, trying to find people he knew. He saw very little of what happened. Paul Holborrow's experience of organising and taking part in demonstrations does not conform with the picture he gave us of what he did in Southall. We questioned him closely on this point, but he maintained that there was complete disorganisation and confusion in Southall on 23 April, and that, if he had been trying to conceal his own involvement in planning an attack on the police, he would have produced a more convincing account. He also pointed out that the attempt to march on the police cordon was clearly doomed to failure and that, in order to organise such an attempt properly, it would be necessary to have 'troops on the ground' and 'proper lines of communication'. It is our view that Paul Holborrow's experience makes it highly improbable that he would have been involved in such a disorganised and unsuccessful exercise. We have also noted that, although Paul Holborrow was in Uxbridge Road at the time of the attempt to break the police cordon, he was not observed by any witnesses playing a prominent role and he was not arrested.

8.24 The other full-time ANL official present in Uxbridge Road, Mike Pearse, was in the crowd when people moved towards police lines, but does not appear to have been near the front. He was not arrested and there is no evidence that he was inciting or leading people to attack the police. Tariq Ali was not in the Uxbridge Road at the time, but in 6 Park View Road, where he was arrested.

8.25 Other attempts to break through the police cordon were made on the Broadway. There were a number of ANL members from East London present on the Broadway during the early part of the evening: as we explained in chapter 2, they included Blair Peach and his friends. No suggestion has been made that any of them were involved in planning or leading an attack on the police and they were not arrested.

Protesters who were arrested

8.26 345 people were arrested during the afternoon and evening of 23 April, and charged with criminal offences. The analysis of the 260 defendants whose charges were heard at Barnet magistrates' court, showed that there were only 16 who neither lived nor worked in Southall or the immediately surrounding area. The evidence of arrests strongly suggests, therefore, that 'outsiders' were not heavily involved in violent incidents and that they did not organise an attack on the police. (See paragraph 5.1).

Conclusion

8.27 As we pointed out earlier (paragraph 8.2), those who support the theory that 'outsiders' were responsible for what happened at Southall ignore the ability of the community itself to demonstrate its anger at the presence of the National Front. As Southall Rights have said, in their report on the events of 23 April: 'It is as stupid as it is condescending to think that Southall's population needed to be provoked by malevolent outsiders before they would show their outrage at the Front meeting and the police protection of it'.

8.28 It seems that the police themselves were surprised by the extent of the turn-out from the local community for the protest against the National Front. A *Daily Mail* reporter, Peter Burden, told the *New Statesman* (4 May) that: 'The high proportion of Asian names surprised people. I was surprised, the police were surprised. It is unusual to suddenly have a tremendous number of Asian names in the detention lists'. Again, the assumption appears to be that, if violence occurs in a place like Southall, it can only be attributable to 'extremist elements' coming from outside the area.

8.29 The evidence we have examined suggests that, even if 'outside extremists' had intended to spark off a violent confrontation with the police, it is extremely unlikely that they would have been able to do so. Once the police cordons were established, fragmenting the would-be demonstrators into different crowds, it was impossible for any group to establish effective control for any length of time, for good or ill, over the conduct of the demonstrations. Stewarding by the organisers was rendered ineffective. An outside organisation would have had difficulty succeeding where the leading organisations and their stewards, known to the crowd, so signally failed.

8.30 In summary, we conclude: first, that the planning and organisation of the protests before 23 April were in the hands of local individuals; secondly, that only a small minority of those hoping to take part in the planned demonstration came from outside Southall and the surrounding area; thirdly, that there was no possibility of any co-ordinated planning on 23 April and that, although attempts were made to break through the police cordon, there is no evidence that this was inspired or incited by 'outsiders'; and fourthly, that 'outsiders' were not disproportionately involved in violence against the police, nor is there evidence that such people were involved in organising, inciting or initiating violence against the police.

9: The Role of the Police

9.1 A number of different explanations have been offered for what went wrong in Southall on 23 April. There is a widespread view in the local community that the police response was altogether out of proportion to the actual threat to public order confronting them; that protesters had been exposed to unprovoked attack by sections of the police; and that much of the violence by some protesters could be explained only as a reaction, in the heat of the moment, to repressive policing tactics. Even more seriously, many people believe that the police behaviour was the result of a decision taken at a high level to 'teach Southall a lesson'. We do not believe that such feelings can be dismissed as the product of an 'anti-police' bias. We have stressed in the Introduction to this report the serious deterioration in community relations which inevitably follows when responsible members of the local community form such a view of the conduct of the police.

9.2 In direct contrast with such diagnoses, both the Metropolitan Police Commissioner and the Home Secretary have taken the view that the violence on the day was caused by unprovoked attacks by protesters on police and property. They have argued that some people came to the proposed demonstration, some of them from outside Southall, prepared for violence against the police and determined to lead an attack on the police in order to achieve their objectives. These charges too are extremely serious.

9.3 In this chapter, we draw on all the evidence available to us to examine the police view that they were the targets of extremely violent, unprovoked attacks, to which they were forced to respond; the general plan for the policing of the proposed demonstration; and the conduct of the police on the day.

Attacks on the police

9.4 We consider first the main attacks on the police which are alleged to have taken place, and then turn to the injuries which individual police officers suffered (see paragraph 9.9 below). According to the Home Secretary's memorandum, the 'first serious attack of the day' took place at around 3 pm on the junction near the Town Hall, as a result of which a cordon was placed across the Broadway. He then goes on to describe the incident with the London Transport bus on the Broadway shortly afterwards and says that 'in the light of the violence which had occurred, it was decided at about 4 pm that the cordoning arrangements to seal off the area should be implemented.' In other words, the decision to form the cordon was taken *as a result of* violence which had occurred.

9.5 Evidence given in court by police officers casts some doubt on the Home Secretary's interpretation. The 'first serious attack', stated to have occurred at about 3 pm on the Town Hall junction, appears to refer to incidents during which six members of the Southall Youth Movement were arrested (see paragraph 2.48). One of them, Mr Aulak, who was charged with threatening behaviour and assaulting three police officers, told the court that police were pushing people towards the Broadway and that he was only trying to join friends in the crowd when he was seized by police officers, pushed to the ground and kicked. Because of serious discrepancies between police and defence evidence, he was acquitted on all charges. In evidence, the police officers said that they had established the cordon across the Broadway, just west of the junction with Lady Margaret Road, *before* the arrests took place. Sergeant Ward told the court that the cordon had broken several times and that there was a 'hostile crowd' of protesters who wanted to get through the cordons. PC Ferguson gave evidence that he was standing on the edge of the pavement and that the cordon was right across the road. He said that they had instructions from a senior officer to form a cordon to prevent the 'rather hostile' crowd from sitting down in the junction 'as had been done earlier in the afternoon'. (We have found no other reference to an attempt to sit down in this part of the road.) There was no attempt, according to PC Ferguson, to use megaphones to order the crowd to move back. He said that the hostility of the crowd increased when the cordon was put in and the arrests started.

9.6 The attempt by protesters to get on to a London Transport bus in the Broadway soon after 3 pm is described in paragraphs 2.50-2.52. Again, there is conflicting evidence about what happened. The Home Secretary's statement that the bus 'was stopped by the crowd' is contradicted by eye-witness statements that it stopped at a scheduled halt. Some people apparently tried to get on to the bus in the hope that the bus would get them through the police cordon to a point nearer the Town Hall, others in the hope that it would get them out of the area altogether. According to the bus driver who gave evidence in court, the bus was immobilised by someone operating the emergency lever on the outside of the bus. Some of those who threw missiles against the bus apparently did so in protest against what they regarded as excessive police force in throwing people off the bus and making arrests.

9.7 The Home Secretary's memorandum says that 'the worst violence of the day' occurred at about 6.20 pm in the High Street, when there was 'a concerted and unprovoked attack on the police cordon'. As we explain in paragraphs 2.78-2.80, this was a deliberate attempt by a number of people in the crowd to break through the police cordon in the hope of getting to the Town Hall. A flare thrown from the Park at the police lines injured one officer, while others, cut off by the crowd from the police cordon, were attacked and kicked by a number of protesters. We describe later (see paragraphs 9.43 and 9.52) the action of the police in repelling the attack on the cordon and dispersing the crowd into Southall Park and Park View Road.

9.8 At approximately 8 pm, according to the Home Secretary's memorandum, 'it was necessary to deal with a large group of youths near Alexandra Avenue' who were throwing missiles at the police. A brick thrown by someone in another crowd in Beechcroft Avenue at about the same time fractured a police officer's jaw in three places. In the operation to disperse the crowd, Blair Peach was fatally injured. These events are described in paragraphs 3.4 and 3.5, and the police action is analysed later in this chapter (paragraph 9.54).

Injuries to individual police officers

9.9 The Home Secretary's memorandum reports that a total of 97 police officers were injured. The *Daily Express* (24 April) referred to 16, and the *Daily Mirror* to 18 officers who were taken to hospital, while TV news reports on the evening of 23 April referred to 21 officers hospitalised. The most serious injury seems to have been to PC Lavercock who was stabbed and was taken off duty for a month afterwards. The Home Secretary's memorandum says that he was stabbed when the crowd moved towards the police cordon in Uxbridge Road at about 6.30 pm. But some police officers on 23 April referred to an officer who had been stabbed in Park View Road (see paragraph 2.79). The Home Secretary has refused to provide further information on the grounds that evidence concerning PC Lavercock may be called at the Blair Peach inquest.

9.10 During the missile-throwing at the police on the Broadway junction of the Broadway and Northcote Avenue, PC Murray was hit by a brick which fractured his jaw in three pieces. Press reports also referred to a police officer with an eye injury and another with an injured leg. The officer with the eye injury appears to have been hurt during the attack on the police cordon on Uxbridge Road, while another officer seems to have been injured on the leg by a petrol bomb or flare thrown in the same area.

9.11 A number of references will be found in chapter 2 to protesters throwing missiles at police officers or police vans (see, for instance, paragraphs 2.53 and 2.55 relating to the Broadway and paragraphs 2.81 and 2.83 relating to the Uxbridge Road). Rev. Roy Smith saw a police officer, who had tripped over as he chased someone out of the Park, 'kicked in the crutch by a young man.' He helped the police officer out of the way. John Clare, reporting on BBC TV news that evening, states that he too witnessed attacks on police officers.

9.12 Evidence given to our Enquiry fully confirms the statement of the Metropolitan Police Commissioner that, on several occasions during the day, in different places, bricks, stones and other missiles were thrown at the police. These barrages were serious enough for the police to consider it necessary to use riot shields for protection. We thoroughly deplore such a resort to violence. Our evidence does not, however, support the view that these attacks on the police by the crowds were premeditated. On the contrary, they appear to have had a random and spontaneous character and to have been responses to the anger and frustration of the moment. Eye-witness accounts, and video-tapes that we have seen, suggest that on several occasions protesters reacted to what they may have regarded as police provocation by reaching for any missile lying conveniently to hand, including bricks, stones and empty cans, and hurling them in the direction of the advancing police lines. (For one such an account, by a witness who himself threw stones, see paragraph 2.55.)

9.13 Once on the Broadway (paragraph 2.55), once on the Uxbridge Road (paragraph 2.79) and twice from 6 Park View Road (paragraph 2.101), what are usually described as 'flares', or by some as 'smoke-bombs' or 'firecrackers', were thrown. Some have stated that a petrol bomb (presumably a Molotov cocktail) was thrown at the police coach involved in the incident described in paragraph 2.55; others have described it as another flare or even as only 'a full, lit box of matches'. We have not been able to establish the exact nature of these objects, which seem to have flared and smoked, but not to explode, nor whether that thrown at the police coach was of the same or a different nature from the rest. They must, in any case, have alarmed the police, just as, when one such flaring object was picked up by a policeman and hurriedly thrown back towards the ranks of protesters, it startled and scared them. In contrast to the other missiles, these flares suggest premeditation on the part of a very small number of pro-testors. It is possible, but it is not likely, that they were improvised on the spur of the moment: the most probable interpretation is that they were brought to the scene by intending demonstrators who anticipated using them in the event of a clash with the police. Although, of course, only one or two such implements may be sufficient to change the character of an episode, by alarming and pro-voking those at whom they are thrown, it nevertheless needs emphasising that only a very few seem to have been used: we have no evidence of more than four. Doubtless their use contributed to inflaming the feelings of the police, and hence to the excesses of which they were undoubtedly guilty; but it does not, in itself, point to the presence of more than three or four individuals engaged in pre-meditated violence.

9.14 Something similar is to be said about the injuries inflicted upon the police, with the single grave exception of the stabbing. Apart from that, all the injuries were caused, so far as we have been able to discover, by the missiles already mentioned, including one of the flares which struck a policeman on the leg. To throw a stone or brick at a line of men is obviously a very dangerous

149

thing to do. It may not involve a deliberate intention to harm a particular individual, but it obviously indicates a general intention to cause injury and a recklessness as to who is injured. We consider that people in the crowds behaved, on occasions, in a reckless fashion which we in no way condone. But we do not think that violence on their part was, in general, either concerted or pre-meditated. They felt themselves to be provoked, and sporadically reacted with short bursts of intemperate violent behaviour. The important question to determine is how far this reaction was due either to misjudgements in the whole police handling of the affair or to improper behaviour on the part of policemen on the ground, and how far to the general situation over which the police had no control. Our answer to these questions is given in the sections of this chapter which follow.

The police plan to cordon off the centre of Southall

9.15 We are not persuaded by the evidence to accept Sir David McNee's suggestion that violence was wholly initiated by protesters and that police action was taken only in response to the violence. As we noted above, the police cordons were put in place before any serious violence had taken place; their presence contributed to the frustration and hostility of the crowd. But there is a more serious respect in which the Home Secretary's memorandum is misleading. Although that memorandum purports to explain why the violence arose, it does not in fact address the question whether the violence against the police was unprovoked, or whether violence by protesters was partly or mainly a response to what was seen as provocation by the police. The memorandum, although it describes something of what protesters were doing to the police, says very little about what the police were doing on these occasions.

9.16 The policing of the demonstration was a vital and active, not merely reactive, factor in the events of the day. It is clear that the plans for cordoning off the central area had been formulated well in advance. The Home Secretary's memorandum suggests that these plans were put into effect only because of violent attacks which demonstrators had launched against the police – implying that the officers in command had intended not to implement the plans for cordons if events had developed in a different way. We find it hard to accept this suggestion. The police had decided, from the outset, not to permit demonstrators to station themselves opposite the Town Hall (the plan to permit a limited number to hold a token protest on the junction confirms that other protesters would have to be kept away from the area; see paragraph 2.70). The first group of arrests outside the Town Hall at about 1 pm resulted from the clash between a fairly small group of SYM members trying to find somewhere to stand as a group, and the police officers who were determined not to allow them to stand anywhere. There does not appear to have been any violence against the police at this stage. But the first cordon on the Broadway was put in place by 3 pm, before the arrests of another group of SYM members took place. Soon after 3 pm, a group of marchers leaving 6 Park View Road found themselves blocked by a cordon on the Uxbridge Road and by a second cordon on South Road (see paragraph 2.97). By 4 pm, police cordons were in place on all approach roads to the Town Hall.

9.17 The establishment of the cordons rendered all the previous plans of the SYM and the Co-ordinating Committee ineffective. Arrangements for stewarding could not be brought into action. Protesters were divided into a number of different, disorganised and leaderless crowds. Those who should have been in positions of leadership spent their time trying to move from one crowd to another (a glance at the map will show what a long way round it was from, say, the Uxbridge Road on the east to the Broadway on the west), trying to find each other and trying to keep frustrated and angry protesters peaceful. Individual protesters were often forced to remain in one part of a road, hemmed-in between police cordons, unable to leave. The purpose of the cordons was achieved: *there was no demonstration.*

9.18 The use of police cordons in this fashion, to prevent a demonstration from taking place and to block off a large part of a town, is extremely unusual. What normally happens is that demonstrators, or those organising a demonstration, take up positions on which they have decided or agreed with the police and, if there is a risk of violent confrontation with some other group, are kept in their position by police lines. On occasions when the National Front has met at Conway Hall in Red Lion Square in central London, protesters have formed up on the pavements, separated from National Front members by rows of police officers. (In 1974, when clashes between the police and anti-National Front demonstrators led to the death of Kevin Gateley and the establishment of the Scarman enquiry, the protesters were *marching* to a meeting point at the far end of Red Lion Square, flanked by police officers, and barred from going too near Conway Hall by a cordon of foot police backed up by mounted policemen.) At Grunwicks, pickets were generally kept on the pavements lining the approach roads to the factories, held back by rows of policemen. On none of these or other occasions did the police decide to *prevent* the demonstration from taking place completely; nor did they cordon off the entire area in which the protesters wished to assemble. Cordons have, of course, been used to prevent a *march* from coming too close to the route of another march or to the building where another group is holding a meeting. In Lewisham in 1977, cordons were used in the attempt to keep a National Front and an anti-fascist march from meeting. In Birmingham in 1978, police cordoned off approaches to the Town Hall where the National Front was meeting. But the use of cordons to ensure that a march sticks to the agreed or prescribed route does not make the march itself impossible.

9.19 The decision to cordon off Southall was not merely a decision about policing tactics. Instead of being a decision about how a demonstration should be policed, it amounted to a decision by senior police officers that no demonstration should be permitted. It was thus a decision with crucial implications for freedom of speech and assembly. As we point out in chapter 6, the National Front's right to freedom of speech was upheld by the local council and the police; the community's right to freedom of speech was destroyed by the police. The gravity of such a decision, the fact that such a cordoning-off operation appears to be virtually unprecedented, and the consequences which that decision had in Southall require that the Home Secretary – as the Police Authority for the Metropolitan area – and the House of Commons to which he is accountable should consider most seriously whether an operation of this nature ought never to take place in future. It is our firm view that it should not.

9.20 In some cases, the crowd was not simply held back by one police cordon. Instead, one cordon faced the crowd, while a second cordon was placed at the back of the crowd, hemming it in. On different occasions in the Broadway, the two cordons moved towards the crowd from different directions, compressing people into an even more restricted area and increasing the tension and risk of violence. Several witnesses objected to what they saw as an arbitrary and unnecessary use of force (see, for instance, paragraph 2.53).

9.21 We do not know what the police 'orders of the day' contained. But we conclude from the evidence available that the police had come prepared to deal with trouble; that they had decided in advance that it would be necessary to cordon off completely the central area of Southall; that large numbers of police would be needed, including all units of the Special Patrol Group and a number of mounted police. 2,750 police officers were on duty in Southall on 23 April, of whom about 200 were SPG officers. We now turn to consider specific aspects of the policing operation: the change of command from the local police to Scotland Yard; the nullification of the stewarding arrangements; the evidence of racism amongst police officers present on the day; the use of snatch squads to make random arrests; the use of riot shields; the evidence of police violence against protesters; and the use of the Special Patrol Group. Finally, we will examine certain general issues which arise from the consideration of these factors.

The change in command

9.22 At some stage before the demonstration on 22 April, responsibility for policing the demonstrations on both 22 and 23 April was moved from the local Divisional Commander, Commander Richardson, to Deputy Assistant Commissioner David Helm, the officer in charge of Scotland Yard's public order branch, with responsibility for policing major public events, including demonstrations. This change in command had a crucial bearing on the events of 23 April.

9.23 The local community organisations involved in planning the protest had had full consultations with the *local* police (see paragraphs 2.20 and 2.36). Although a representative of Scotland Yard was present at one of these meetings (paragraph 2.20), he appears to have had little or no part in the discussions. No indication – apart from some observations to the effect that 'we won't be in charge on the day' — was given to the local organisations about the shift of command. They were left without any idea of the way the police in fact intended to handle the affair.

9.24 The SYM and the Co-ordinating Committee were therefore led to believe by the local police that their respective plans for a picket and a sit-down demonstration had been accepted. Members of the Co-ordinating Committee were indeed told, as they had expected, that they would be arrested if they sat down, and replied that they would not resist arrest; indeed, they were at pains to make sure that this was clearly understood, even informing the Home Secretary himself (see paragraph 2.22). It is likely that the community leaders did not appreciate how much the police disliked this projected train of events. But since no attempt was made by the police either to dissuade them from their plan or to suggest any alternative form of demonstration, it is not surprising that they assumed that the police would allow them to go ahead with their plan and had, in this sense, acquiesced in it. The SYM planned a demonstration which, depending on the numbers involved, would have been lawful and were given the impression that this would not be impeded. In their case, agreement was reached with the local police liaison officer who had been kept closely in touch with their plans but who, on the day, found his authority disregarded by police officers from outside.

9.25 Only when the arrests began and the cordons went up did the community leaders learn their mistake. We regard this failure to inform the community organisations that their plans were unacceptable, or to discuss alternatives with them, as evidence of the contempt in which Scotland Yard appeared to hold the local organisations. Even after 23 April, when Sir David McNee had taken the unprecedented step of publishing an open letter to the people of Southall, stressing the need to restore good relations between the police and the community, Scotland Yard invited representatives of the national and local Anti-Nazi League to a meeting to agree plans for the Blair Peach memorial march. Representatives of the main local organisations only found out about this meeting when they arrived at Scotland Yard for a different, and later meeting, at which they were told of the agreed route — and asked to change it!

9.26 Scotland Yard's refusal to deal straightforwardly with the community organisations or to treat their leaders as responsible people is significant not only for its effect on police-community relations. It directly affected the breakdown of liaison between the local organisations and the police in the very early stages of the demonstration on 23 April. When the police began to arrest SYM members outside the Town Hall, the natural reaction of SYM representatives was to seek out Chief Inspector Gosse, with whom their negotiations had been conducted, in order to agree terms on which a peaceful picket could be conducted. When they finally found Mr Gosse, he apparently agreed that the protesters would be allowed to form a single-line picket on the pavement. But when the SYM representatives communicated this agreement to the officer actually in charge of the Town Hall area, he refused to take any notice. The remark he is said to have made — 'Who the fuck's Gosse? I'm in charge here' — which rapidly became known amongst the crowd and which has passed into Southall folklore, is a pertinent reminder of the consequences of the shift in command. The officers now in charge of the demonstration had deliberately deprived themselves of the obvious benefit to be gained from the mutual understanding between the community and the local police which had been built up over a lengthy period.

9.27 Even from the point of view of Scotland Yard itself, faced with having to police what they believed would be a difficult and possibly violent occasion, the failure to work closely with the local police and, through them, the local organisations, was a serious mistake. Given the size and scale of the policing operation envisaged and the strategy adopted of using a substantial force of police officers, the shift to Scotland Yard command was understandable. But from a broader perspective, the wisdom of the decision is questionable. Relations in a borough like Southall are inevitably delicate and much depends on the measure of understanding and trust developed over a long period of patient work on both sides. The local police, the Community Relations Council and the local organisations had, despite all the problems involved, persisted in maintaining a creditable level of liaison, with a significant degree of mutual respect and trust. The view was strongly expressed to us on several occasions that the local police, who knew the community, its geography and people, and who had been in regular contact with the organisations involved, could and should have played a positive, restraining influence on the day.

9.28 On a practical level, the police cordons sometimes seemed to have been placed in ignorance of the local geography. The cordons in the Broadway, for instance, allowed access to Beechcroft Avenue which is a cul-de-sac (running into Herbert Street which, in turn, runs back on to the Broadway, within the area confined by the police cordons). Some of the protestors who fled from the police in the Uxbridge Road ran into Park View Road, another cul-de-sac, from which they could only escape by trespassing in private gardens and crossing walls into an alleyway which emerges near the police station, also behind the police cordon. More importantly, officers who had been brought into the area for one day's operations had no particular commitment to maintaining regular, good, day-to-day relations with the community once the event was over. One result of events on 23 April was that community organisations immediately withdrew from the Police Liaison Committee. It is the local police, not Scotland Yard, which suffers from this loss of regular contact. At the time of writing, nearly a year later, the Liaison Committee has not been re-established. Community organisations and protesters not only faced a very considerable force of largely unfamiliar police officers, but their leaders found themselves dealing with officers in command with whom they had previously had no contact whatsoever. The decision to transfer command of the day to Scotland Yard, and the failure of Scotland Yard to create a command structure which fully involved the senior officers of the local division, cut the police off from the community. It made the police appear, in the eyes of the protesters, an external and alien force, occupying their town and destroying the plans they had agreed with the local police. We believe that the change in command – epitomised by the Scotland Yard officer's reference to Chief Inspector Gosse – contributed significantly to the rapid degeneration of relations between the police and the demonstrators.

The breakdown of stewarding arrangements

9.29 Scotland Yard itself encourages organisations holding marches or meetings to make proper arrangements for stewarding. Experience of demonstrations suggests that it is easiest to preserve public order when the demonstrators themselves are responsible for stewarding and disciplining their own forces, leaving the police to adopt a more neutral role of enforcing agreements as to the course of the demonstration, rather than replacing the self-discipline of the demonstrators with the aggressive, large-scale policing used on 23 April.

9.30 The Co-ordinating Committee had agreed to appoint four chief stewards to be identified by armbands. A briefing meeting for stewards was arranged for 1 pm on that day. Not all the plans materialised. The local police had turned down a request for four stewarding lorries, and given permission for only one. The Committee had planned to have a number of loud-hailers, but only one materialised. The briefing meeting started late. Balwinder Singh Rana, the chief steward, had been held up in Leicester and had to be temporarily replaced; Vishnu Sharma, who had been at an immigration appeals hearing in the morning, did not arrive in time to meet the stewards. Anticipating that the road immediately in front of the Town Hall would be kept clear by police, a few individuals decided to put their own loud-hailers on top of a shop opposite the Town Hall, thinking that this would give them a means of communication to demonstrators in the four approach roads to the Town Hall. Had the sit-down taken place as planned, with a very large number of people involved, these somewhat sketchy stewarding arrangements would have been placed under very severe pressure. It is noteworthy, however, that at the memorial march on 28 April when feelings against the police were running high, stewarding arrangements which were also somewhat sketchy worked quite satisfactorily.

9.31 In the event, however, it did not matter whether the stewarding arrangements were adequate or not. They made no effective difference because the police ensured that they were never allowed to become effective.

9.32 Throughout the whole of the afternoon and evening, there appears to have been no contact between the police and the chief steward or any of his assistants. The cordoning off of the central area, breaking the crowd into different groups may have facilitated police control, but it effectively cut the protesters off from each other, making it impossible for the stewards to get any clear view of the overall pattern or impose on it any semblance of coherent order. Having received the first reports of the early arrests outside the Town

Hall, the stewards agreed to meet again at 4 pm outside the Town Hall. This meeting did not, of course, take place. Before that time, Southall Rights, one of the few points where responsible members of the organisations involved could have met to take stock of events, was sealed off by the police.

9.33 The Home Secretary's Memorandum notes that 'a stewards' meeting was hurriedly called at 1 pm. It is not clear what tactics emerged from that meeting. However, it is clear that the main co-ordinating body, including the older Asian leadership, did not gather together during the day nor did they seem to be aware of the tactics to be employed by those at the stewards' meeting.' This statement is somewhat less than forthright and may even be misleading. The stewards' meeting was 'hurriedly called' because events had taken a sudden and (to them, though not to the police) unexpected turn, as a result of the scuffles in front of the Town Hall. The police were 'not clear' what tactics emerged from the meeting. But it is pertinent to ask whether they made any effort to discover what had been agreed. If it had been the intention of the police to sustain the stewards, as far as possible, in their role of disciplining the crowd, it would have been crucial to discover what the responsible community leadership intended to do. But the police made no attempt to make contact with the stewards or with the leaders of the community organisations. Indeed, the decision of the police to cordon off the area − of which the stewards and community leaders were completely ignorant at 1 pm − rendered any tactics they might have decided utterly irrelevant.

9.34 The Memorandum suggests that the failure of the main co-ordinating body and the 'older Asian leadership' to gather during the day, and their ignorance of the stewards' tactics, might have had something to do with the violence that occurred. It is a little difficult to understand precisely what is being insinuated (that the stewards' tactics were unwise or even themselves provocative or violent?); but in any case the suggestion is contradicted by the evidence. The decision to cordon off the centre of Southall made it impossible for the leaders or stewards to meet or to exercise any control. The attitude of police officers in charge of different areas suggests that they were determined to render the stewarding useless. For instance, Balwinder Singh Rana, the chief steward, said in his evidence to us that, when stone-throwing began on the Broadway, he tried to exert his influence to bring it to a halt and impose some order. The officer in charge approached him and said 'Leave the stewarding to me'. Other policemen nearby told him to 'Fuck off!' The brick-throwing continued and, shortly afterwards, the police advanced on the crowd with riot shields. His view is that, after about 2.30 pm, all attempts to steward the demonstration were impossible. For good or ill, the protesters were without visible leadership and the police themselves were in charge.

Racist attitudes of police officers

9.35 Evidence has been given to this Enquiry of disturbing manifestations of racism by police officers on duty in Southall on 23 April. Father Thomas Lloyd says that, as early as around 3 pm 'signs of obvious contempt were shown by the police. For instance, police moved people on with words like: "OK. You folks move along. A bit of exercise does you good. Stops you being constipated after all those curries you people eat".' He saw some people being arrested and kicked in the process and commented that 'both the police and younger immigrant population seemed to be ready for trouble'. Father Thomas Lloyd also noticed, as he walked down South Road, that a policeman sitting in a parked bus 'held up the ace of spades against one of the bus windows. and wrote the letters "NF" on the steamed-up glass' of the coach window. Other complaints of racist abuse are referred to in chapter 2 (see, for instance, paragraphs 2.66, 2.88 and 2.90).

9.36 If the complaints are true that police officers were using racial abuse against protesters, before as well as after arrests started, then the police themselves are partly to blame for the violence from which they suffered. We condemn the violence which individuals used against the police. But we must note that many of the people who threw stones, bricks or other missiles at police or police vehicles felt themselves to be reacting to gross provocation. Racist attitudes and behaviour are entirely unacceptable in a disciplined force charged with the duty of policing a multi-racial community; they are particularly unforgivable on an occasion such as a demonstration against the National Front, when insults by the police, added to the insult offered by the National Front's presence, are peculiarly likely to trigger off violence. It is sometimes suggested by senior police officers that the police, like any section of society, will reflect attitudes, including racist attitudes, which are held by many other people. This may be true. But senior police officers are not so complacent when it comes to criminal behaviour amongst the police, nor do they suggest that a police force, like any other section of society, will contain its share of thieves, blackmailers, the violent and the corrupt. It is our view that the Metropolitan Police should, at the highest level, make it known that racist behaviour or the expression of racist attitudes will no more be tolerated than corruption, and should take every possible step to eradicate racism from within its force.

Random arrests and the use of 'snatch squads'

9.37 A number of witnesses complained to us that the police seemed to make arrests at random, often using 'snatch squads' to do so. A small group of police officers may act together to snatch someone out of a crowd; or part of a police line may form a wedge which moves into the crowd in order to seize someone standing in the middle or at the back. The use of the wedge and of snatch squads was common during the Grunwick picket.

9.38 It may appear uncontroversial for the police to form up in a group in order to make an arrest of someone who could otherwise be protected by others in a crowd. But the matter is not so simple. The arrest of one person from within a crowd of demonstrators appears to be arbitrary, and often must be. On some occasions, the police may have had reason to believe that the person they were arresting had been throwing missiles at them. But on other occasions, the person arrested seems to have been selected for no particular reason, as one of a 'hostile crowd', and charged with obstruction of the highway (an offence with which anyone in the crowd could, technically, have been charged) or with the use of threatening words or behaviour. When the police decided to disperse the crowd who were sitting on the bridge at the southern end of South Road (see paragraph 2.117), they picked out individuals who must have been chosen at random, who did not appear to have been committing any offence other than obstruction of the highway, but who were chosen in preference to others who were allowed to go free. Malcolm Hurwitt, a local solicitor, said that the arrests happened so quickly that there was not enough time for anyone to have committed an offence (see paragraph 2.119).

9.39 In addition to the risk that the use of snatch squads to effect an apparently arbitrary arrest will anger the crowd, the effect of the snatch squad is to bring the advancing wedge of police into direct physical contact with a section of the crowd. This may be justifiable if a single individual has been identified as persistently inciting the crowd to violence or as responsible for throwing missiles at the police. But we are not satisfied that the technique was always used on 23 April in such circumstances and we believe that sections of the crowd reacted to what they saw as indiscriminate and unjustified violence by the police by abusing or physically attacking the police.

The use of riot shields

9.40 The Scarman Enquiry into the events in Red Lion Square on 15 June 1974 was told by Counsel for the Enquiry (i.e. the lawyer appointed to assist Lord Scarman in gathering and sifting evidence) that the Metropolitan Police 'does not use or seek to use special riot equipment'. Three years later, the Metropolitan Police decided to equip itself with what are commonly known as 'riot shields', but which the police describe as 'protective shields'. These were first used during the policing of the National Front and anti-racist marches in Lewisham in south London in 1977 and have been used on a number of occasions since. The shields, which are made of reinforced plastic, are curved and sufficiently high to be held in front of the body, reaching from about the knees to face-height. The justification for riot shields is, of course, that when the police are faced with a hail of cans, stones, bricks and other objects, they must be able to protect themselves from injury. The use of riot shields can, however, have extremely unfortunate effects. By suggesting that the police expect to remain under attack, they may actually encourage protesters to throw missiles, thus becoming a factor in the escalation of the violence. By depersonalising police officers, and making face-to-fact contact with the demonstrators more difficult or impossible, they make normal crowd control methods ineffective. Moreover, it appears that at Southall some policemen succumbed to the temptation to use their protective shields as offensive weapons. One young protester was injured on the hand by a riot shield (see paragraph 2.105), as was Amanda Leon in Beechcroft Avenue (see paragraph 3.8).

9.41 The decision of the police to use riot shields is due to the recent increase in violence against police officers on duty at demonstrations. We condemn this violence. Nevertheless, we believe that the Metropolitan Police were right in their former policy of preferring to deal with demonstrators without special equipment; and we think that the recent decision to acquire such equipment may, in the long run, make difficult situations even more violent. We hope that the Police Authorities outside London, the Home Secretary and the police themselves will reconsider the decision to use riot shields.

Police violence against protesters

9.42 We have dealt earlier (see paragraphs 9.9-9.14) with violence against the police and the injuries police officers suffered. In this section, we consider allegations of violence against protesters. Because we have more evidence of police violence, the description of injuries suffered by protesters is more complete than that of injuries suffered by police. This in no way indicates any view that the injuries inflicted on the police are less important, but reflects the decision of the Metropolitan Police not to give evidence to this inquiry.

9.43 On two occasions, police efforts to disperse the crowd led to serious violence against protesters. The first was on the Uxbridge Road, at about 6.30 pm, when an attempt was made to break through the police cordon (see paragraphs 2.78-2.80 and 9.7). The police cordon parted to let through foot police carrying riot shields and mounted police officers, who proceeded to disperse the crowd into the Park to the south and Park View Road to the north. Many witnesses have vividly described the violence which police used against protesters. Judith Power saw 'people with blood on their faces' and 'six to twelve people led away holding their heads' (paragraph 2.80). Martin Craxton was hit on the head, pushed to the ground and kicked (paragraph 2.83). The cut on his head was two inches long and penetrated to the bone. In the police coach, he saw a police officer trying to kick another arrested person in the face. John Hall saw five police officers kicking a black youth in the back and chest, and David Greaves saw a police officer hit a by-stander on the back of the head (paragraph 2.84). Christopher Bolton, a member of Peoples Unite, was trapped in the Holy Trinity Churchyard, along with a number of others who were fleeing from the police charge. He was overtaken by police officers, pushed to the ground and hit 'all over my body and face . . . One officer had me in a stranglehold . . . I kept blacking out and coming round again'. A witness said that he 'looked in a pretty bad way, almost in a state of collapse. His face was a horrible colour, his eyes were staring and his tongue was hanging out' (paragraph 2.87). The *Daily Telegraph* (24 April) summed up the scene in the churchyard: 'Within three minutes police had cornered about 50 demonstrators against the walls of Holy Trinity Church-

yard . . . several dozen, crying, screaming, coloured demonstrators were dragged
. . . to the police station and waiting coaches. Nearly every demonstrator we
saw had blood flowing from some sort of injury; some were doubled up in pain'.

9.44 As the crowd were pursued by the police into Park View Road, missiles
and two flares were thrown from the roof and first-floor windows of No.6 (the
house occupied by Peoples Unite) at the police who were lined up on the road
opposite. Some police officers who gave evidence in court said that they had
been ordered to enter the house, make arrests and evict its occupants; other
officers said that the decision to evict the house was made by individual officers
on the spot, and one officer said that it would be fair to describe the scene as
a 'free for all'.

9.45 The police gave no warning that they were going to evict the house. As
they entered the house, they broke down the door of the room marked 'Medical
Centre'. Although the doctor, the ambulance-man and the lawyer in there
identified themselves to the police, they did not escape injury (see paragraph
2.104-2.106). John Witzenfeld, the solicitor, was hit on the back of the head with a
truncheon. He saw Richard Bunning, the ambulance-man, 'holding his head from
which blood was pouring'. Richard Bunning fainted from his blow and had to be
taken to hospital, where he remained for a day. Dr Nehmad was hit on the head,
and John Witzenfeld noticed the wound bleeding badly. Eve Turner, one of the
stewards who was also in the Medical Centre, had 'a bloody bandage on her head'.

9.46 The police moved upstairs to arrest others in the house. They found the
top of the stairs blocked by a table behind which a number of Peoples Unite
members were sheltering. The Home Secretary's memorandum states that 'police
officers came under heavy attack from missiles thrown from the top floor. The
stairs were heavily barricaded and paint and other articles were thrown at the
police as they negotiated the stairs'. We have received evidence from some
people who went to the house earlier in the evening and said that the upper floor
was virtually empty of furniture or other loose fittings which might have been
used in this way. Since the middle floor had recently been decorated, however,
it seems likely that tins of paint were still there. We do not doubt that missiles
were thrown at the police by some occupants of the house. We are certain that
other occupants were in no way involved in this and were unaware that it was
taking place; this applies in particular to those in the medical room and to
members of Peoples Unite.

9.47 The Home Secretary's memorandum states, correctly, that 'the occupants
of the top floor were persuaded to surrender and they were arrested'. (Amongst
them were John Knight and three others who were present at the barricade; they
were acquitted on all charges.) The memorandum does not mention what a
number of witnesses, including John Witzenfeld and Richard Bunning, have
attested to, that having promised those on the top floor that they would be
unmolested if they came down, the police formed a gauntlet down the stairs

of the house and on either side of the stairs leading from the front door, and subjected all those who passed to kicks and blows.

9.48 One of the women who was evicted from No.6 but not arrested, described 'a long line of police down one side of the staircase on the right hand side as you were going down. As we were made to go down stairs one by one this row of policemen kicked each person's legs . . . I saw (the man in front of me) get either a fist or a boot in his side . . . Then the policeman at the top of the row got me by the hair. He pulled my head back. He then brought his truncheon down on my forehead. It was a heavy blow and I was completely stunned. I did not lose consciousness however. My head hurt a lot. The blow was to the centre of my forehead and on my nose towards my left eye. He then shouted to the other "Get this one". He said this just as soon as it happened.

'By this time blood was pouring down my face and was in my eyes. I shut my eyes. I held my head down and tried to protect it with my right arm . . . As I went down the stairs I was being kicked and my hair was pulled. They seemed to be trying to get my head up again. Some of my hair came out because they were pulling it so hard. I suffered more blows to my head which I think came from fists . . . I was kicked in the stomach with someone's knee. This was a hard blow. I received another knee in the back.' A man who was arrested and charged with threatening behaviour, but who was acquitted in court, says that 'when I reached the first landing someone got hold of my hair and pulled it so hard that it was quite clear that he wanted to pull it out . . . I think apart from kicks and punches I was hit with truncheons as well. I did not really know what was happening to me. The next thing I knew I was lying on the bottom step and there were five officers kicking and punching me.'

9.49 Amongst those arrested and injured in No.6 was Clarence Baker who went into the ground-floor room on the left, where there a number of 'little kids and young ladies'. A brick came through the window. According to Clarence Baker, a crowd of police came in to the room, one said 'Get him' and he was hit with truncheons by about six police officers. 'I felt one blow. I did not really feel anything after that. I was knocked out'. After being released from the police station (where he was charged with assaulting the police, threatening behaviour and possession of an offensive weapon), he was taken to hospital. The X-ray showed a fractured skull, and a brain scan revealed a blood clot on his brain. He remained in hospital for 15 days, and was under hourly observation for one day. For four days, Clarence Baker was so concussed he did not realise he was in hospital; six months later, he still suffered from head pains. All charges against him were dismissed by the magistrate without any defence evidence being heard (see paragraph 2.107).

9.50 The Enquiry knows of 32 people arrested in 6 Park View Road. Of the 28 results known, 14 defendants were acquitted on all charges. Some others were acquitted on some of the charges against them. (For instance, Tariq Ali was

161

acquitted of threatening behaviour inside the house, but convicted of obstruction after he had been arrested and taken outside.) Of the 32 defendants, 26 complain that they were assaulted by the police. A further five people who were in the house, but who were not arrested, were also assaulted by the police. In all 31 cases where police violence is alleged, there is corroborating evidence in the form of witness statements and/or medical reports.

9.51 In chapter 2 (see paragraph 2.114), we refer to the fact that after evicting all its occupants, the police occupied the house, refusing to let anyone enter until after 3 pm the following day. Gareth Pearce, a solicitor who was the first to enter the house, found a scene of complete destruction. Photographs taken at the time bear out the allegations that, between 6.30 pm when the house was cleared and 3 pm the following day, speakers and mixers belonging to the musical groups had been destroyed, guitars had been broken, a telephone ripped from the wall and other equipment damaged.

9.52 The police were entitled to enter 6 Park View Road in order to arrest without warrant those reasonably suspected of throwing missiles. They were entitled to use force to make the entry, if those inside the house refused to let them enter. (Although one police officer yelled out a request to people inside to open the door, there was no time for those inside to comply with the request even if they had wished to.) They were also entitled to search the property. In making an arrest, the police are entitled to use 'reasonable force'. Neither these legal powers, nor the missile-throwing to which the police had been subjected, could possibly have justified the violence with which the police attacked the occupants of the house and evicted everyone present, regardless of whether or not they were being arrested. Nor can the power to *search* the premises justify the length of time for which the police occupied the house, refusing to allow anyone else in. And nothing can justify the wanton destruction which took place of all the contents of the house.

9.53 On two occasions on the Broadway, the crowd was frightened and angered by the use of police vehicles. On the first occasion, at about 7.30 pm, a police coach was driven extremely fast through the crowd. Although the police have claimed that the coach had been attacked by a 'fire bomb' and that the driver was only trying to get away, other evidence suggests that the coach was only attacked *after* being drived at high speed through the crowd (see paragraph 2.55). Soon afterwards, a number of Ford Transit Vans, apparently used by the Special Patrol Group units on duty that day, drove at considerable speed up and down the Broadway. (Witnesses estimated the speed variously at 15-20 and 30-40 mph, but all stressed that, in the very crowded street, where the road as well as the pavements were occupied by protesters, the vans were driving far too fast for safety.) No justification has been offered for this action which, in the circumstances, was both dangerous and provocative. If it was part of a planned move to disperse the crowd, and not simply a piece of irresponsible brinkmanship undertaken by individual officers on their own initiative, the judgement of the officer who gave the order must be seriously questioned.

9.54 On the Broadway, a decision was made shortly before 8 pm to disperse a crowd which had formed at the top of Beechcroft Avenue. (The circumstances are described in chapter 3.) Once again, the police had come under attack from protesters throwing cans, stones and bricks. At about 8 pm, PC Murray was hit by a brick which fractured his jaw in three places. The Home Secretary's memorandum refers to this injury as the reason for the order to disperse the crowd, but it may be (see paragraph 3.5) that the order was given before PC Murray was injured. But, even if the injuries suffered by PC Murray, and possibly other officers, took place before the order was given to disperse the crowd, the undeniable gravity of the injuries does not justify the violence used by the police. Foot police carrying riot shields, followed by two SPG vans, chased the crowd down Beechcroft Avenue. Witnesses described seeing police officers laying about them with truncheons (see paragraphs 3.6-3.11). A number of people were injured, including Amanda Leon who was hit on the head with a truncheon and whose hand was cut by a riot shield (see paragraph 3.8). The most serious injury was, of course, that suffered by Blair Peach, who was struck on the head near the corner of Beechcroft and Orchard Avenues and died in hospital four hours later.

Summary of injuries to protesters

9.55 The Home Secretary's estimate of 64 protesters injured is clearly incomplete; indeed, it is hard to see how the police could have claimed to know of all the injuries suffered by protesters. Our own analysis of 243 statements given to the Enquiry or to solicitors shows that, of 146 people charged with criminal offences, 83 complained of being assaulted by the police, including 36 who complained of injuries to the head. Of those not charged with an offence, 10 complained of an assault, including 6 who said they had been hit on the head. Even this figure of 93 people injured, including 42 who had suffered head injuries, is likely to be incomplete. Many who had suffered only minor injuries from kicks, hair-pulling or truncheon blows did not go to see a doctor and not all gave statements to Southall Rights, to solicitors or to this Enquiry.

9.56 At least three protesters were hit so hard on the head that their skulls were fractured. One was Blair Peach, who died from the blow. One was Clarence Baker, who suffered a blood clot on the brain. The third was a 35 year old man who said he was walking home and sustained his injury in Waverley Road. Many other people also suffered severe blows on the head. They included Vincent Conway, who was arrested in 6 Park View Road and acquitted on all charges and who had three stitches in his head, and Martin Craxton, arrested in Southall Park, who had two stitches to a wound which penetrated to the bone. Charges against him were dropped on his agreement to be bound over. Paul Seligman, who was arrested and taken to the police station but not charged, was kicked in the face and his teeth chipped. Gareth Pearce, who went to Southall Rights late in the evening to give legal advice, was appalled by the number of people she saw with head injuries and commented that 'they needed a doctor, not a lawyer'. One of the stewards, Inderjeet Singh Kohli, who was cornered in the Holy Trinity Churchyard, suffered a fractured pelvis and a young member of Peoples Unite suffered a severe eye injury in 6 Park View Road.

9.57 Press reports in October 1979 referred to another protester who had lost a testicle. This report was given in good faith to the *Guardian* (6 July 1979) by a solicitor, and was repeated by the chairman of this Enquiry in an article in the NCCL journal, *Rights* (January 1980). As far as we have been able to establish, however, the person concerned did not lose a testicle as a result of injuries received on 23 April, but from some other, and unrelated cause.

The use of force by the police

9.58 A number of extremely serious issues are raised by this summary of the police use of violence against people in the crowd. The first is the use of truncheons. We do not have a copy of the current Metropolitan Police instructions relating to the use of short truncheons. However, in 1974 Assistant Commissioner Gerrard of Scotland Yard gave evidence to the Scarman Enquiry in which he quoted the instructions then current:

'Truncheons are supplied to the police to protect themselves if violently attacked. In using them officers should aim at the arms and legs as those parts of the body are least likely to suffer serious injury and avoid the head as much as possible. The use of the truncheon is to be resorted to in extreme cases, when all other efforts to arrest have failed and a prisoner is likely to escape through the officer being ill-used or overpowered. When used, the fact must be mentioned when the prisoner is charged, and also given in evidence at Court. In every instance where a truncheon is used it is to be submitted to the Station Officer for inspection as soon as possible.'

In the absence of any statement by the Metropolitan Police or the Home Secretary suggesting that these instructions have been changed, we take them as the standard by which police use of truncheons on 23 April should be judged. The evidence we have received leads to the inescapable conclusion that, on 23 April, police officers used their truncheons, not for self-protection but as offensive weapons against people in the crowd; that truncheons were used randomly against people who were running away from the police and not offering any violence to them; that in many cases those injured were *not* arrested and no attempt was made to arrest them; and that truncheons, far from being used against the arms and legs of those hit, were repeatedly used to hit people on the head.

9.59 It was not only short truncheons which were used to attack members of the crowd. When the mounted police were used in the Uxbridge Road to help disperse the crowd into Park View Road and South Park, they drew their long truncheons. According to eye-witnesses, many mounted police officers used those long truncheons to lay about people who were trying to escape. In evidence to the Scarman Enquiry, Assistant Commissioner Gerrard said that, in 28 years' service, he had never seen a long truncheon used by a police officer. When asked if they could be dangerous weapons, he agreed that 'they must be very effective' and that an officer using the long truncheon would be liable to injure somebody quite badly. The use of a long truncheon can be justified only in the most exceptional circumstances, when a police officer has no other way of protecting himself or another person from serious injury. We do not believe that their use was justified in the circumstances of Park View Road and the Park when the crowd was *dispersing* and when most or all of those injured, far from trying to attack the police, were running away from them as fast as they could.

9.60 If the instructions given to the Metropolitan Police concerning the use of short and long truncheons have been changed, then Members of Parliament and the public should be told what the new instructions are and what justification there is for the changes. If the instructions have not been changed, then there is evidence that they were disobeyed, not by one or two individual officers, but on a massive scale. Far from being used for self-protection or as a last resort to effect an arrest, both short and long truncheons were used on a number of occasions in Southall as an instrument of arbitrary, violent and unlawful punishment.

9.61 Both in the Uxbridge Road and on the Broadway/Beechcroft Avenue junction, the police were ordered to *disperse* the crowd. Once again, we draw on Assistant Commissioner Gerrard's evidence to the Scarman Enquiry for information concerning the nature of dispersal. Mr Gerrard said then that dispersing a crowd 'should be so done as to cause the minimum of damage to persons, firstly; secondly, the minimum of damage to property; and thirdly the minimum of damage to public relations between the police and the public.' Counsel for the Enquiry, describing police practice, said that 'dispersal should be in directions where the crowd can find exits. In other words, *the primary aim is not to corner and arrest, but to make people move away and to let them get away.* Secondly, that the first step in dispersal should be, if possible, by public announcement.' (our italics.)

9.62 We consider these statements of the aim and nature of a dispersal operation sensible and acceptable. But the dispersals carried out on the Uxbridge Road and the Broadway on 23 April bear little resemblance to them. As far as we can establish, no attempt was made at a public announcement ordering the crowd to disperse. The Home Secretary's memorandum does not refer to a megaphone announcement on either occasion, and no witness has been able to recall such an announcement. We think that, given the violence which had erupted in Uxbridge Road, it might have been very difficult or impossible to make an announcement heard. In the Broadway and in 6 Park View Road, however, we think that a megaphone announcement would have been both possible and desirable.

9.63 Counsel for the Scarman Enquiry referred to the fact that the crowd should be dispersed in directions where they can find exits. In the case of Uxbridge Road, some of the crowd were pushed through a narrow gate into the Park from which it was easy to leave. But those who were chased into Park View Road found themselves in a cul-de-sac, from which the only exit was through private gardens into an alleyway leading back towards the police station. If the commanding officer was unaware of this fact, it underlines our earlier point that Scotland Yard would have benefited from closer liaison with the local police; if he knew that there was no exit from Park View Road, then the decision to force the crowd into Park View Road is open to serious question. Again in the case of the Broadway and Beechcroft Avenue, the crowd was pushed into a road from which the only exit by road (via Herbert Street) would bring them out behind the police cordon on the Broadway. The evidence of Martin Gerald and others (see paragraph 3.9) suggests that officers at the end of Orchard Avenue directed people to an alleyway which led to South Road. Nonetheless, the operation was likely to cause confusion.

9.64 More important, however, is the discrepancy between the description of a dispersal as designed to allow people to get away, not to 'corner them and make arrests', and what actually happened on the Uxbridge Road and in Beechcroft Avenue. It is quite true that very few arrests were made in either operation (this fact underlines our earlier conclusion that the use of truncheons was excessive and unjustified). But a larger number of people trying to flee from the police found themselves cornered and beaten. A number of protesters leaving Uxbridge Road took refuge, as they thought, in the churchyard on the corner, where they were pursued by police officers on foot and on horseback. Others were followed up Park View Road and along the alleyway leading back to the police station. Evidence from eye-witnesses suggests that people *running* away from the police into the Park were singled out for pursuit and many, once again, found themselves trapped by mounted officers. (People who remained calm enough to walk through the Park were, it seems, less likely to be pursued or injured.) In the Beechcroft Avenue operation, we have evidence that people running into an alleyway leading off Beechcroft Avenue were pursued by the police and some of them attacked with truncheons, while others running down the road towards Orchard Avenue found themselves followed by foot police and by SPG vans. It is hard to think of a situation more likely to cause 'damage to persons' and 'damage to public relations between the police and the public'.

The treatment of people who were arrested

9.65 In addition to complaints of excessive violence when people were arrested, many witnesses have complained of the way they were treated in the police van and the police station. For instance, someone arrested in the Broadway at about 4.30 pm says he 'was grabbed from behind, one took my right

166

arm, one my left and one or two took my legs and threw me into the van. They did not say they were arresting me and I had just been standing there. I was taken to Harrow Police Station. In the van I was put between the seats lying on my face. There was one officer sitting on my neck and one on my legs and one was punching me.' A woman stated that she lost her temper after seeing a police van drive rapidly towards the crowd, forcing her to jump out of the way, and that she pulled a wing mirror off the van. She was arrested, 'pushed into the van and made to lie on the floor face down. They put their boots on me. They shouted abuse at me like "You Commie slag, we'll get you".' Another man arrested on the corner of Broadway and Northcote Avenue at about 8 pm complained that he was made to lie down between the seats and 'other prisoners sat on the seats with their feet on me. Then about five or six policemen sat on me and started hitting me and punching me.'

9.66 Many of those arrested complained of verbal abuse. Martin Craxton, who had been hit on the head by a truncheon, had blood dripping from his wound in the police van. He complained that a police officer in the van 'looked at the wet patch on the top of the seat and said "What's that claret, is it yours?" He then said "Yes, it's claret, if you don't wipe that off with your sleeve quick you'll get another thump on the head". I quickly wiped it off.' He said that when two Indians were bundled into the van, the police started shouting "You black scum you've no right to be in a country like this. You Commie agitator, you Commie scum, you only cause all this trouble." When he pointed out that he was a Labour Party member, they said "you're not Labour, you only hide behind the Labour Party".' Another man who was arrested in the Broadway at about 6.15 pm said the police officer asked him what he was doing at the demonstration; when he replied, the police officer called him 'a lying black cunt'. The officer asked him where he was born. He said, in India. The officer said 'What the fuck are you doing here? If there were enough of us, we'd get hold of you and ship you back where you belong.' Another witness who saw police officers hitting people in the van with truncheons said that the police officers 'were saying things like "How does that feel, you bastard? Why don't you go back where you came from?"'

9.67 Some of those arrested said they had no trouble at the police station, or complained only of not being able to contact their families. Others complained of physical violence and racial abuse. A supporter of SYM, who was arrested in the Broadway, was taken to Southall police station. 'On the way into Southall police station there is a door with a glass panel on the way to the cells. They banged my forehead hard against it before we went into the police station. . . . I was later taken to Ealing police station and when they took my shoes off, the policemen trod hard on my feet.' Paul Seligman, who was released from Southall station without being charged, said that 'horrible things were going on all around the crowded lobby' of the station. 'In front of me a policeman was examining the possessions of an Asian youth with an injured face and abusing him: "That's unusual for someone of your race – none of you lot are civilised. Don't you know only monkeys throw bricks – you should be back in the trees." There were many similar remarks. A white lad was brought in doubled over. He collapsed semi-conscious, his face a ghastly pale green. A policeman and a policewoman were shaking him and shouting "Get up, there's nothing wrong with you, you bastard." I said to the police officer "He should see a doctor." He did nothing. An Asian boy was holding his hand at a strange angle. His wrist looked broken. Another Asian was brought in with a severe head wound, holding a completely blood-soaked piece of clothing to it. Police were jabbing prisoners in the stomach etc. I saw none of these people get medical attention before they were taken away to buses.' Vincent Conway was also denied prompt medical attention. At about 8 pm, he was seen by the police surgeon at Rochester Row, who apparently said that he needed stitches which should be done 'before 12 o'clock'. At 11 pm, he was taken to Lambeth station. At 12.30, he complained about his head, which was still dripping blood, and the lack of treatment. It was not until 4.30 am that he got to New Ealing Hospital, where his head wound was stitched.

9.68 At the police station, some defendants were allowed to contact a friend or solicitor. (The Criminal Law Act 1976 provides that a defendant is entitled to have the police contact a person of his request, unless hindrance would be caused to police investigations as a result. In addition, the Judges Rules provide for an arrested person to be allowed to contact a lawyer.) Father Thomas Lloyd says 'I was treated politely (at Harrow police station) and my solicitor was contacted immediately, possibly as a consequence of the fact that I am a priest. A friend who was arrested was not so fortunate.' Another man who was taken to Rochester Row police station asked the police to phone his children, who had seen him being dragged away on television, but the police refused either to let him telephone them or to do so themselves. He and others in the same cell asked for water, but were told 'you're not supposed to have a drink'. Eventually, they were given a drink out of 'a dirty plastic cup'. (The Judges' Rules provide for reasonable refreshments to be given to people detained at the police station.) Another man taken to Rochester Row (who was acquitted on all charges) was asked detailed questions about 'where I was born, where I went to school, where I lived and who lived there with me. Many questions relating to passports were asked. No detail was spared.' Other witnesses have said that similarly detailed, and irrelevant, questions were asked of people in the police vans.

9.69 A number of those arrested complained to the Enquiry that they were forced to give fingerprints and have their photographs taken, or were led to believe that they had no right to refuse. One witness says: 'Although I had a slip in my hand which mentioned at the bottom that we had the right to refuse (I did not read this until later) I was not told this verbally.' A social work student saw another man, who had refused to be fingerprinted, led off to a cell. He himself was told 'and you'll stay there for seven days too'; having been told that he would be released after being charged and 'not wanting to be subject to coercion of this form I agreed, very much against my will, to have my fingerprints taken.'

9.70 In many cases, the decision about which offence to charge an arrested person with seems to have been entirely arbitrary. 'While we were in the bus, two policemen asked each other what they should charge me with. They asked if they should charge me with throwing a bottle or throwing a brick or with swearing at them.' One of the arrested people taken to Hayes police station said that, when they arrived at the station, the arresting officer said 'I think a charge of threatening behaviour would suit you very nicely. If you want something else however I will give you the opportunities'. Another man taken to Hayes police station refused to take off the religious bangle which he wears on his left wrist. 'A policeman said to the other one who had arrested me that I would not take off my bangle. The other officer said that in that case the policeman would report that I had assaulted him in the police van. This was completely untrue.'

9.71 At Rochester Row police station, another protester was told to remove his bangle. When he refused to, saying that it was against his religion to do so, the police officers forcibly removed it. He was then told to take off his turban, which he also refused to do. 'Two police officers tried to forcibly pull my turban off, but they did not succeed'. He was kept at the station for about 10 hours, spending much of the time in a cell with 14 other people. He complained that he was refused water with which to take medication he was carrying with him.

9.72 Because so many people were arrested, the police vans transported many of them to police stations a considerable distance from Southall. Some were taken on a round of police stations before one was found with sufficient cell-space. Although some people were detained at the station over-night, others were released in the early hours of the morning. For instance, D.S. Ghiani, a former president of the IWA (Southall) was taken to Southall Police Station, then to Rochester Row, then to Lambeth, before being returned to Rochester Row from where he was bailed at some time after 4 am. 'We had to make our own way home. Some people did not have any money'. (Mr Ghiani was charged with obstructing the highway, and was bound over to keep the peace by Ealing Magistrates' Court.) Another man who was taken to Harrow police station was bailed at just after midnight, but stayed at the station until 1 am when a van from Southall Rights came to collect him and others.

The use of the Special Patrol Group

9.73 Although SPG officers formed less than 10% of the police on duty in Southall, the SPG appears to have played a prominent role in the worst scenes of violence, particularly in 6 Park View Road, the Broadway and Beechcroft Avenue. Much public criticism of police behaviour singled out the SPG for special mention. Sir David McNee responded to these criticisms by expressing his full confidence in the Group. This hasty declaration could not assist public confidence in the enquiry established by Sir David, at Mr Whitelaw's request, into the SPG. The report of that enquiry, carried out by a senior Metropolitan police officer, has not been published. It has, however, led to a decision that the SPG should be reorganised on an area, not a Metropolitan, basis, in order to integrate it more closely into the local command structure of the police, and that no officer should serve in the SPG for more than four years. As a result, a very high proportion of its current membership is being transferred to other duties.

9.74 All six units of the SPG were on duty in Southall on 23 April. Two of these units were involved in the dispersal operation in Beechcroft Avenue, and the evidence suggests that it was one of their number who struck Blair Peach (see paragraph 3.4). It was SPG officers who drove their vans at such alarming speed along the Broadway (see paragraph 2.55). And SPG officers were amongst those who entered and evicted 6 Park View Road.

9.75 The SPG was first formed in London in 1965 in response to the rising rate of urban crime, as a mobile squad which could give aid to divisional forces. The Metropolitan Police has six SPG units, with a complement of 204 officers. Each unit has three sergeants, 28 male and two female police constables, under the command of an inspector. Until the recent reorganisation, the SPG had its own independent command structure through the A9 branch of Scotland Yard, headed by a Chief Superintendent. Each unit is equipped with three Ford Transit vans, with a driver and radio operator. Officers are identifiable by the 'CO' flash worn on the shoulder. SPG vans carry arms and riot control equipment which are issued on instruction.

9.76 We believe that there has been a significant shift in the use to which the SPG is put. Instead of being a mobile anti-crime group, acting in support of local police divisional forces and under local command, it has become a quasi-independent 'fire brigade' force, brought in to swamp identifiable 'trouble spots' or to help in policing industrial disputes and demonstrations. The SPG appears to have been at the forefront of a move away from the traditional role of an unarmed police force, policing by consent, towards what John Alderson, Chief Constable of Devon and Cornwall, describes as 'a quasi-military reactive concept' where the police 'see themselves as mobile respondents to incidents'. Mr Alderson points out, rightly in our view, that the main casualty in this organisational and technological change is public confidence and community trust. So far as the SPG is concerned, the shift can be identified with the decision in 1972 to revise police training for public order operations, after a thorough review of British police tactics in the light of American and Western European riot-control techniques.

9.77 The police have always denied that the SPG is a riot control force. Counsel for the Scarman Enquiry in 1974 said that: 'First of all, the Metropolitan Police does not possess, and I think does not wish to possess, a special riot squad.

Secondly, it does not use or seek to use special riot equipment . . . Thirdly, by and large, most of the police on duty in demonstrations are ordinary police officers called in to do the job . . . it is believed . . . that this is the best way to maintain good relations with the demonstrators and with the public and to keep violence to a minimum and *that the use of special squads or riot equipment will tend to exacerbate the violence*' (our italics). We agree with this judgement. Officially, successive Governments have decided against the creation of a third 'para-military' force, of the kind which is common in Continental countries. Although the SPG carries special equipment, to the best of our knowledge they have not yet used any equipment on a demonstration other than truncheons and riot shields. (Whatever the weapon which killed Blair Peach, it does not seem to have been part of the equipment issued to the SPG.) But they have been singled out by the police, and identified by the public, as a special squad to be used against demonstrators. In 1972, for instance, the report of the Metropolitan Commissioner spoke of the group's activities at demonstrations 'at which militant elements were thought likely to cause disorder'. A Southern Television documentary in 1976 (*The Men in the Middle*) showed the SPG practising the 'wedge' and the 'snatch' (see paragraphs 9.38 above), techniques of unarmed combat, the use of riot shields as both defensive and offensive equipment and the use of CS gas. We believe that the SPG has, in practice, adopted the role of a special riot squad in public order situations, with precisely the effects which were feared by counsel for the Scarman Enquiry. The use of the SPG in circumstances such as those which existed in Southall on 23 April is a major factor in converting a tough but traditional policing operation into something approaching an urban riot or a staged battle between protesters and the police.

9.78 It is not within our remit to examine the use of the SPG as an anti-crime squad, although we are well aware of the concern about its use in Lewisham in 1975 and in Lambeth in 1978, where black people in particular were the victims of their operation. We believe that the Government should establish a public enquiry into the role and operation of the SPG and similar forces in other parts of the country; in default of this, we think the task could usefully be under-taken by the new House of Commons Select Committee on Home Affairs. We think that the SPG has no place in the policing of demonstrations. Whether it should be disbanded altogether or retained for its original purpose is outside the scope of our enquiry.

The accountability of the police

9.79 There are, in theory, a number of mechanisms for ensuring that the police are held accountable for any misbehaviour on their part. In 1976, the machinery for dealing with police complaints was revised with the establishment of an independent Police Complaints Board. Very few formal complaints against the police appear to have been made by those who have criticised the police action at Southall. We believe that there are several reasons for the low level of complaints. First, since no complaint is investigated until after the outcome of criminal proceedings against the complainant, those who were arrested and charged, but who complained of police violence against themselves, had little incentive to make a complaint. Secondly, the fact that a complaint against the police continues, even under the 1976 Act, to be investigated by another police officer does not enhance confidence in the impartiality of the system, particularly when the complainant belongs to a group which feels that it has been deliberately picked on by the police. The independent Police Complaints Board does not affect this lack of confidence, since it takes no part in the investigation, and receives the investigator's report only after the DPP has decided whether or not to institute criminal proceedings against the police officer and after the Chief Constable has decided whether or not to bring a disciplinary charge. Thirdly, the investigation of an *individual* complaint cannot take into account the general allegation of a breakdown of discipline on the part of the police, of which the individual incident was only a small part.

9.80 A police officer who is suspected of a criminal offence may be prosecuted at the instigation of the Director of Public Prosecutions. Very few complaints lead to criminal proceedings and the difficulty of identifying a police officer responsible for an alleged assault on a protester makes it unlikely that complaints arising out of Southall would have led in many cases to criminal proceedings against a police officer. Whether justified or not, the decision of the DPP not to prosecute any officer for the assault on Blair Peach did nothing to enhance the confidence of potential complainants in the system for making complaints. More generally, in view of the evidence of grave police misconduct, we think it highly regrettable that the police have given no sign of recognising that their behaviour on 23 April was less than impeccable. Cynicism is not surprising when, although more than 300 private citizens were prosecuted, no action — criminal or disciplinary — is seen to be taken against any police officer. We think that public confidence would have been restored, rather than weakened, by a franker attitude on the part of the police and by evidence of a determination to enforce discipline.

9.81 Outside London, the Police Authority should exercise some control over the operations of the local force. In London, the Police Authority is the Home Secretary himself. Both Mr Rees, the Home Secretary in the last Government, and Mr Whitelaw, the present Home Secretary, have refused to establish a public enquiry into the events in Southall on 23 April under section 32 of the 1964 Police Act. It is also possible for the new Police Complaints Board to establish its own enquiry under section 8 of the 1976 Police Act. Neither the Home Secretary nor the Board has used its powers.

9.82 Commander Cass's report of his investigation of Blair Peach's death has not been made public. It has been suggested that the report contained evidence which would have formed the basis for charges of affray against police officers who had been present in Beechcroft Avenue, and charges of obstructing the course of justice against officers who had tried to thwart the enquiry, as well as evidence pointing to one officer responsible for Blair Peach's death (*Sunday Times*, 16 March 1980). We deplore the fact that Commander Cass's report has neither been published nor made available to parties represented at the inquest. We do not accept the argument that publication would be unfair on the suspects against whom the DPP has decided that there is insufficient evidence to prosecute, since those suspects will be identified in any case when they are called to give evidence at the inquest.

9.83 According to the *Sunday Times,* the Director of Public Prosecutions did not obtain counsel's opinion before deciding whether or not to prosecute officers as a result of Commander Cass's investigation. It is our view that the DPP should reconsider his decision on that report and, if he has not already done so, should obtain counsel's opinion on the question of prosecutions. Furthermore, an investigation should be established into the conduct of the officers who entered 6 Park View Road, and a report submitted to the Director of Public Prosecutions who should consider whether charges of affray or assault should be laid against any of the officers concerned.

9.84 Concern has been expressed about the willingness of the DPP to prosecute police officers, not only in relation to Southall but also in the Operation Countryman corruption enquiry. A refusal by the DPP to prosecute not only means that no criminal proceedings will be brought: it also means that no disciplinary charge can be brought arising out of the same incident. This rule, introduced to avoid placing a police officer under 'double jeopardy', has the effect that a police officer suspected but not prosecuted for a criminal offence is never brought to account at all.

9.85 We explain in paragraph 3.44 why the inquest into Blair Peach's death cannot be, and is not intended to be, a substitute for a public enquiry or for criminal proceedings. Only a public enquiry can consider all the events that occurred in Southall on 23 April as a whole; only such an enquiry can have the power to summon witnesses and order the production of evidence, including the police orders and the detailed commands given to police officers during the day. We therefore urge the Home Secretary to establish such an enquiry without further delay.

Was there an alternative to the policing operation?

9.86 According to the Home Secretary's memorandum, the Metropolitan Police Commissioner believed that the police had no choice but to implement the plans to cordon off the centre of Southall. Although the police may, by the afternoon of 23 April, have left themselves with no alternative but to implement their plans for a cordon, we cannot accept that there was no alternative to the original plan. Having criticised the police operation in its original planning and its execution, we now set out the alternatives which we think should have been considered.

9.87 As we suggested earlier (paragraph 7.20), we believe that the police should have allowed the picket and the sit-down demonstration to take place. We accept that such a course of action would have presented real problems. It would have been necessary to divert traffic from the centre of Southall. Since, however, this was one consequence of the decision to cordon off the area, no additional inconvenience to motorists and bus passengers would have been caused. It would have been necessary to reach an agreement with the SYM about where the pickets would stand, and how many there would be; and with the Co-ordinating Committee about where the sit-down demonstration would take place. It would have been necessary to ensure access to the meeting in the Town Hall. That could have been done in two ways: either by taking National Front members to the meeting through a back door; or by keeping open a pathway past the demonstrators to the front door of the Town Hall. The arrival of National Front supporters at the front of the hall would undoubtedly have been a signal for violence on the part of some people present at the demonstration and the picket. The police would have had to form a cordon between the demon-strators and the path which was being kept open for the National Front mem-bers. The desire of at least some demonstrators to prevent the National Front from reaching the Town Hall would have placed a severe strain on the police lines. But facing a line of demonstrators who are trying to break through a police cordon in order to reach a target beyond is a situation with which the police are well used to dealing. It is not a pleasant or desirable situation, but it rarely results in serious injuries or death. We think that the conflict would have been lessened if the meeting had been a genuinely public one (see our recom-mendations in chapter 6) and the demonstrators had known that members of the community were present in the meeting room. This course of action would not have removed the risk of violent conflict between some demonstrators and the police. But it would have had two real advantages over the plan that was adopted: it would have confined the risk of conflict to a fairly small space and to a much shorter period of time (primarily when the National Front supporters arrived); and it would have ensured that the stewards and community leaders were able to use their authority to assist the police in maintaining order.

9.88 Allowing a picket and sit-down demonstration to take place would have respected the choice of the community as to the form of protest and for that reason it is the course of action we should have preferred. But it was not the only alternative open to the police. If senior police officers had persisted in their judgement that they could not have prevented serious public disorder had the demonstration and picket been allowed to take place, they could and should have consulted with the community organisations involved about alternative forms of protest. Had such discussions taken place, they might well have ended in agreement on, for instance, a limited picket on the pavements outside the Town Hall, combined with a protest march past the Town Hall in the afternoon or early evening culminating in a rally in the Park. Again, such a plan would not have completely avoided the risk of violence from, for instance, some of the people on the picket or from some marchers as they passed the Town Hall. But it would have limited the likelihood of violence to a specific place where police lines should have been able to cope, and would again have ensured that community leaders and stewards, fully informed of police plans, would be helping to maintain discipline and order amongst the demonstrators.

9.89 Far from being the only alternative available, the decision to cordon off the centre of Southall and the way that decision was carried out was the worst possible alternative open to the police. It alienated the police from the local community, depriving the police of the benefit of assistance from stewards and community leaders and leading many of the protesters to feel that they were being confronted by a force of hostile and sometimes racist outsiders. It divided the protesters into a number of confused, disorganised, leaderless and frustrated crowds, making communication between protesters and between the stewards virtually impossible. It established a number of flash-points where violence was likely to occur repeatedly over a longer period of time. In its execution, the plan not only destroyed the possibility of a demonstration and hence destroyed the right to freedom of speech of the protesters; it involved severe and unjustified violence on the part of the police. We utterly condemn those who used violence against the police and deplore the injuries which occurred to nearly 100 police officers. But we do not consider that the gravity of those injuries, the hostility of the crowd or the attempts made to break through the police cordon justified the measures which were used in retaliation by the police or the injuries suffered by many protesters. The violence used by the police in their eviction of 6 Park View Road was so serious, arbitrary and unjustified as in itself to constitute grounds for an enquiry into the behaviour of the police. But the eviction of 6 Park View Road was not the only occasion when police discipline appeared to break down completely. The pursuit of protesters into Park View Road, into Southall Park, and into Beechcroft Avenue was carried out with shocking, unnecessary and unlawful violence. If such violence was ordered, then those responsible for giving the orders should be publicly identified and called to account. If the violence was the result, not of orders, but of a breakdown in the discipline of a larger number of individual officers, then it demands an enquiry into why such behaviour occurred and how it can be prevented in future.

9.90 The outcome of the police operation on 23 April could hardly have been worse. Many police officers and members of the public suffered serious injury. One person died, apparently at the hands of the police. And the confidence of many people in Southall in the police, and the institutions of the law, was shattered. Those protesters who, deliberately or in the heat of the moment, used violence against the police must carry their share of the responsibility for what happened. But we do not accept that the responsibility was wholly or even mainly theirs. We regard the decision to prevent the demonstration and to cordon off Southall as entirely misconceived, and the failure to communicate the decision to the community organisations as disastrous. Those who regard our proposed alternatives as unsatisfactory should seriously consider whether such unacceptable consequences would have flowed from a police operation which respected the community's right to protest; which kept them informed of the police plans; which limited the time and place where violence conflict might erupt; and which enabled stewards and community leaders to exercise authority over the protesters in order to ensure that, as far as was humanly possible, the demonstration remained the peaceful protest which had always been intended.

10: Summary of Conclusions

The Death of Blair Peach

10.1 The coroner of the inquest into the death of Blair Peach should make available in advance to all parties represented at the inquest copies of the statements obtained by Commander Cass's investigation. If necessary, the law should be changed as a matter of urgency to require the coroner to make this information available. The Anti-Nazi League should continue to be represented at the inquest (see paragraphs 3.48, 3.49).

10.2 The jury which sits with the coroner when the inquest resumes should be randomly selected from the electoral registers for the coroner's district. There should be no vetting of jurors, whose selection should be carried out not by a police officer but by independent officials under the direct supervision of the Lord Chancellor's Department. (3.50)

10.3 The Director of Public Prosecutions should reconsider his decision not to prosecute any officer as a result of the investigations into Blair Peach's death and, if he has not already done so, should take counsel's opinion on prosecution. (9.83)

10.4 There is reason to believe that Blair Peach was killed by an SPG officer, and no evidence to suggest that he was killed by anyone else. It is a matter for astonishment that the police investigation into his death has resulted in no criminal or disciplinary proceedings. (3.51)

The Courts

10.5 The decision to hold the court hearings in Barnet was at best inept and insensitive. Trials of this kind should be held locally and the Lord Chancellor's Office should have tendered advice to this effect. (5.10)

10.6 Legal aid should, as a rule, be refused only on financial grounds in demonstration cases. Applications in such cases should be considered with expedition. The dilatory administration and initial refusal of applications in the Southall cases was regrettable. (5.14)

177

10.7 Rules should be made under the Criminal Law Act 1977 (section 48) so that prosecution statements are available in all contested cases where requested by the defence. Such statements should in any event be available in demonstration cases. The Memorandum of the Metropolitan Solicitor covering this question should be amended to this effect. The Royal Commission on Criminal Procedure should note defects in the operation of the present guidance. (5.17)

10.8 The tendency to remove a defendant's right to elect trial by jury is to be regretted. In particular, serious offences involving the allegation of violence against police officers should carry a right to jury trial. Defendants in demonstration cases, as in others, should, if charged with possession of an offensive weapon, be so charged under the Prevention of Crimes Act 1973 which gives such a right. (5.18)

10.9 Apparent variations in conviction and sentencing patterns between different magistrates were not an indication of deliberate policy, but reflect variations normally found between magistrates' courts. (5.19)

10.10 Remarks reportedly made by Mr Canham during Southall cases were open to the unfortunate interpretation of bias. They should be the subject of investigation by the Lord Chancellor's Office. (5.25, 5.27)

10.11 The power to bind over a witness who has not been charged or convicted of a criminal offence should be abolished. (5.26)

10.12 Magistrates sitting in demonstration cases should take particular care to avoid charges of bias through injudicious comment and should pay particular heed to the standard of proof in matters of identification. In some cases heard at Barnet, substantial injustice may have occurred; in general, justice was not seen to be done. (5.27)

The National Front meeting and the Representation of the People Act

10.13 Ealing Council had no power to require the National Front candidate to hold his election meeting elsewhere in the constituency or in another part of the borough. (6.4)

10.14 The Representation of the People Act 1949 should be amended so that a 'public meeting' is defined for electoral purposes as one to which members of the public are admitted on a 'first come, first served' basis. (6.10)

10.15 Ealing Council should have taken steps to ensure that the meeting was genuinely open to the public. In the absence of such a guarantee they could and should have refused permission for the meeting. (6.11)

10.16 No attempt should be made to outlaw the National Front and similar groups. (6.15)

10.17 Sections 82 and 83 of the Representation of the People Act 1949, requiring the local councils to make premises available to candidates, should not be repealed. (6.20)

10.18 The amount of the electoral deposit (£150) should be increased to discourage small parties putting up candidates and thereby exploiting the electoral process through free postal delivery of election addresses etc. (6.21)

10.19 The Director of Public Prosecutions should, if he has not already done so, examine whether the speeches at the National Front meeting in Southall were in breach of the law against incitement to racial hatred. (6.22)

10.20 The present law against incitement should not be amended by outlawing the advocacy of repatriation. (6.25)

10.21 Consideration should be given to extending the police power to demand the speaker's name and address, or to arrest, to cases of incitement to racial hatred. Stronger directives should be given to the police to enforce the present law. (6.26)

10.22 Consideration should be given to removing the necessity to obtain the Attorney General's consent before a prosecution can be brought for incitement to racial hatred, and allowing the police and possibly the Commission for Racial Equality to bring such prosecutions. (6.27)

10.23 The power of organisers of an election meeting to refuse admission should be removed. Stewards should thus have powers only to ensure orderly queuing and admission until the hall is full. Stewards should have no right of search. (6.32)

10.24 There is a need for a fundamental change in the attitude of political leaders, government and authorities, and a real commitment to combatting racism on every level. (6.28).

The response of the community and the law relating to demonstrations

10.25 The community had a right to organise a peaceful protest against the National Front. But their right to protest was not protected by the law nor recognised by the authorities, and their freedom of speech and assembly was therefore nullified. (7.3, 7.8)

10.26 The assertion by Mr Whitelaw that differences 'between the young Asians and their elders' helped to precipitate the violence on 23 April appears entirely without foundation. (7.5)

10.27 The offence of obstructing the highway under the Highways Act 1959 should be amended to ensure that an arrest and prosecution can only take place when there is an actual obstruction caused which makes it impossible or very difficult for other users of the highway to go about their business. (7.13)

10.28 The cordoning-off of Southall by the police (although its lawfulness would probably be upheld by the courts) contributed significantly to the violence which occurred, made a peaceful protest impossible, and was unreasonable and unjustified. (7.18, 7.19)

10.29 The police should have permitted a picket and sit-down demonstration to take place. Alternatively, had they remained unwilling to allow that form of protest, they should have advised the community organisations of their view and discussed other forms which the protest could have taken. (7.20)

10.30 The law relating to public order should be amended to provide a statutory right to demonstrate peacefully. (7.21)

10.31 The power of the police to take action when they reasonably fear a breach of the peace should be restricted to circumstances when a breach of the peace has already taken place or is imminent. (7.21)

The Role of Outsiders

10.32 It seems likely that the meeting of community organisations called by the Indian Workers Association (Southall) on 11 April would have decided in any event to hold a demonstration. Their decision was however influenced by the report of a previous Anti-Nazi League broadcast announcing a demonstration. The planning and organisation of the protest was in the hands of local individuals. (8.7, 8.30)

10.33 The Home Secretary's Memorandum gives no ground for believing that there was a substantial proportion of non-local protestors and makes it clear that 'outsiders' were not involved in the clashes with the police which took place between about 1 pm and 4.30 pm. (8.12)

10.34 The use by the ANL of 6 Park View Road as an office and distribution centre may have involved discourtesy towards Peoples Unite, a local community organisation, but is no evidence of any intention to create a violent confrontation with the police or to incite the local community to do so. (8.18)

10.35 There is no evidence to suggest that the ANL or its members and officers present on the Uxbridge Road or the Broadway were involved in planning or leading an attack on the police. (8.22)

10.36 The evidence of arrests strongly suggests that 'outsiders' were not heavily involved in violent incidents and that they did not organise an attack on the police. (8.26, 5.1)

The role of the police

10.37 Evidence given to this enquiry confirms that, on several occasions during the day, missiles were thrown at the police. It does not, however, support the view that most of these attacks were premeditated. On three occasions, flares or smoke-bombs were thrown at the police; on one occasion, it appears that a petrol bomb was thrown at a police coach. Unlike the other missiles, these objects point to premeditation on the part of a very small number of protesters. We thoroughly deplore any such resort to violence, which resulted in injuries to 97 police officers. Those who used violence against the police must carry their share of the responsibility for what happened. (9.12, 9.13, 9.90)

10.38 In the Uxbridge Road at about 6.20 pm, there was a deliberate attempt by people to break through the police cordon, in the course of which a number of police officers were injured. But the dispersal of the crowd by the police involved excessive and unnecessary violence. (9,7, 9.43)

10.39 The decision to cordon off the entire centre of Southall was virtually unprecedented. It amounted to a decision by senior police officers that no demonstration should be permitted. Cordons were put into operation before any serious violence had occurred; the evidence suggests that the officers in command had decided to implement the plan for cordons regardless of the conduct of the protesters. We regard this decision as entirely misconceived and propose that the Home Secretary and the House of Commons should consider most seriously whether an operation of this nature ought ever to take place in future. It is the Enquiry's firm view that it should not. (9.19, 9.21, 9.90)

10.40 Scotland Yard's failure to inform the community organisations that their plans for a protest were unacceptable, or to discuss alternatives with them, is evidence of the contempt in which Scotland Yard appears to hold these bodies. The failure to inform community leaders of the police plans for a cordon was disastrous. (9.25, 9.90)

10.41 The change of command from the local police to Scotland Yard, and the failure of Scotland Yard to create a command structure which fully involved the local police, contributed significantly to the rapid degeneration of relations between the police and demonstrators. (9.28)

10.42 The use of snatch squads to effect apparently random arrests caused the crowd to react to what they saw as indiscriminate and unjustified violence by the police. They should only be used in exceptional circumstances. (9.39)

10.43 The Metropolitan Police were right in their former policy of preferring to deal with demonstrations without special equipment; such equipment may, in the long run, make difficult situations even more violent. The Home Secretary, the other Police Authorities and the police themselves should reconsider the decision to equip the police with riot shields. (9.41)

10.44 The missiles thrown by some occupants of 6 Park View Road towards the police cordon do not justify the violence with which the police attacked and evicted the people in the house. In the view of the enquiry, the violence used, the length of time for which the house was sealed off by the police and the wanton destruction of the contents of the house after the eviction, were unlawful. An investigation should be established into the conduct of the officers who entered 6 Park View Road, and a report submitted to the Director of Public Prosecutions who should consider laying charges of affray and assault. (9,52, 9.83)

10.45   The rapid driving of a police coach through the crowd on the Broadway, and the forays of SPG transit vans which followed, were dangerous and provocative. (9.53)

10.46   The serious injury sustained by a police officer on Northcote Avenue, and the throwing of missiles by some people, do not justify the violence with which the police dispersed the crowd down Beechcroft Avenue, in the course of which a number of people were injured, Blair Peach fatally. (9.54)

10.47   The number of protesters injured significantly exceeds the Home Secretary's estimate. Many of the injuries were very serious, and one was fatal. Most disturbing is the large number of head injuries suffered by protesters. (9.55)

10.48   On a number of occasions, the evidence shows that police officers used their truncheons, not for self-protection but as instruments of arbitrary, violent and unlawful punishment. Such use of short truncheons violates the instructions given to the Metropolitan Police, published to the Scarman Enquiry in 1975. If those instructions have been changed, Members of Parliament and the public should be told what the new instructions are and what justification there is for the change. The use of long truncheons by mounted police in dispersing the crowd on the Uxbridge Road was unjustified and appears contrary to long-established police practice. (9.58-9.60)

10.49   There is disturbing evidence of racist behaviour by police officers on duty on 23 April. The Metropolitan Police should, at the highest level, make it known that racist behaviour or the expression of racist attitudes will not be tolerated, and take every possible step to eradicate such attitudes from the force. (9.36)

10.50   The Special Patrol Group, although providing only a small proportion of the officers on duty, was prominent in the worst scenes of violence, on the Broadway, in 6 Park View Road and in Beechcroft Avenue. Although established as a mobile anti-crime squad, the SPG has in practice taken on the role of a special riot squad in public order situations. We believe that the SPG has no place in the policing of demonstrations. The Government should establish a public inquiry into the role and operation of the SPG and similar forces; in default of such an enquiry, the House of Commons Select Committee on Home Affairs should conduct its own. (9.77, 9.78)

10.51   There is disturbing evidence of racist abuse and unnecessary violence against people who had been taken into police custody. (9.65)

10.52 In view of the evidence of grave police misconduct, public confidence in the police would have been restored, rather than weakened, by a franker attitude on the part of the police and by evidence of a determination to enforce discipline. (9.80)

10.53 The Home Secretary should establish a public enquiry into the events in Southall without further delay. (9.85)

Appendices

APPENDIX I: STATEMENT BY THE HOME SECRETARY TO THE HOUSE OF COMMONS, WEDNESDAY 27 JUNE 1979

With permission, Mr Speaker, I should like to make a statement to the House on the events which occurred at Southall on 22 and 23 April 1979. I have now received and considered the report from the Commissioner of Police of the Metropolis that my predecessor requested.

That report did not and could not deal with the inquiry being conducted by Commander Cass into the circumstances surrounding the death of Mr Blair Peach. His investigation is continuing and the outcome will be submitted to the Coroner and to the Director of Public Prosecutions. Nor did the Commissioner's report deal with individual complaints against the police. These will be dealt with in accordance with the statutory procedure; that includes a reference to the Police Complaints Board which may, if it thinks fit, make to me a special report on any matters which by reason of their gravity should be brought to my attention.

I have already placed in the Library of the House a factual account of the disturbances.[1] My statement will deal with the conclusions of the Commissioner's report, and the lessons to be drawn from the incident.

Mr Speaker, there were two reasons for expecting violence on this occasion. The first was the National Front's decision to hold a meeting in Southall on 23 April. It is the Commissioner's view that, from the moment the National Front was given permission to hold an election meeting at Southall Town Hall, there was a real threat of serious public disorder. Many of those whom the Commissioner subsequently interviewed argued that the meeting should not have been allowed to take place. But the law does not allow election or other meetings to be banned on public order or any other grounds, nor does it permit a local authority any discretion in making premises available for election meetings on the grounds that the views likely to be expressed are offensive.

The second reason was divisions within the Asian community in Southall.

1. See Appendix 2.

184

Despite the deep apprehension of the local Asian community, there were, in the days preceding the disturbances, useful and continuing discussions between the police and community leaders. Regrettably, however, the preparations for opposition to the National Front meeting revealed a growing difference of view between the young Asians and their elders, which as events turned out, was easily exploited by extremist elements, not all of them from Southall, some of whom seemed determined to bring about a confrontation with the police.

I should like to deal with the main criticisms levelled against the strategy and tactics of the police. First, it is said that there were too many police on duty. The Commissioner rejects this. I share his view. It is difficult to conceive that any number significantly less than the 2,750 deployed could have handled the situation better. Information available to the police in advance indicated that there might be several thousand demonstrators, and indeed some 3,000 are estimated to have taken part. Moreover, it has been and will remain the Commissioner's policy, which I fully support, that defensive containment by numbers of police on foot is more likely to be successful, and is certainly more within our traditions, than deliberate, offensive tactics by smaller groups equipped in the style of some foreign police forces.

Second, it is said that the Special Patrol Group should not have been deployed at Southall. The Commissioner does not accept this. Nor do I. They formed only part, and that a very small part, of the deployment at Southall. As the Commissioner made clear in his recent annual report, the Special Patrol Group is used on a wide variety of tasks including crime and traffic, as well as public order. Indeed, most of their arrests in 1978 were crime arrests. A mobile reserve has considerable tactical value, but its work needs to be kept under review and the Commissioner has asked the Deputy Commissioner to conduct an examination of the Group.

The Commissioner has told me of his proposals for restoring and improving relations between the police and the local community in Southall. He will also be making renewed efforts to attract more Asians from the area as regular or special constables. He intends to review his whole community relations organisation and, where necessary, will allocate further resources to it.

The events in Southall inevitably raise questions about the adequacy of the law in relation to public order. I have already indicated to the House that I wish to consider whether changes in the law are required. The Government is, therefore, undertaking a review of the Public Order Act 1936 and related legislation. I shall welcome the views of Members of this House and of interested organisations. On any matters touching the Representation of the People Act 1949, there will be consultation with the Parties in the normal way.

In conclusion, Mr Speaker, I should like to emphasise certain general points. The Government firmly sets its face against extremist organisations, whether to the left or right, who seek to divide society and exploit racial tension. All who live in this country are equal before the law and should be treated as such. Anyone, private citizen or policeman, who breaks the law should be brought before the courts and, if found guilty, properly punished. If the police find it impossible to maintain public order under the existing law, then it is for Parliament to decide whether and how a new balance has to be struck.

But whatever the law may be, it is the duty of the police to uphold and enforce it impartially. That is what they were trying to do in Southall in very difficult circumstances. In my view no police force in the world does it better. We ask much of our police, Mr Speaker, in carrying out the duty which we lay upon them; I believe that we in this House owe them a reciprocal duty of wholehearted support.

APPENDIX 2: THE FACTS OF THE DISTURBANCES AT SOUTHALL ON 22 AND 23 APRIL 1972

A Memorandum placed in the Library of the House of Commons by the Secretary of State for the Home Department following the Report to him by the Commissioner of Police of the Metropolis

On Sunday 22 April 1979, the Indian Workers Association, Southall, and others, organised a march to protest against the National Front meeting to be held in the town hall on Monday 23 April. The organisers hoped to have between 10,000-15,000 people on the march. In the event, approximately 2,000-2,500 people took part, but as a result of the call for larger numbers and uncertainty as to the intentions of the organisers, approximately 1,200 police officers were on duty. *2.24-2.25*

The Commissioner tells me that the march was disorganised and there was obvious friction between the participating groups. As the marchers passed Southall police station, two young West Indians were arrested for obstructing the police and the march did not continue until they were released half an hour later. The marchers continued to argue amongst themselves and eventually the march split into two different sections. During the course of the march a number of arrests were made for minor offences. Although the events of 22 April were not therefore without incident and foreshadowed to some extent the events of the following day, there was no serious disorder. *2.26-2.31*

The disturbance on Monday 23 April were of a different order. It is estimated that some 3,000 demonstrators took part. 2,756 police officers were deployed. 345 people were arrested. 97 police officers were injured. 64 members of the public were injured, and one of them, Mr Blair Peach, subsequently died. *9.9-9.14 9.55-9.56*

The Commissioner's report makes clear that the police had carefully prepared for the demonstrations on 23 April. It was proposed that the National Front meeting would be policed by cordoning the area and allowing a limited number of demonstrators into pre-arranged positions within sight of the town hall. It was intended to allow demonstrators *2.44 2.46 9.22-9.28 9.16*

186

to take up three positions, at the west footway of Lady Margaret Road, the west footway of South Road, and on Avenue Road at the junction of High Street — see attached map. Arrangements were made to seal off the area if it became necessary at the following points:

    i. The Broadway, at the junction of Greenford Avenue;
    ii. Lady Margaret Road, at the junction of Shackleton Road;
    iii. High Street, at the junction of North Road; and
    iv. South Road, at the junction of Beaconsfield Road.

The police arrangements were originally to commence at noon, with mobile reserves patrolling the area, but, as a result of information that young Asians might take some form of action at 1 pm, two inspectors, four sergeants and 40 constables were brought on duty at 11.30 am. The organisers had originally planned for a 'sit down' demonstration at about 5 pm and the leadership in the community were expecting an organising meeting to be called for about 4-4.30 pm. In fact, a stewards' meeting was hurriedly called at 1 pm. It is not clear what tactics emerged from that meeting. However it is clear that the main co-ordinating body, including the older Asian leadership, did not gather together during the day nor did they seem to be aware of the tactics to be employed by those at the stewards' meeting. *2.35 2.41- 2.42 2.45, 9.17, 9.29- 9.34*

Shortly after 1 pm a number of young Asians gathered near the town hall. By the time the group had numbered about 150, the police decided to move them away from that area. There was a gradual build-up of police on all corners of the junction, and police attempted to keep the footways open to pedestrians. At about 1.50 pm, a youth was arrested outside the town hall for being in possession of an offensive weapon, a stiletto knife. By 3 pm there were approximately 300 demonstrators on the south west corner of the junction and a further 100 or more on the north west corner. They were extremely excited and shouted and waved placards. Although at first the demonstrators were persuaded to move relatively calmly away from the town hall, the group suddenly attacked the police using poles and placards in the first serious attack of the day. *2.35- 2.40 2.48, 9.5* *2.48, 9.5*

The next major incident occurred shortly after 3 pm when a London Transport bus was stopped by the crowd of people facing the police cordon which had been put in place after the first attack. When the doors of the bus were opened, demonstrators boarded it causing serious damage. Demonstrators on the footpath threw bottles, bricks and stones at the bus. The polive moved the bus, and the people they had arrested were taken to Southall police station. Further violence then took place. *2.50- 2.52 9.6*

In the light of the violence which had occurred, it was decided at about 4 pm that the cordoning arrangements to seal off the area should be implemented. Crowds gathered at the cordons in The Broadway, South Road and the High Street. They totalled about 2,000 and the *2.46, 2.48, 2.49* vast majority were of Asian ethnic origin. The Commissioner accepts that the cordoning arrangements enhanced the frustration of some of the demonstrators, but, as he has pointed out to me, the police at the time had little choice but to take that action. For the next five hours at various points in the vicinity of the town hall the police were subjected to a number of unprovoked and often extremely violent attacks.

9.86-
9.90

At about 6.20 pm in the High Street, the worst violence of the day occurred. The police cordon in the High Street was placed a few yards east of North Road to protect Southall police station which is in the High Street at the junction with North Road. The number of demonstrators at this cordon varied throughout the day from 500 to over 2,000. They included a number of young men who were seen to kick down a brick wall to provide ammunition to be thrown at the police. At about 6.30 pm, there was a concerted and unprovoked attack on the police cordon in the High Street. Bricks, stones and smoke cannisters were thrown at the police. There was a strong attempt to breach the police cordon and a number of police officers were injured, including one who was stabbed. Some of the police officers were cut off by the crowd and were in serious danger. Two groups of mounted officers were brought forward to disperse the crowd and protective shields had also to be used.

2.74-
2.90
9.7

9.43,
9.61-
9.84

Some of the demonstrators went into Park View Road, adjoining High Street which runs north from the High Street. The crowd in Park View Road started stoning police from the garden of No.6. As police attempted to move this crowd they were attacked by a shower of missiles from the upstairs windows of the house. It was decided to enter and secure these premises. This proved to be very difficult and the police officers came under heavy attack from missiles thrown from the top floor. The stairs were heavily barricaded and paint and other articles were thrown at the police as they negotiated the stairs. Eventually, the occupants of the top floor were persuaded to surrender and they were arrested. Over 70 people were arrested either in or outside the house. Seven motor vehicles were damaged and 12 police officers were injured.

2.92-
2.115,
9.44-
52

Some way from these disturbances an elderly National Front supporter was found in the siding of Southall Railway Station. He had been seriously injured after being attacked by a group of young Asians.

2.120

The police in The Broadway had a difficult crowd to deal with from shortly after 5 pm until almost 9 pm. From 5.30 pm until 6.30 pm the police cordon in The Broadway was positioned at the junction of Herbert Road. West of the cordon was a crowd of over 1,000 demonstrators. The front lines of demonstrators were little trouble and on reasonable terms with the police, but there were a number of troublemakers 20 yards back in the crowd. On three or four occasions, stones, cans and wood were thrown at police. There were several attacks on the

2.53-
2.57

cordon by individuals or groups who pushed through from further back in the crowd.

At about 6.25 pm, the window of the Co-operative Stores on the north side of The Broadway was broken by demonstrators. The crowd was informed by loudhailer that the police cordon would be moved forward. The new cordon was positioned at the junction of St Georges Avenue. Sporadic attacks continued to be made on the police.

At about 6.40 pm, 20 youths managed to get on to the roof of "Safeway's" in The Broadway, and again it was necessary to push the police cordon west along The Broadway. Demonstrators were informed of this by loudhailer. But on this occasion more determined opposition was met. Demonstrators broke "Safeway's" window, but they were removed from the roof and the cordon was established west of St Georges Avenue. — *2.54*

At approximately 8 pm, it was necessary to deal with a large group of youths near Alexandra Avenue. The throwing of missiles increased and it was necessary for police to use protective shields. It was at this time that an officer at the junction of Northcote Avenue and The Broadway was hit by a brick, which was thrown by someone in a crowd which had gathered in Beechcroft Avenue opposite. His jaw was fractured in three places. Assistance was then summoned to disperse the crowd and Mr Blair Peach was seen at the junction of Beechcroft Avenue and Orchard Avenue having sustained an injury to his head. An ambulance was summoned by telephone from 71 Orchard Avenue and at 8.12 pm Mr Peach was conveyed to Ealing Hospital where he later died. His skull was fractured. — *3.4-3.12, 9.8, 9.54, 9.61-9.64 3.14-3.16*

The intensity of missile throwing in The Broadway began to increase and shop windows were being broken. At about 8.20 pm, police advanced along The Broadway in a controlled and disciplined way. The crowd was dispersed and no further serious trouble was encountered in The Broadway. 19 shop windows in the area had been broken by demonstrators. — *2.58-2.63*

National Front members began to arrive at 7.30 pm. Ealing Borough Council instructed the National Front that no more than 60 people should be allowed into the hall and 20 of these should be members of the public. From the people who wished to attend the meeting, five were selected at random from each of the four main police cordons. The meeting was attended by the press and a number of Asian members of the public. The meeting ended at 9.30 pm. Following the departure of the National Front, the demonstrators started to disperse, the police cordons were removed, and at 10 pm traffic was allowed into the area. — *2.70-2.73 6.8*

Home Office
Queen Anne's Gate
LONDON
June 1979

APPENDIX 3: SOME OTHER NATIONAL FRONT FUNCTIONS DURING THE 1979 ELECTION
This chronology is based on national press reports.

April 18th Battersea Town Hall election meeting (permission granted by Conservative-controlled Wandsworth Borough Council). *Daily Mirror* (19 April) reported eight non-National Front members attended. Counter-demonstration, but no incidents, arrests or injuries reported.

April 20th Islington Town Hall election meeting (permission granted – for the first time since 1974 – by Labour-controlled Islington Borough Council). 2,000 police deployed (including 60 mounted police). 300 demonstrators held on the side of Upper Street opposite the Town Hall. Police refused permission for non-National Front members to enter the meeting. Incidents: one policeman reported injured (*Guardian*, 21 April).

April 21st Leicester St George's Day march to election meeting at girls' school, Wyggeston Collegiate, in town centre. Labour and Conservative Parliamentary candidates, churches and other groups petition for the march to be banned. Counter-demonstration opposed (Chief Steward: Ray Sutton, Anti-Racist Co-ordinating Committee). Leicestershire Chief Constable, Alan Goodson, deploys 5,000 police from 21 police forces. 12 coach-loads of National Front members bussed in to the city to join 1,100 on the march. 2,000 counter-demonstrators. Collisions between demonstrators and police. Police dogs used to pursue demonstrators on the university campus. Demonstrators throw cobblestones at police. 39 injured (including 25 policemen), 40 arrests (*Daily Telegraph*, 23 April) (*Daily Mirror* reported 60 police injured and 82 arrests). John Tyndall address: the National Front must emulate the heroes of H.G. Wells' *The Time Machine* and defeat the 'dark skinned, hook-nosed dwarfs'.

April 23rd – Southall

April 24th Plymouth election meeting. Before the meeting began, anti-racialist demonstrators filled the hall, whereupon the Front cancelled the meeting. No injuries or arrests.

Binas Powys, South Wales election meeting. Six National Front members arrived for the meeting, plus 200 demonstrators. Police bundled Front members away by car. No arrests or injuries.

April 25th Newham Town Hall election meeting. Deputy Assistant Commissioner David Helm deployed 4,000 police, including members of the Special Patrol Group (*Daily Telegraph*, 26 April, reported 3,000 police with 2,000 in reserve, 'at least' 24 mounted police and 'scores' of plain clothes police mingling with the demonstrators. The *Daily Mail*, 26 April, reported 4,000 police with 3,000 in reserve). 400 National Front members admitted to the meeting, plus 20 others. Some incidents, 15 arrests, no injuries reported.

April 26th Lewes Town Hall election meeting – four arrests.

National Front national television election broadcast.

April 27th Crawley. Labour Council refused permission for the use of the Town

Hall (*Daily Express,* 26 April) but the National Front held a rally in the town centre. Rally broke up after 15 minutes heckling.

April 28th West Bromwich election meeting. 5,000 police deployed, permitted 150 non-National Front members into the meeting. National Front stewards tried to evict hecklers; police cleared the hall of non-Front members; fighting, some injuries, 20 arrests, including the Rev. Richard Thompson (*Observer,* 29 April).

East London — 4-5,000 anti-racialist march diverted by police order from passing the National Front headquarters. 8,000 police deployed. Nine arrests after the march.

April 29th New Brighton (Merseyside), National Front election rally for John Tyndall. No national press reports.

April 30th Bradford election meeting. 800-1,000 police deployed, 200 demonstrators; fighting, some injuries (including, according to the *Guardian,* 1 May, four policemen), 13 arrests.

Bristol election meeting, 40 National Front members attended, 200 demonstrators. No national press reports.

May 1st Caxton Hall, London, final national election rally. 300 National Front members attended, 23 demonstrators admitted to the meeting by the police. Press report very tight police control. No incidents reported.

Glasgow election rally. 700 demonstrators, 1,000 police (*Morning Star,* 2 May).

Appendix 4: INDIVIDUALS AND ORGANISATIONS WHO GAVE EVIDENCE TO THE ENQUIRY

ALI, Tariq
ANTI-Nazi League
ASGHAR, Mohammed
ATWAL, Jaswant

BADHAN, Satman
   Singh
BAKER, Clarence
BAKER, Peter
BARTON, James
BHASSI, Prem
BHATIA, Krishnan
BIDWELL, Sydney; MP
BOLTON, Christopher
BRAMALL, Sir Ashley
BRARD, Gurmail Singh
BRICE, Martin

BRONNERT, Rev
   David
BRUNNING, Rev Tony
BULKLEY, Rip
BUNNING, Richard
BURNETT, Danny
BUTT, Azher

CALAY, Kaljeet Singh
CHANA, Dilbagh
CHANA, Jasbirs
CHANA, J.S.
CHATTERJEE,
   Prokash
CITY of Manchester
   (Deputy Town
   Clerk)

COHEN, Phil
CONWAY, Vincent
COOK, Eileen
COTTER, Councillor
CRAXTON, Martin
CRICK, Rev Benjamin
CROFT, Paul

DAVIES, Mak
DEWJEE, Audrey
DHANJAL, Beryl
DHESI, Gurdev Singh
DROMEY, Jack
DUNBAR, Donald

EALING Community
   Relations Council

EARLINGTON, Owen
EZRA, Yinnon

GARGE, V.
GAVIN, Stephen
GHIANI, Darshan
  Singh
GILL, Balbir
GILL, Bhupinder
GREAVES, David
GRUBB, Martyn

HAIN, Peter
HALL, John
HIBBS, Gavin
HOLBORROW, Paul
HUDSON, Councillor
  Brian
HUNDAL, Navtej Singh
HURWITT, Malcolm

IMRAY, Malcolm
INDIAN Workers
  Association
  (Southall)
INDRA

JONES, P.E.
JUNG, Sher

KHERA, Amarjit
KOHLI, Inderjeet Singh

LAMBERT, Diane
LEWIS, James
LEWIS, Councillor
  Robert

LLOYD, Father
  Thomas
LONDON Borough of
  Ealing (Town Clerk)
LOURIE, Councillor
  Michael

MAHER, M.
MONAGHAN, Eileen

NORY, Stephen

O'DWYER, Michael
O'REILLY, Carolyne

PARKINSON, Rev Jim
PATHAK, Councillor
  Rabindra Nath
PEARCE, Gareth
PEARCE, Sue
PEARSE, Mike
PERHAR, Anita
PERHAR, Mahendra
PLAHA, Manohar
POST, Peter
POWER, Judith
PUREWAL, Belraj

RAI, Kulwant Singh
RANA, Balwinder
  Singh
ROBINS, Colin
RUDDER, Joan

SAMUELS, Rev Theo
SANDHU, Tarlochan
  Singh

SEHGAL, Ajay
SELIGMAN, Paul
SHARDA, Anita
SHARMA, Naresh
SHARMA, Vishnu
SHARPE, J.
SHAW, Belinda
SIHRA, Mohan Singh
SMITH, Rev Roy
SOCIALIST Workers
  Party
SOCIETY of Friends
SOUTHALL Rights
SOUTHALL Youth
  Movement
SUMAN, S.
SUTTON, Martin

TAYLOR, Mark
TAYLOR, Reg
THOMAS, Jeanette
THOMPSON, Rt Rev H;
  Bishop of Willesden
TURNER, Eve
TWENTYMAN, Anna
TYSON, Delvin

UNGPAKORN, Giles

VINCENT, Rev K.
VIRDEE, Parveen
  Singh

WALSH, Rob
WATSON, Rosalie
WEBBER, Frances
WITZENFELD, John
WOODIN, Sarah

In addition, we received from solicitors information in statistical form concerning 188 defendants, some of whom allowed disclosure of their statements provided they remained anonymous. Observers on behalf of the enquiry attended more than 70 contested cases concerning alleged offences in Southall on 22 and 23 April. The Defence Committee who attended all the hearings in Barnet Magistrates Court allowed us free access to the detailed notes which they took.